DEGREES OF FRE

Prison Educati
The Open Univ

Edited by
Rod Earle and James Mehigan

P ◖ The Open University | **50** YEARS

First published in Great Britain in 2020 by

Policy Press
University of Bristol
1-9 Old Park Hill
Bristol
BS2 8BB
UK
t: +44 (0)117 954 5940
pp-info@bristol.ac.uk
www.policypress.co.uk

North America office:
Policy Press
c/o The University of Chicago Press
1427 East 60th Street
Chicago, IL 60637, USA
t: +1 773 702 7700
f: +1 773-702-9756
sales@press.uchicago.edu
www.press.uchicago.edu

in association with

The Open University, Walton Hall, Milton Keynes MK7 6AA, UK,
www.open.ac.uk

British Library Cataloguing in Publication Data
A catalogue record for this book is available from the British Library

Library of Congress Cataloging-in-Publication Data
A catalog record for this book has been requested

978-1-4473-5306-5 hardback
978-1-4473-5307-2 paperback
978-1-4473-5310-2 ePub
978-1-4473-5309-6 ePDF

Cover design by Andrew Corbett
Front cover image: Original cover art donated by the artist who is serving a prison sentence and wishes to remain anonymous
Printed and bound in Great Britain by CMP, Poole
Policy Press uses environmentally responsible print partners

This book is twice dedicated: to teachers and learners in prison and to the egalitarian vision of social justice that propels The Open University.

Contents

Notes on contributors

Stephen Akpabio-Klementowski is Regional Manager in the Students in Secure Environment team at The Open University. He completed his undergraduate degree with The Open University while serving a prison sentence and is now a PhD candidate at The Open University.

Abdulhaq Al-Wazeer is self-employed and completed his degree in Politics, Philosophy and Economics with The Open University.

Rod Earle is Senior Lecturer in Youth Justice at The Open University and a founder member of the British Convict Criminology group that supports and develops criminology informed by personal experience of imprisonment.

Margaret Gough is a former prisoner who completed a series of degrees with The Open University and other universities.

David Honeywell started his studies with The Open University while serving a prison sentence. He has a PhD from the University of York and is a teaching fellow at Manchester University.

Michael Irwin is a former prisoner who studied criminology with The Open University and at Queen's University, Belfast. His memoir, *My life began at forty* (LR Price), was published in 2017.

Erwin James Monahan FRSA, Dip. EH., BA (Open), MUniv (Open) was made an Honorary Master of The Open University in 2008. He is Editor-in-Chief of *Inside Time*, the national newspaper for people in prison, and has been a columnist and contributor to the *Guardian* since 1998. He is the author of three books, and is a Fellow of the Royal Society for the encouragement of the Arts, a trustee of the Prison Reform Trust and a patron of the prisoner rehabilitation charities Create, Human Writes, and the Prison Phoenix Trust.

Gabi Kent is a member of the Open University Ireland Time to Think oral history project team.

Kris MacPherson recently completed a prison sentence at HMP Kilmarnock in Scotland.

Ruth McFarlane is the Senior Manager of the Students in Secure Environments team at The Open University.

Laurence McKeown was a prisoner in Long Kesh during the Troubles. He completed his undergraduate studies with The Open University before doing a PhD at Queen's University Belfast.

James Mehigan is a barrister at Garden Court Chambers and a former lecturer in criminology at The Open University. He is now Senior Lecturer in Law at the University of Canterbury, New Zealand.

Philip O'Sullivan is Senior Lecturer and Lead Staff Tutor in the Faculty of Arts and Social Sciences at The Open University in Ireland. He is a member of the Open University Ireland Time to Think oral history project team.

Anne Pike is a visiting fellow at the Faculty of Wellbeing, Education and Language Studies at The Open University.

Edwin Schreeche-Powell is a PhD candidate at the University of Kent. He completed his undergraduate degree with The Open University while a prisoner.

Dan Weinbren is Curriculum Manager in the Faculty of Arts and Social Sciences at The Open University. He is the author of *The Open University: A history* (Manchester University Press, 2014).

Vignette authors responded to an open call to contribute short accounts of their OU experiences at events organised by The Open University Students in Secure Environments (SiSE) team and their contacts in various prisons. Biographical notes were not requested and so are not included here.

Acknowledgements

Rod Earle is grateful for the support of colleagues at The Open University, but most especially Ruth McFarlane, whose vision, energy and enthusiasm for this project has been central to the completion of the book. She identified authors, inspired and cajoled contributions, and secured the donation of the image on the front cover. Gill Gowans provided helpful support in negotiating with publishers and steering the project through a variety of gates that we, as editors, sometimes didn't even know existed. Clare Charlton's early recognition of the book's potential to contribute positively to the efforts to celebrate the 50th anniversary of The Open University gave us the confidence to continue. She delivered the institutional support we needed. I'd also like to pay tribute to the diligence, calmness and good humour of my editing partner, James Mehigan. As with all academic work, there are invisible frameworks of support preventing the collapse of all and any academic ambitions. Charlotte Pearson continues to provide me with these and I am grateful to her and all the other members of my family for helping me realise this project. Finally, I'd like to thank my father, Eric Earle, for his love of books and universities.

James Mehigan would like to thank everybody at The Open University who has contributed to this book. Though too many to mention them all, it is easy to say that the book could never have happened without the support of Ruth McFarlane, who helped us again and again to get the raw material for the book. It would have been very difficult or maybe impossible without her. I would also echo Rod's acknowledgement of Gill Gowans and Clare Charlton, whose work was invaluable. Rod himself also deserves heartfelt thanks. It would have been impossible without Rod, whose understanding of the issues, easy temperament as a colleague and empathy for Open University students (both inside and outside the prison walls) has made working together a pleasure. Gill Gowans and Clare Charlton's support from so early on made it possible to get the book done in time for the 50th anniversary celebrations and their expertise made our lives infinitely easier. I would also like to thank all my colleagues in the Social Policy and Criminology Department at The Open University. In particular, Deb Drake has been an invaluable adviser throughout the project. My wife, Isabelle Guitard, had to put up with a lot during the production of the book and I'm grateful to her for her patience and to our twin 2-year-olds for their lovely smiles and late-night 'suggestions' that we had been getting too much sleep. Finally, I would like to give a special thank you to all the prison students I have taught criminology to over the last 10 years. I have learnt so much from you all, about prison, education and criminology itself. I would never have been able to do this project without that experience.

As one reads history ... one is absolutely sickened,
not by the crimes that the wicked have committed,
but by the punishments that the good have inflicted;
and a community is infinitely more brutalised by
the habitual employment of punishment, than
it is by the occasional occurrence of crime.

Oscar Wilde, 1987: 1088, *The soul of man*
under socialism

Even in the darkest of times we have the right to
expect illumination, and [...] such illumination
may well come less from theories and concepts than
from the uncertain, flickering, and often weak light
that some men and women in their lives and their
works will kindle under almost all circumstances.

Hannah Arendt, 1968, *Men in dark times*

Openings and introductions: education for the many, prison for the few

Rod Earle and James Mehigan

They say you shouldn't judge a book by the cover but we are more than happy for this book to be judged that way. The cover art for this book was given to us by an artist in a Scottish prison. He got to hear about the book through the regular outreach work conducted by the Open University's (OU's) Students in Secure Environments (SiSE) team. His work has been acclaimed and displayed by the Koestler Trust, a charity that promotes arts and humanities activities in prisons across the UK. Ruth McFarlane (see Chapter 2) invited 'Ben' to produce an image for the cover of the book. Without much briefing – except that it was about the OU's work in prison – he produced the stunning image on the front cover. We could not have asked for a more life-affirming image. As one of our contributors, Erwin James (see Chapter 14), a former prisoner himself, has said, 'in prison you live in your head' (James, 2013, p 3). Anyone who has been imprisoned knows the truth of that. Here, in 'Ben's' artwork, that quality of imprisonment is invoked and subverted. The light of learning pours out of a radiant and smiling face. You can judge our book by the way it measures up to this image. It is not all about hope, transcendence and liberation, but the opening of life's potentials that Ben's image evokes has driven the OU's work in prison and propelled the contributors to this book, most of whom have been imprisoned themselves.

Academic publishing houses, such as Policy Press, invite independent academics to critically evaluate the strength and viability of the book proposals they receive. One of the academics reviewing our proposal commented "it reads a bit like a love letter to the OU". We stand guilty as charged. Although the real history of The Open University is one of a tangled and contested mesh of competing narratives, as Dan Weinbren's Chapter 4 shrewdly attests (see also Weinbren, 2014), there is much to be loved and cherished about the OU. However, reaching its 50th anniversary in 2019 it can look back over a time of neoliberal ascendancy in higher education that has seen its fees quadruple following the withdrawal of tax-generated government subsidies in 2010. As a result student registrations have fallen dramatically. Since 1969, the OU's singular position as the one and only 'university of the air' has been transformed. It is now jostled in a rowdy new marketplace for higher education, distance and online learning, and studying throughout the life course. Our affection for the OU is undoubtedly conditioned by nostalgia for less embattled times, but our love for it comes from a sense of what is sacred about it. As Hannah Arendt (2006 [1961], p 196) argues, 'education is the point at which we decide whether we love the world enough to assume responsibility for it'.

Education appeals to what the novelist Doris Lessing (1998: ix) describes sympathetically as 'a deep and terrible need within us all to systematise and make order'. Writing an introduction to a small 'pocket canon' edition of *Ecclesiastes or, The preacher*, Lessing warns of the way 'the living springs of knowledge, of wisdom, become captured by institutions, and by churches of various kinds'. Lessing points to the tangled and obscure origins of the figure that speaks through this 'book' of the Old Testament Bible with such mysterious beauty. How and what do we know of the provenance of this figure who is claimed by many but known by few, asks Lessing: 'this "Preacher" was no churchman, and nowhere does he mention a church'. The figure of the 'Preacher' in Ecclesiastes is perhaps a retrospectively imposed term, assigned by 'organized Christianity' rather than the image Lessing prefers to reclaim for the voices she reads in the book: 'Should that "Preacher" have been "Teacher!"? – a very different thing' (Lessing, 1998, p xi).

The Open University is certainly not a church, but it has been driven by teaching and teachers, most of whom have a fierce and profound faith in its foundational principles; open to ideas, to people, to places and to methods, and the need to argue about them. In Chapter 4 Dan Weinbren reports on a student who, after studying with the OU, laments that he 'has been unable to see less than six sides to any question'. The 50th anniversary has involved championing the OU's principles and returning to the question of what a university can do and who it should be for, sometimes with positively Old Testament zeal, as a former Vice Chancellor, Peter Horrocks, discovered when his cavalier approach to the task of re-structuring the OU led to a staff revolt, culminating in his resignation. Nowhere is the OU passion for teaching and learning more obvious or more urgent than in its work with prisons and prisoners. In this book you will find not only first-hand testimony to the value of that work but also arguments, ideas and, most specifically, love for The Open University.

The first five chapters of the book bring together academic and other OU staff to provide historical, sociological and organisational context for the development of The Open University's work in prisons. The remaining nine chapters are from prisoners and former prisoners who have themselves completed OU studies while on the inside. Interspersed among the 14 chapters are some short reflective pieces, or 'vignettes', by prisoners about studying with the OU while incarcerated. Each one is a personal view of the experiences and challenges of studying while serving a prison sentence. There are nine of these vignettes and we hope they add a further idiosyncratic dimension to the longer chapters comprising the book.

Following this chapter, Ruth McFarlane and Anne Pike in Chapter 2 discuss how the work in prison and with prisoners has developed over the last 50 years. It looks at the prison student's journey and the practical issues involved in developing and delivering the OU curriculum in prisons. The digital divide may be threatening to leave behind prison students (and others with access difficulties) but it also has interesting potential. The chapter introduces these exciting digital opportunities. They may be just emerging but they have the potential to enable many more students in prison to transform their lives. The gap between the mainstream and prison student experience may never be completely bridged, but with the right technology and commitment, it may well be significantly reduced.

Chapter 3 offers a singular and focused account of the extraordinary circumstances of prison education in Northern Ireland. Drawing on the OU's oral history archive Time to Think, Philip O'Sullivan and Gabi Kent discuss the development of prison education in the context of the conflict. Prisoners from both sides of the political divide were educated throughout the Troubles, but this policy would not have come about without the impressive work of OU staff and some insightful state functionaries who could see the value of higher education to prisoners, regardless of any political motivation to their offending. The OU's prison education helped prisoners from both sides to develop their intellectual interests while serving sentences for offences committed during their political struggles.

In 2014 Dan Weinbren wrote the definitive history of The Open University (Weinbren, 2014). For this volume he has focused on the history of prison education. While O'Sullivan and Kent looked at the early development of a very specific part of the OU's prison education development, Weinbren takes a broader perspective. He looks at the OU's prison education across the regions and nations to locate the development of the OU's work in prison in historical context. The OU has to be seen as a product of the unique historical moment of its creation. The influence of the Cold War and the need for a social democratic bulwark or counterpoint to communism tied in neatly with the university's modern industrial-scale curriculum development in disseminating enlightened cultural values. While we may romanticise the motivations of the OU's founders, it is important not to forget the times, society and geopolitical reality of which they were a product.

This opening series of chapters is concluded with the fifth, in which Rod Earle and James Mehigan ask searching questions about the recent convergence between the expanded new university sector and the ever expanding prison complex. The OU's pioneering work has laid a path up which many have travelled and, while we would never decry the achievements of individual students or their teachers, we query the benefit of finding virtue and opportunity in prison expansion. Universities must ask critical questions of prisons and the work they do. The measure of success, argue Earle and Mehigan, would be prison shrinkage and the warning signs of failure, growth.

The rest of the book is written entirely by people who have been imprisoned and studied with The Open University. In the first prisoner-authored chapter Kris MacPherson takes us through the literature on desistance and rehabilitation from the perspective of a serving prisoner. There is a lot of research on desistance and it is a thriving specialism, but MacPherson's contribution here is unique in that it connects a deep understanding of that literature with a thoughtfully reflexive application of that theory to his own relationship with the criminal justice system generally and the road to release more specifically.

The desistance pathway as a journey of introspection and realisation is also present in the chapter by Margaret Gough. Receiving a 15 year sentence was a low point in her life, but she threw herself into education, passing exams and building the confidence to apply to the OU. She had, all her life, thought that degrees were for 'clever people', but took a chance on a free introductory course. Her road to first class honours is a clear illustration of many of the challenges described by McFarlane and Pike (Chapter 2) including the difficulty of accessing the internet and communicating with tutors. The hopefulness provided by studying and academic success is also tempered by the prejudicial attitude to prisoners upon release, a theme sadly returned to by many of the contributors to this volume.

Working in the OU's Students in Secure Environment's team, Stephen Akpabio-Klementowski supports prison education as someone with deep experience of it. Having graduated from the OU while in prison, he then undertook a Master's degree, also while in prison, and went on to commence his PhD at the OU. These studies, on rehabilitation and prison education through the prison gate, are conducted part-time alongside his full-time work supporting prison students. For Akpabio-Klementowski the education of prisoners is almost all consuming in deeply personal, as well as professional and academic ways. In his chapter he discusses the changes he experienced in himself in the course of his sentence and their relationship with his OU studies. The frank contrast of his pre-prison life and his life today is a testament to the impact the OU can have in the prison environment.

Starting out at the OU is not always easy for any student and it was not until Michael Irwin transferred from a prison in England to one in Northern Ireland that he was able to get over the 'false starts' he had been experiencing in his studies. Irwin is clear that his OU studies helped him survive in prison and grow in confidence. In this chapter he describes that road and the influence of many of the academics whose work helped him along the way. Having found a fascination for convict criminology while doing his OU degree in prison, he published his memoir *My life began at forty* upon his release (Irwin, 2017).

Unlike Irwin who began his sentence at 40, Abdulhaq Al-Wazeer received a lengthy sentence as a young adult. Like many of the contributors to the volume, he had negative experiences of formal education and a lack of confidence in engaging in university-level studies. His journey to an OU degree is not one of a planned, targeted, steady graft, but almost of an accidental progression through his prison educational opportunities. It led him to 'develop an acute, yet quite accidental interest in politics'. His story of personal development and study during his time inside finishes with a plea for the role of education in the rehabilitation of prisoners to be taken more seriously.

Since Edwin Schreeche-Powell was released he has gone on to commit to forging an academic career. A PhD candidate at the University of Kent, he completed his OU BA while in prison. Schreeche-Powell's chapter begins with the judge's sentencing remarks (the same moment Gough, in Chapter 7, described as the lowest point in her life). He then takes the reader through his story by looking at his sentence in three stages, as they relate to his OU studies. This unique take begins by looking at his life inside before his studies, a period he describes as 'ante/anti-' the OU, when he was resistant to the idea of studying. He then looks at his studies and postgraduate life. He concludes by telling the reader of his great regret that his father is not around to see the progress he has made.

Far from Schreeche-Powell's life in the south-east of England and separated by years as well as distance, Laurence McKeown lived out one of the more unusual lives of an OU student. Having been convicted for offences related to the Troubles in Northern Ireland, he was imprisoned in the H–Blocks in the Maze Long Kesh Prison. The story of students in prison as a result of the conflict in Northern Ireland is an unusual one, and some historical context is discussed by O'Sullivan and Kent (Chapter 3). McKeown brings out his distinctive personal and political experience of study and discusses how his OU education shaped him, his time in prison and his perspective on political struggles in Ireland. His experience is from the Nationalist side of the conflict, but many prisoners from the Loyalist side were also able to benefit from OU study while serving their sentences. Although we were unable to include their voices in this collection, we hope further publications of this kind will afford them this opportunity. O'Sullivan and Kent's chapter offers some insights into the experience of prisoners from both sides, and they are also extensively explored in the OU's oral history archive Time to Think. The archive has an online presence where sections of interviews with prisoners, tutors and others involved in prison education at the time can be explored online.

The penultimate chapter is by another convict criminologist, David Honeywell, who has been studying desistance as part of his PhD at the University of York. Honeywell's experience with the OU was relatively brief. He completed a foundation course while a prisoner and this gave him the capacity to enter undergraduate studies at a traditional university upon his release. Even this small contact demonstrates one end of the spectrum of means by which prisoners have used the OU to help them advance their lives. In this chapter he draws upon his research to bring a different perspective on the desistance literature. Through a series of qualitative interviews with prisoners and former prisoners, Honeywell looks at the quality of 'liminality', a sense of ambiguity that anthropologists describe in rites of passage. The motivation for the research was to find out if his own sense of stigma and liminality were widespread. It is clear from the chapter that they are. This liminality may pose many challenges to those on the desistance pathway, and education can help with this, but the conflict between past and present will remain for many prisoners.

Perhaps the highest profile contributor is Erwin James, a former prisoner who had a column in the *Guardian* while still serving his sentence. James' contribution is in one sense a classic 'redemption script' one could imagine reading about in the desistance literature discussed by other contributors such as MacPherson and Honeywell. Yet it is also a deeply personal account of what the OU has given to the author, with tangible examples of where higher education could, and did, help him progress from prisoner to writer. It provides the perfect way to round out the chapters and bring together the sense of what the OU contribution can be for a prisoner with the hunger to learn.

Throughout the book there are references to module names and codes. While most universities have their own acronyms and phrases to help navigate their organisational structures and academic practices, it often seems that the OU has taken to this parallel language with a phenomenal enthusiasm. To some degree this is inevitable as traditionally closed practices were opened up and produced at scale, although sometimes it can seem a bit unnecessary ('modules' were called 'courses' until recently and webpages still contain the word 'course' as it is better for internet search engines). We have tried to edit in a way that respects the student's experience of their own studies, remembering that for years the student will have known the module by its number more than its name.

While the technology and course or module titles have changed over the years, the basic principles of OU teaching have remained reasonably consistent. Central academics and a wider team of advisers and external contributors design the teaching and learning materials for a module. Once they have been produced, in all their diverse and changing forms of media, they are presented to students by associate lecturers (also known as tutors) who support regionally based tutor groups. Students in secure environments, such as prisons, cannot participate in these groups and are allocated a dedicated tutor to support their learning. There are some references to 'tutor-counsellors' from among the contributors to this volume and this reflects an earlier role, which involved both tutoring and some pastoral advisory support. We have avoided altering these descriptions as they reflect the linguistic experience of the student at the time of their studies and it did not feel appropriate to 'update' or homogenise the terms across the book.

Tutors allocated to support a student in prison will have different levels of access to their students, depending on the distance of the tutor from the prison, the teaching requirements of the module or course, and other aspects of the learning design developed by the team. Each prison's capacity and willingness to facilitate such access is a further factor influencing the student's learning journey. Many students have benefited from face-to-face tutorials, but others have had to make do with telephone tutorials and others have had no verbal contact with their tutors at all. This has meant that different prisoners have had different experiences of different modules throughout their studies as well as compared to similar students in other prisons. Providing a consistent experience is difficult for all forms of distance education, but it is even more complicated for prison students, given their unusual status as both student and prisoner, living for the future and suffering for their past.

In this collection not every contributor wants to disclose their offending history or the offence(s) which led them to serve the sentences where they studied with the OU. For some students their offence may be central to the account they want to present in their chapter or vignette while for others, putting it (or them) behind them may be more important to their narrative. This might occasionally leave some readers feeling like they are missing a bit of context, or some important detail about the author but, as editors, we respect their decision about how much to discuss their 'index offence'. Having tutored and mentored prison students for many years we feel that higher education in prison is about the student's future and not necessarily all that much to do with their past. In many ways this perspective fits with the OU's mission, to provide educational opportunity to anyone who is willing to commit to it, regardless of their background, race, gender, status or previous educational experience. We are happy to carry that lack of prejudice into the field of prison education and we trust that most readers can as well.

Indeed, resisting a rush to judgment based on an offence category is, in many ways, essential for prison education to be a success. Not all tutors are so comfortable with this approach and even some of those who elect to support students in prison struggle with their relationship with students because of their past criminal history. However, this is unusual and unsurprising. Tutoring prison students at the OU is an 'opt-in' experience for which tutors are not paid very much. Tutors come at it with an open mind, a commitment to open access to education and a professionalism which is widely admired by prison staff and students alike. Throughout this book there is reference to the excellent work of tutors and we would like to acknowledge it here. It is for this reason that we have dedicated this book to those tutors who have gone into prisons, or taught prison students by other means over the last 50 years.

It is also very important to acknowledge the work done by prison staff in facilitating the prison student experience. Not every case has been perfect and not every prison has embraced the challenges of distance learning equally, but the last 50 years have provided many examples of prison staff going the extra mile for OU students. In assembling this book it was important for us to focus on the stories of the prisoners themselves rather than the prison staff. Their accounts of the OU are important, but, to echo the current vernacular in higher education, for us it was a case of 'students first'. The stories of education and other prison staff's role in enabling the OU to accomplish its mission in prisons are crucial and waiting to be heard but they are for another book, another story for another day.

To bring this chapter back to where it began, with the front cover and the visual impact of a book cover, we are as concerned about the future of higher education as we are about the state of prisons. The image on our cover, so beautifully painted by the artist and gifted to us, is of the radiant potential of education and its capacities to extend the mind, to free the soul of the prisoner. Universities do not routinely invoke such ambitious images even in their most expensive marketing strategies for fear of seeming ridiculously, implausibly and abstractly idealistic. And prisons certainly don't. The Open University, 50 years on from its establishment, can still, we believe, work with such an image and such an idea because that is how it started, and how we hope it will go on.

References

Arendt, H. (2006 [1961]) *Between past and future*, London: Faber and Faber.

Irwin, M. (2017) *My life began at forty*, London: LR Price.

James, E. (2013) *Free to write: Prison voices past and present*, West Kirby: Headland Press.

Lessing, D. (1998) 'Introduction', in *Ecclesiastes or, The preacher*, Edinburgh: Canongate.

Weinbren, D. (2014) *The Open University: A history*, Manchester: Manchester University Press.

2

From prisoner to student

Ruth McFarlane and Anne Pike

Introduction

The Open University (OU) has a long history of championing access to higher education for people whose prior experiences of education have not always been positive. In particular, almost since its inception, the OU has supported people who wish to study for a degree while serving a prison sentence, many of whom have had troubled pasts and been excluded from school. In 1974 HMP Wakefield celebrated the first OU prison graduate and since then thousands of students have gained a degree while in prison, with thousands more gaining certificates and diplomas or simply beginning their learning journeys. There are currently almost 1,800 OU students in prisons and secure hospitals across the UK, with degree pathways in all faculties. For many of these students, the OU is life-changing, providing a new perspective on life and an opportunity to become a valued member of society upon release.

This chapter discusses the benefits of OU study in prison, stressing the importance of developing the whole person and of having a positive, pro-social student identity. However, there are huge challenges to studying in prison which are also discussed. Key milestones over the last 50 years highlight how legislative changes and rapid advances in digital technologies have influenced delivery over that time. Despite some advances, there is still limited access to digital study materials in prison, most students use offline printed packs, often amounting to several hundred pages, which they study within the confines of a small cell. Yet their academic achievement is on a par with mainstream students, with many earning exceptional results. Continuing to provide a learning experience which is comparable with mainstream students, while still adhering to the strict requirements of the secure estate is extremely challenging for the OU. This chapter explores the students' journey and the practical issues involved in developing and delivering the OU curriculum in prisons and introduces some of the exciting digital opportunities just emerging which may enable many more students in prison to transform their lives.

OU in prison: the benefits

Students first, not prisoners: positive personal and social identity

Many prisoners come from socioeconomically disadvantaged backgrounds having experienced family breakdowns, periods in care, physical abuse, drug and alcohol abuse (Ministry of Justice, 2010; Williams et al, 2012; Light et al, 2013). Consequently, prisoners have often had disrupted educations with 63 per cent of adult prisoners having been suspended or temporarily excluded and 42 per cent permanently excluded or expelled from school (Williams et al, 2012). Added to which, a third self-identify as having a learning disability (Coates, 2016). So, a prison sentence can offer a second chance for an education. However, prison populations are diverse, and education brings different benefits for some prisoners. Acknowledging education as a basic human right, the Council of Europe states that education in prison should aim to develop the whole person; to limit the damage done by prison, to provide support to address educational disadvantage and to support them turning away from crime (Council of Europe, 1990).

Prison education departments prioritise literacy and numeracy programmes which are clearly important to address basic skills deficits, where necessary, but often do not adequately provide prisoners with the skills and qualifications required to address personal and social development needs, essential for social integration and sustainable employment (Clark, 2016). Since a lack of previous education does not equate to a lack of intelligence, many prisoners excel at their studies, rising quickly to higher levels, if provided with the opportunity and the necessary support to progress (Pike and Hopkins, 2019).

Prisoners may start their learning journey for many reasons – survival of a long prison sentence, boredom, making loved ones proud and using time usefully (Hughes, 2012). Some prisoners work their way through all the basic education available and OU study is then a natural progression. Other prisoners may already have previous qualifications and need to study for their wellbeing or to re-skill for a change of employment on release (Champion and Noble, 2016). Interest in OU study may be sparked by seeing other prisoners studying, by participating in a general OU promotional seminars, or by being involved in other university-led activities such as Prison University

Partnerships, many of them developed by the Prison Education Trust. The initial reason to start studying rarely matters but progression is vital. With progression comes confidence and with higher-level learning comes the ability to critically reflect on a situation; the life that led to prison. Eventually, students can develop a new perspective on life and begin to see a different future:

> Never in a million years would I have thought I would undertake a degree – yet here I am, doing it! What is most striking is how it turns from something to do with my time in prison into something I do with the rest of my life. (Nic, HMP Parc, 2018; taken from *Guardian* Awards submission)

Studying with the OU enables prisoners to develop positive personal and social identities, to redefine themselves and develop new horizons. They learn to partition themselves from the more damaging effects of prison (Behan, 2014). They belong to a learning community and develop an identity as students, not prisoners, seeking different interests and conversations from their fellow inmates:

> It's opening up my eyes to a lot of things. It's changing me as a person. It's giving me the way out. My interests are different. I don't necessarily entertain certain conversations as I'm not in that frame of mind. (Andrew, in Pike and Hopkins, 2019, p 57)

The potential for a crime-free future post-release

Positive student identity, along with realistic hope and resilience are key benefits for improving post-release outcomes for students, negating the undesirable labels commonly encountered by ex-prisoners on release. Longitudinal research, which investigated the impact of higher-level learning and explored factors that contributed to a readiness for learning (Pike, 2014), found that prisoners who fully engaged with their studies in prison had high hopes and strong, realistic aspirations for a different life upon release. Their sense of hope was raised as they were provided with the means of realising their aspirations. However, by comparison, those students who expressed an interest in OU study but had not progressed, often due to being unprepared for higher level study, had very few aspirations or protective factors.

OU students in prison also develop resilience through successfully overcoming the challenges in completing distance learning in a prison environment (Hughes, 2012). That resilience is found to help them to overcome the immense difficulties faced in the early weeks and months after release. First, it enabled them to seek out support that was needed but not immediately forthcoming. Second, it helped them to 'tread water until that support arrived' and, third, it 'stopped them from taking the easy option of going back to prison' (Pike, 2014, p 285).

Positive identity change or cognitive transformation can lead to lasting or 'secondary' desistance from crime (McNeill, 2014) and therefore the potential for a crime-free life upon release, not least because higher education increases prisoners' employment prospects and rates of pay in employment upon release (Costelloe, 2014; Duwe and Clark, 2014). The Longford Trust reports that the targeted financial support it provides for serving and ex-prisoners to undertake higher education courses at universities, results in fewer than 5 per cent of recipients of its awards re-offending (Coates, 2016, p 38). Also, a Justice Data Lab report highlights that receiving a grant from the Prisoners' Education Trust to undertake an OU course in custody leads to a reduction in re-offending of between 4 and 8 percentage points (Ministry of Justice, 2014).

OU in prison: the challenges

Milestones over 50 years

There are immense challenges to providing a learning experience which is comparable with mainstream students while still adhering to the strict requirements of a secure environment. Those challenges for both prisons and the OU have evolved over the last 50 years and Table 1 shows key milestones during that time, from the prison and the OU perspective, indicating how legislative changes and rapid advances in digital technologies have influenced delivery of education.

Developments in technology over the last 50 years have led to major changes in the way distance learning study materials are prepared, shared and utilised, and as a result the gap between the learning experience for students in prison and that of mainstream students has widened. In the early 1970s, OU course materials were mostly books with additional television programmes, tutorials and residential schools (Forster, 1976). Prisoners received the same paper-based materials as other OU students. Obviously, prisoners could not attend residential schools or indeed view live television programmes since in-cell television was not introduced until the late 1990s (Knight, 2016) but all other study materials were the same and very few alternatives were required. The OU, as a global university, embraced the rapidly developing technologies and by the 1990s had a growing number of online, interactive courses, in a gradual move towards a 'digital by design' methodology. Prisons, on the other hand, were slow to manage security implications of new technologies. As more courses required the use of digital technologies, the OU devised a 'traffic-light system' with 'green' courses fully available in prison, 'amber' courses difficult to study in prison and 'red' courses unavailable in prison, mostly due to being interactive or online. This system enabled staff and students in prison to make appropriate course choices, by explaining requirements for digital study which was not accessible from prison. Research in 2007 (see Adams and Pike, 2008; Hancock, 2010) highlighted significant inconsistencies in student experiences as the number of 'red' courses (which were not accessible from prison) grew rapidly, leading to a review of OU provision and support, as well as a bespoke prospectus being published in 2009 and now updated annually.

Changing responsibilities for prison education over the 50 years have also had an impact on OU studies. The Prison Service Instruction (PSI) on Higher Education (Ministry of Justice, 2012) requires that all communication between the OU and its students must be via an intermediary within the prison, often the education manager. In the 1970s prison education was run by different local education authorities, which meant inconsistent education across prisons, but with good support often available for 'extra-mural' activities such as OU study (Forster, 1976). Conversely, the introduction of the Offender Learning and Skills Service's (OLASS) contracted college providers in 2006 led to improved technology for learning and greater consistency across prison education departments but, as OLASS focused on lower-level study, less support for OU students.

The strict and diverse prison regimes: learning and working

Forster (1976) suggested there were discrepancies between distance learning provision in different prisons and that some participants appeared misinformed about how much face-to-face support they could expect. While his study was more than forty years ago, many researchers have since found that the learning environment varies significantly across different prisons. The concept of 'learning' and 'working' prisons was introduced by Pike and Adams (2012) as two ends of a spectrum of different learning environments. A 'learning' prison reflects the students' perceptions of a good supportive environment which actively supports independent learning. A 'working' prison describes a prison in which work, or prison-based interventions, take priority and where there

Table 1: Key milestones in delivering OU services in secure environments

Date	Government policy	Prison technology	OU technology	OU prison education management
1970s	Home Office prison education scheme developed		TV/radio programmes to support printed teaching materials Residential schools	1971 – first courses available 22 students in two prisons. By 1976, 142 students in 14 prisons in England and Wales (Forster, 1976)
1980s	Prison governors control their own education budget Education run by local education authorities		TV/radio programmes supplemented by video/audio-cassette Residential schools	150 students in 31 prisons (Weinbren, 2014). Printed materials and video recordings of TV programmes Regional links with prisons and visits from tutor-councillors
1990s	Prison Service Instruction (PSI) defines delivery of higher education	TVs in cells. Some computers in education and libraries. Education prioritised (min. 10 hours per week)	Emails to facilitate tutor contact Internet Web 1.0; interactive integrated multi-media Virtual Learning Environment (VLE)	300 students in 80 prisons Printed materials and video/audio cassettes Regional management of tutor visits
2000+	Local colleges responsible for prison education	Good intranets (such as those in HMP Whitemoor) and other inconsistent, ad hoc technological solutions	Social media; internet Web 2.0; Virtual Worlds, enhanced VLE	1,500 students in 120 prisons Printed offline study packs and CDs Prison Liaison Group works across the country
2005	Reducing reoffending through skills and employment (Green Paper) published. Offender Learning and Skills Service (OLASS) formed	Technology more controlled. Polaris (proof of concept) in eight London prisons	Increased use of discussion forums for collaborative activities	Traffic light system developed to identify which OU courses can be offered in prison
2006–7	OLASS rolled out (see Halsey et al, 2006)	Virtual Campus trialled in East region (with offline Access courses)	Additional software requirements for many OU modules	Rapid reduction of courses available. OU review of prison education provision and new government contract for higher education delivery in prison

(continued)

Date	Government policy	Prison technology	OU technology	OU prison education management
2008–9	Government report *Meeting needs?** OLASS Phase 2	Virtual Campus rolled out across most prisons		Central coordination for prisons and OLASS. OL Development Group and first bespoke prison prospectus
2010–11	New PSI for higher education: PSI 33/2010: Open University, higher education and distance learning OLASS Phase 3		Secure version of VLE developed as 'Walled Garden' – online Access courses available via Virtual Campus	Introduction of tuition fee loans (end of subsidised study except for Access modules) OU moves to centralised administration and closes regional offices
2012–13	PSI updated for new funding, six-year rule restriction on loan eligibility OLASS Phase 4		Increased use of online tutorials to replace face-to-face delivery in regional centres	New OU team refers to students in prison as 'students' rather than 'offender learners' and offers specialist study support from registration through to graduation
2014–15	Prisons Minister, Chris Grayling, bans books being sent into prisons – overturned after appeal by prisoner in HMP Send		Learn7 platform developed to host secure VLE	OU prison student numbers fall below 1,000 due to funding changes
2016–17	Coates (2016) review of education in prison	Stand-alone laptops made available to some OU students for use in education centres	Free OpenLearn short courses made available in offline format in some prisons	Central team (Students in Secure Environments) grows to 12 staff. New Scholarship funding for first level 1 module. 1,450 students in 120 prisons
2018–19	New Prison Education Framework with greater governor control of budgets and expectation of use of technology in education	Investment in IT infrastructure across the estate to make it fit for purpose	120 modules available on Learn7 20 OpenLearn short courses on Virtual Campus	Commitment to provide laptops for students once Ministry of Justice approval for devices is agreed. 1,800 students in 120 prisons

*House of Commons Committee of Public Accounts (2008).

is little time or space for learning. OU students consider themselves almost invisible in such an environment; usually they are required to attend workshops during the day and are unable to use libraries as they are rarely open in the evening or at weekends.

Understandably, the ethos of a prison is also heavily dependent on the senior management team. Some governors acknowledge the importance of education, some are OU graduates themselves and others encourage their staff to study, thus reducing the divide between staff and prisoners (Worth, 1996). However, much of the good work in prison education is carried out by individuals who work 'in an atmosphere of good will and cooperation, often in spite of rather than because of prevailing regimes' (Hurry et al, 2012, p 28) and OU coordination is no exception.

Distance learning can be a lonely activity and students in prison may experience severe isolation. Researchers (for example Hughes, 2012; Pike, 2014) have identified that the support of 'significant others' can help to overcome this isolation and alleviate some of the many difficulties of studying in prison. These 'significant others' may be family, friends, peers, staff within the prison or OU tutors. McFarlane and Morris (2018) found that when students were actively involved in a study community or a student council, which allowed them to suggest improvements to the system, their levels of engagement increased, leading to increased confidence and higher overall assignment scores. Hopkins and Farley (2014) identified a wide set of social and cultural issues associated with learning in prison and with prior experiences of learning, recognising that social interaction is fundamental to learning, but is often missing in a prison setting due to security restrictions.

This interaction is offered in part by the OU tutor, the main academic contact for the prison student. The distance learning model adopted by the OU allocates a tutor to every student so although prison students are not able to participate in group tutorials, either online or in the community, they do receive individual support from a tutor, with detailed feedback on each assignment and, depending on the module, through face-to-face or telephone tutorials. Students on many level 1 modules can typically expect three or four tutorials and these visits can help them to feel part of a wider learning community.

Key challenges for tutors relate mostly to communication, as contact with their student is always via an intermediary in the prison. Arrangements for face-to-face visits can take a long time to organise and, with many students still hand-writing their assignments, tutors sometimes need to adjust the way they mark assignments and provide feedback. Many tutors go to great lengths to support their students in prison, even when students are transferred across the country with little warning. The importance of this support is fully acknowledged by students:

> the drive and determination of the Open University tutors I have had during my studies. Without a doubt, without them and their constant, active engagement with me and their encouragement when I wanted to give it all up I would not have completed my studies. (Liam, former OU prison student)

Further social interaction may be offered through Prison University Partnerships (Prisoners' Education Trust, nd), in which university students, including some OU students, join with prison students for seminars and short courses. These have been running in different forms for many years and are increasing in popularity, as institutions recognise the mutual benefit for participants. The OU offers accreditation pathways which enable prison students to build on the learning they gain from these partnerships and help them to select appropriate progression opportunities.

Learning in a digital world

Prisoners are a group that remains almost entirely disconnected from the 21st-century digital 'network society' described by Castells (2004). Most prisoners still have no direct access to internet-enabled computers, although there have been moves to improve access in prisons for many years. Digital skills are vital for everyday existence; without them prisoners are significantly disadvantaged, and less likely to successfully integrate back into society upon release.

It is understandable that prison policy makers prioritise security concerns and therefore adopt a risk-averse approach to the use of technology. However, the ubiquitous use of technology in modern life has led to a competing agenda for policy makers, who are also required to consider how people in prison are equipped to lead law-abiding lives upon release. Johnson and Hail-Jares (2016) cite this risk-averse approach as contributing to an increasing digital 'isolation' among prisoners with limited access to technology.

In the 1990s (and early 2000s) there was ad hoc development of technologies for learning, dependent on individual governors and technology-enthusiast staff in their employment. Pike and Adams (2012) found that, counter-intuitively, high security prisons were more supportive of access to technology than the lower security prisons. For example, the Whitemoor Wide Web was an intranet in a very high security prison. It provided, for a short time, a learning environment which looked very much like the internet but was totally secure, even allowing students to use the Moodle forums (internally), which encouraged a learning community (Pike, 2009). However, these ad hoc technologies were gradually closed down as the prison service sought a more consistent (secure) system. The first iteration of this was POLARIS, a 'proof of concept' trial of online computers in London prisons with an external server (Schuller, 2009). The system worked well but was considered difficult to roll out across the estate because it required implementation over multiple prisons. Instead, the Virtual Campus (VC) was developed to provide secure access to selected employment and education websites. After initial trials it was extended to most prisons and intended to streamline and modernise the system of delivery for education, training and employment (Turley and Webster, 2010). The value of the VC has been undermined by outdated technology and inadequate infrastructure in prisons which render many websites unusable. Access to the OU's secure Virtual Learning Environment (VLE) (Learn7) which is hosted on the VC is often restricted by OLASS provider priorities and regime requirements. However, there are early indications that recent upgrades and developments in secure solutions will facilitate improved digital access and the OU is instrumental in driving these changes.

Post-release challenges and support networks

Longitudinal research (Pike, 2014) found that, although OU students expected some difficulties upon release from prison, they were unprepared for the intensity of those difficulties, and the challenges of maintaining the positive benefits of their prison education. The stigma of being labelled an 'ex-con' can severely challenge a student identity and homelessness can reduce newly built confidence. Other difficulties included a lack of structure to life, lack of easily accessible information, and lack of technology and the skills to use it. Since 21st-century living is digital, from job applications and shopping to claiming benefits, lack of digital skills is a major barrier to integration into society. Some students become alienated from their family and social background but have not yet fitted into a life to which they aspire, with one foot in and one foot out of their previous life. Belonging to a learning community post-release, helps to maintain a positive student identity and eases integration into society (Forster, 1976; Hughes, 2012; Pike, 2014).

In order to continue studying post-release, students require much support 'through the gate' and a support network is vital (Pike and McFarlane, 2017). This support should start before release and continue for as long as required after release. Peer mentoring both in prison and post-release is found to be especially successful as the mentor values the responsible role and the mentee has trusted support. The OU has recently developed a scheme to lend laptops to released prison students and the OU Students Association has dedicated support for its ex-prison students. The opportunity to belong to a learning community can also develop via the Prison University Partnership pathway (Prisoners' Education Trust [PET], nd) and successful schemes such as the PET Alumni group, are demonstrating good practice in this area. Indeed, the academic voice of those who have studied in prison is increasingly recognised as offering an informed perspective on the criminal justice system based on first-hand experience (Honeywell, 2013; Aresti and Darke, 2016); the Prisoner Policy Network, coordinated by the Prison Reform Trust, is an example of how such experiences are starting to influence government policy (Wainwright et al, 2019).

The student journey: from enquiry to graduation and beyond

Distance learning is a complex activity, requiring many stages of input and support to guide the student through initial enquiry, course choice, funding applications, development of study skills, assignment submission and eventually to graduation and celebration. For students in prison, all these stages of the journey must be completed via an intermediary, staff within the prison who act as gatekeepers, advocates, administrators and often timekeepers for the student journey. The vital role of these staff is often under-acknowledged, and yet this support can be crucial to students' success. Moreover, the rapid change of responsibility for prison education and the numbers of different organisations involved, has often resulted in confusion in staff roles and an inconsistent level of support to students.

Becoming a student

The journey to becoming a student is a long and often emotional one, requiring a level of self-belief, plenty of support and encouragement from 'significant others':

I soon realised that for once in my life, I took the right course of action and made the correct decision to study. Furthermore, with the OU, it changed my life and suddenly I felt better inside. It made all my everyday problems, prison and other adversaries easier to accept and solve. I had a purpose. (Student A)

Prisoners applying for OU study, must first seek permission through the Sift (the prison's complex screening procedure). Then, they must either fund themselves or apply for funding through charitable trusts such as the PET or, since 2012, for a government tuition fee loan, as they are required to pay the same tuition fees as mainstream students. This raises several issues relating to higher education provision within the secure estate (Champion and Edgar, 2013) including the range of courses available, access to learning materials, and value for money, as well as the requirement for additional support to complete the funding paperwork since this can be daunting and cannot be done online.

Not all students can apply for a loan. Current loan repayment requirements dictate that students must be within six years of their release to be eligible for a tuition fee loan. This government restriction reduces the possibilities for prisoners serving longer sentences to gain access to higher education and is being strenuously challenged.

However, the introduction of tuition fees has led to students in prison developing their identities as discerning consumers with high expectations around levels of study support and access to library resources. This presents further challenges for the OU in trying to meet these expectations within the designated security restrictions. Creative solutions have been developed which build on the benefits of collaborative working and seek to minimise the difficulties of studying in prison. One example is OU research events, in which OU academics deliver a short seminar and Question and Answer session with a group of students in prison. Feedback from all participants has been very positive, with one academic describing it as 'one of the most profound educational experiences I have been involved in'. Increased understanding of restricted educational environment in prisons also helps academics to consider how they write teaching materials to meet the needs of this diverse student body.

Since 2009 there has been a dedicated OU prospectus for students in prison which provides details of the pathways and qualifications available across all faculties. There are currently 130 modules offered for study in prison, with the most popular being social science, business management and maths.

Learning how to study

Once the learning journey has begun, the student must learn how to study at a distance. Historically, study materials were provided in print format and today many students continue to express a preference for books (Ellis et al, 2017). The OU is a global university, its distance learning model is designed for scale and, as there is no entry requirement, is designed to cater for a variety of educational needs. This has led to a Universal Design for Learning approach to develop learning environments, including online programmes, to meet the diverse needs of students (Seale, 2014). This enables accessibility issues to be factored in to the study materials design (Galley, 2015) but also leads to a competing agenda to deliver a technology-enhanced learning experience while not excluding those students with restricted access to technology (Cross et al, 2015). This is particularly relevant in the prison setting. While paper-based activities lend themselves easily to offline study; collaborative, online and research-based activities are a huge challenge, with alternatives required to ensure OU students' experience in prison is comparable with that of mainstream students.

Most OU students in prison are now offered study materials both in print and via a reduced version of the VLE (Learn7), hosted on the VC (see Table 1). This is based on the original materials but adapted to remove activities deemed inappropriate or requiring external internet access via hyperlinks, student forums or collaborative activities.

In a study carried out before the introduction of the VC, Hancock (2010) tested the provision of alternative activities to students in prison, with encouraging results, concluding that it enabled students to succeed in the course without disadvantage compared to their peers. Hancock adapted her study materials in direct response to student feedback, capitalising on her role as a tutor, having particular success with the incorporation of anonymised forums to allow students to participate. Alternative collaborative activities are now sometimes provided to replicate online forum discussions which help to provide a sense of learning community (McFarlane and Morris, 2018).

Study skills sessions, to assist groups of students with note taking, essay writing and exam techniques, are also now being offered in a number of prisons by OU tutors. This brings the benefits of a face-to-face teaching session, as well as helping to establish a learning community within the prison in which peer-support can be offered. Provision of these sessions is encouraging more students to take up higher-level study and improving the assignment scores of participating students.

A particular concern of the discerning student consumer in prison is the lack of access to the OU online library and to address this, a library support scheme has been developed in partnership with the OU Students Association. Student volunteers respond to written requests from students in prison for assistance in sourcing articles from the online library. Some of the volunteers are ex-prisoner students who are acutely aware of the situation, are keen to support their peers, and are seeing benefits to their own study too.

Some prison education departments employ an OU Orderly, an OU student in the prison, who assists with administration and promotion of distance learning activities. These roles offer students a responsible position and a greater sense of ownership of their learning, which has led to increased study success (McFarlane and Morris, 2018). Assignment submission dates are tracked and reminders given, meaning all students are more likely to submit on time and to ask for help when needed.

In learning how to study, there are many barriers to be overcome and a key factor in determining future success is 'readiness for learning' described in 'OU study: The benefits'. This highlights the importance of initial assessment to establish the most appropriate level of education and Coates (2016) describes how a rigorous assessment process, subject to regular review, can help to set aspirational targets. It is right to be aspirational, because in spite of the challenges of prison-based study, success rates are equivalent to those for general population students, with some prison students achieving distinctions (over 85 per cent) even on modules which are largely digital in content. This is how one student described their experience:

> My new addiction was studying and the adrenaline coupled with that meant I was now experiencing a new high. Every time I opened an envelope from the OU containing the results of my coursework or essay, I felt good within myself.

Successful students adopt a range of strategies to allow for their personal circumstances, such as completing assignments a week before deadline to allow time for postage or choosing to study at 4 am when the wing is quiet. Any contact with OU tutors is highly valued and students normally relish the opportunity to ask questions and discuss their thoughts.

Progressing and moving on

Within the prison estate, transfers between establishments, sometimes with very little prior notice, are common and can cause additional challenges for OU students and their tutors, especially if the student's printed study materials do not move with them. Since the support for distance learning can vary so much across the prison estate, some students have been known to try to refuse a move when they have an assignment or an exam due imminently.

Preparing for release while engaged with OU studies can be similarly problematic. OU data indicates that module pass rates for released students are about half those for students in prison, when they do not benefit from pre-release information and the learning community support described in 'OU study: The challenges'. A range of additional support has recently been introduced for released students including the loan of a laptop to support development of digital skills, additional tutor support to facilitate integration into the tutor group, and use of the inter-library loan scheme, which allows access to a local university library.

Support and recognition of the individual circumstances of each student is vital, as highlighted by this OU student:

> I had served 15 years ... feeling that no-one cares and I did not know where or even if I would fit into society. I have been released just over a year now and it has been difficult at times. I found the readjustment after so long overwhelming.

However, many students manage to complete their studies in prison. In the 2017/18 academic year, 213 achieved higher education qualifications (certificates, diplomas or degrees) and 17 degree ceremonies were held in prisons to celebrate these achievements. Some students were permitted to attend a public OU degree ceremony (for example at the Barbican in London) as part of their day release arrangements, while others chose to delay their celebrations until they were released. As with all OU students, this is a momentous occasion, often with friends and family present, and students wear their gowns with pride. It is an important way of recognising their achievements, as reflected in this extract from a speech made by a student at his degree ceremony:

> Open University study has coincided with radical change in the trajectory of my life since I started in 2008 ... Now I have a first-class honours degree proudly displayed on the wall, years of consistent 'model' prisoner behaviour behind me and a progressive transfer imminent as I work towards release ... My degree has given me confidence to believe

I can yet claim a place in the world and thrive. Those are Open University lessons I will never forget.

Conclusion: onward and upward

As the OU celebrates its 50th anniversary, there is inevitably consideration of what the future holds for the institution and for its students. A key priority for students in prison is the development of secure in-cell technology which will enable students to access the same high quality, digital study materials as all other registered OU students. Developments in this area are gathering pace and there is an optimistic view that within the next year laptops will be provided to OU students in prison, albeit on a small scale to begin with. This will have benefits to the OU, as well, enabling a greater focus on developing digital skills and moving away from the costly process of adapting materials to a printed format.

When in-cell technology becomes more widely available, it will be possible to offer OpenLearn courses on a range of subjects. These free short courses are available on open licence so that others, including colleges and other providers, can copy and re-use the content for their own teaching and learning. They might serve as a taster, an introduction to higher and distance education, or just to bridge the gap between compulsory- and post-compulsory-level learning, and will be delivered in partnership with the education providers under the new contract arrangements starting in April 2019. In particular, the development of new Everyday English and Maths courses which cover Functional Skills level 1 and 2 will offer an experience of supported digital learning to a much wider group of students.

The OU is a proud member of the Prisoner Learning Alliance, representing the voice of the prison education sector, including small organisations, charities and people with lived experience of prison. This alliance is campaigning for better use of technology within prisons for educational and social purposes. It is also supporting staff training, seeking improved ways to share good practice across establishments and will be monitoring impact of the new funding arrangements on education provision in prisons.

Many hundreds of OU students will testify to the benefits of higher-level study in prison, as evidenced by the chapters in this book. Higher education has an important place in the prison education system just as it does in mainstream society. Increasingly, the academic voice of these students is contributing to policy debate and influencing change, bringing a new dimension to the benefits of a positive student identity.

> Study with The Open University has given me the sense of new direction, a new future. All the years of struggling and perseverance have paid off. Knowledge is power, and I know that I can go a lot further than I ever imagined I could. I know I can fulfil any ambition.

Currently only about 2 per cent of the prison population are studying at university level, and it is hoped that the eagerly anticipated developments in technology, as well as changes to funding regulations, could allow OU study to be 'opened up' to many more students, with the introduction of OpenLearn courses meaning that this is not restricted to those at higher education level.

Meanwhile, many of the challenges of navigating the delivery of higher education across inter-organisational barriers remain. It is likely that a study experience completely equal to that of mainstream students will never be fully achieved, but as the use of technology develops and attitudes change, there is the potential for the gap to reduce, with an increased focus on compensating for the disadvantages of being in prison. Pursuing this ambition is consistent with the OU's mission to be 'Open to people, places, methods and ideas'.

There are some clear milestones to aim for over the next ten years, notably the introduction of in-cell devices, including connectivity to allow more established links with family members; use of an online study library; access to free OpenLearn courses to offer pathways into formal learning; and improved learning communities. There is a lot to be optimistic about, as well as much to celebrate.

References

Adams, A. and Pike, A. (2008) 'Evaluating empowerment and control of HE e-learning in a secure environment', paper presented to British Educational Research Association (BERA) conference, Edinburgh. http://oro.open.ac.uk/24174/.

Aresti, A. and Darke, S. (2016) 'Practicing convict criminology: lessons learned from British academic activism', *Critical Criminology*, 24.

Behan, C. (2014) 'Learning to escape: prison education, rehabilitation and the potential for transformation', *Journal of Prison Education and Reentry*, 1(1): 20–31.

Castells, M. (2004) 'Informationalism, networks and the network society: a theoretical blueprint', in M. Castells (ed.) *The network society: A cross-cultural perspective*, Cheltenham: Edward Elgar, pp 3–45.

Champion, N. and Edgar, K. (2013) *Through the gateway: How computers can transform rehabilitation*, London: Prison Reform Trust.

Champion, N. and Noble, J. (2016) *What is prison education for? A theory of change exploring the value of learning in prison*, London: Prisoners' Education Trust, www.prisonerseducation.org.uk/wp-content/uploads/2019/04/Theory-of-Change-Report.pdf.

Clark, R. (2016) 'How education transforms: Evidence from the experience of Prisoners' Education Trust on how education supports prisoner journeys', *Prison Service Journal*, 225: 3–8.

Coates, Dame Sally (2016) *Unlocking potential: A review of education in prison*, London: Ministry of Justice.

Costelloe, A. (2014) 'Learning for liberation, teaching for transformation: can education in prison prepare prisoners for active citizenship?', *Irish Journal of Applied Social Studies*, 14(1): 30–6.

Council of Europe (1990) Education in Prison: Recommendation No. R (89) 12 adopted by the Council of Ministers of the Council of Europe on 13 October 1989 and explanatory memorandum, Strasbourg: Council of Europe. www.epea.org/wp-content/uploads/Education_In_Prison_02.pdf.

Cross, S., Sharples, M. and Healing, G. (2015) *E-pedagogy of handheld devices 2013 survey: Patterns of student use for learning*. http://proxima.iet.open.ac.uk/public/2015-01-RI-E-Pedagogy-of-handheld-devices-2013-survey.pdf.

Duwe, G. and Clark, V. (2014) 'The effects of prison-based education on recidivism and employment', *The Prison Journal*, 94(4): 454–78.

Ellis, E., Gallagher, A. and Peasgood, A. (2017) *Study behaviours in an increasingly digital world: Learning habits, top tips and 'study hacks' questionnaire survey*, Milton Keynes: The Open University.

Forster, W. (1976) 'The higher education of prisoners', Vaughan Papers in Adult Education No. 21. Leicester: University of Leicester.

Galley, R. (2015) *Learning design at The Open University: Introducing methods for enhancing curriculum innovation and quality*, Milton Keynes: The Open University.

Halsey, K., Martin, K. and White, R. (2006) *The Implementation of OLASS: An assessment of its impact one year on*. Research report No. 810. Nottingham: Department for Education and Skills.

Hancock, V. (2010) 'Essential , desirable or optional? Making distance e-learning courses available to those without internet access', *European Journal of Open, Distance and E-Learning*, 2010(1): 1–11.

Honeywell, D. (2013) 'Doing hard time in the United Kingdom', in S. Richards (ed.) *Prisoners in solitary confinement: USP Marion and the Supermax movement*, Carbondale, IL: Southern Illinois University Press.

Hopkins, S. and Farley, H. (2014) 'A prisoners' island: Teaching Australian incarcerated students in the digital age', *Journal of Prison Education and Reentry*, 1(1): 42.

Hughes, E. (2012) *Education in prison: Studying through distance learning*, Farnham: Ashgate.

Hurry, J., Rogers, L., Simonot, M. and Wilson, A. (2012) *Inside education: The aspirations and realities of prison education for under 25s in the London area*, London: Centre for Education in the Criminal Justice System, Institute of Education.

Johnson, R. and Hail-Jares, K. (2016) 'Prisons and technology', in Y. Jewkes, B. Crewe and J. Bennett (eds) *Handbook on Prisons*, Oxford: Routledge, pp 278–92.

Knight, V. (2016) *Remote control: Television in prison*, London, Palgrave Macmillan.

Light, M., Grant, E. and Hopkins, K. (2013) *Gender differences in substance misuse and mental health amongst prisoners: Results from the Surveying Prisoner Crime Reduction (SPCR) longitudinal cohort study of prisoners*, London: Ministry of Justice Analytical Services.

McFarlane, R. and Morris, A. (2018) 'Developing the learner voice', *Advancing Corrections Journal*, 6: 151–60.

McNeill, F. (2014) 'Three aspects of desistance', Workshops. http://blogs.iriss.org.uk/discoveringdesistance/2014/05/23/three-aspects-of-desistance/.

Ministry of Justice (2010) *Compendium of reoffending statistics and analysis*. www.justice.gov.uk/downloads/statistics/mojstats/compendium-of-reoffending-statistics-and-analysis.pdf.

Ministry of Justice (2012) *Prison Service Instructions 2012: Open University unclassified*. www.justice.gov.uk/offenders/psis/prison-service-instructions-2012.

Ministry of Justice (2014) *Justice data lab re-offending analysis: Prisoners' Education Trust*. https://assets.publishing.service.gov.uk/government/uploads/system/uploads/attachment_data/file/270084/prisoners-education-trust-report.pdf.

Pike, A. (2009) 'Developing online communities to support distance learning in secure environments', in 7th International Conference on Education and Information Systems, Technologies and Applications: EISTA 2009, Orlando, FL, USA. http://oro.open.ac.uk/24175/.

Pike, A. (2014) *Prison-based transformative learning and its role in life after release*. Unpublished PhD thesis, The Open University, Milton Keynes, UK. http://oro.open.ac.uk/44618/.

Pike, A. and Adams, A. (2012) 'Digital exclusion or learning exclusion? An ethnographic study of adult male distance learners in English prisons', *Research in Learning Technology*, 20(4): 363–76.

Pike, A. and McFarlane, R. (2017) 'Experiences of post-secondary learning after prison: reintegrating into society', in P. Crane (ed.) *Life beyond crime: What do those at risk of offending, prisoners and ex-offenders need to learn?*, London: Lemos & Crane, pp 258–62. http://oro.open.ac.uk/52294/

Pike, A. and Hopkins, S. (2019) '"Education is transformational": positive identity through prison-based higher education in England and Wales', *International Journal of Bias, Identity and Diversity in Education*. http://oro.open.ac.uk/57143/.

Prisoners' Education Trust (nd) PUPiL Network. www.prisonerseducation.org.uk/what-we-do/work-with-universities/prison-university-partnerships-in-learning/.

Schuller, T. (2009) 'Crime and lifelong learning', IFLL thematic paper 5, Leicester: NIACE. www.learningandwork.org.uk/wp-content/uploads/2017/01/Crime-and-Lifelong-Learning-Thematic-Paper-5.pdf.

Seale, J. (2014) *E-learning and disability in higher education: Accessibility research and practice*, 2nd edn, Abingdon: Routledge.

Turley, C. and Webster, S. (2010) *Implementation and delivery of the testbeds virtual campus*, London: National Centre for Social Research.

Wainwright, L., Harriott, P. and Saajedi, S. (2019) *What incentives work in prison? A Prisoner Policy Network consultation*. www.prisonreformtrust.org.uk/Portals/0/Documents/PPN%20Incentives%20Report.pdf.

Weinbren, D. (2014) *The Open University: A history*, Manchester: Manchester University Press.

Williams, K., Papadopoulou, V. and Booth, N. (2012) *Prisoners' childhood and family backgrounds: Results from the Surveying Prisoner Crime Reduction (SPCR) longitudinal cohort study of prisoners*, Ministry of Justice Analytical Services Research Series 4/12.

Worth, V. (1996) 'Supporting learners in prison', in R. Mills and A. Tait (eds) *Supporting the learner in open and distance learning*, London: Pitman Publishing, pp 177–90.

VIGNETTE 1

Choosing my journey

Kamal Abdul

"I've reached page ten thousand and fifty-nine. Completed. I must do this. This is my life in front of me. Hold on, what does this all mean? Not a Skooby!" This is the very beginning of my time in prison, all those 11 Ramadans ago. Remand. Belmarsh. Trying to understand the case against me: "Joint Enterprise" and case-papers stacked up to my shoulders. Then the realisation my reading age was 11.

Once the post-conviction smoke had dispersed, a remedy for ignorance became paramount. I proudly became a student, of Education, Religion, Legal Studies and many other subjects. However, I faced a crossroads: continue straight as a conventional student, GCSE, A-level; or jump onto the (final charity funded) express motorway – Open University, ill-prepared for the long journey ahead. I knew this was an opportunity I could not lose. And, as one teacher reassured me, "Your tenacity will pull you through." Motivation and drive were certainly my strengths.

At the time the destination was clear, an earlier ambition, Structural Engineering. However, prison is never simple. Engineering courses were deemed a security risk within the high security estates. Thus, I had no choice but to study all the peripheral subjects related to Engineering. Mathematics, once an old enemy, now became an ally.

My studies began very nervously, unsure and always second guessing myself. However, deadlines would force me to overcome nerves and execute the task in hand. Just as the reputation that precedes it, mathematics proved to be very difficult. Nevertheless, learning had to be in layers, taking incremental steps which continuously reinforced itself, expanding my knowledge and ability. This was all very well; but my English needed some attention. Fortunately, I was able to enrol for an English A-level in my prison, alongside my OU studies. English became an escape from maths (a paradox), and today it remains a destination of creativity away from the 'shackles of mathematics'.

The journey into mathematics and engineering was very difficult within the secure environment. The lack of fellow students in the same subject really forced me to confront some tall walls alone. Equations which would keep me up days on end. However, perseverance would be rewarded, understanding would unveil itself, and a flood of confidence, enthusiasm and passion would return (stronger). I learnt to become very resourceful. Eventually I was permitted to study an engineering course and in an aim to bridge theory with practice, I joined the welding workshop, which proved to be equally as important as the OU course material. The workshop gave me access to materials, industry practices, and processes. In fact, we constructed small structures, magnifying my understanding.

Although my subject was uncommon, being around other students who had worked equally as hard, and had faced similar issues, reassured and encouraged my resolve. In spite of this, nothing would have been possible without all the wonderful librarians (non-prisoners) who have encouraged, supported and provided the security of a close OU community – something not easily achieved in prison. I will mention particularly HMP The Mount library and its diligent, hospitable librarians. (I may be biased, as I currently enjoy the OU coordinator role here at The Mount library; and boastfully count 38 OU students.)

From this unexpected choice, mathematics began to take a central role in my life. Unconsciously at first. My day-to-day activities became very methodical, analysing all things around me with a new lens. I discovered I had a new ability to understand multiple (entangled) complex ideas. Undeniably, I had changed; this surprising revelation at that very moment felt like I had been given a super power. Thus, the very fact I am able to communicate here with relative ease, my story (this being my first draft), demonstrates the vast change that I recognise in myself. One upon a time, a general application (to the wing office) would take numerous rewrites. Be it ability, confidence, or experience, all of which have given me the framework to continue to study, learn and develop many more skills for the future. Opening, I hope, doors, windows and gates.

Upon reflection, was it prison which gave me this opportunity? I do not see it that way, I have always dreamt of university. However, I am resoundingly grateful higher learning was not prevented within the prison environment. Rather, many barriers were removed and it was encouraged with support. I truly believe prison without higher learning would be a grave loss; not only to individuals but also to our society. Awareness is responsibility and motivation. Thereby I am optimistic Degrees of Freedom (those who have completed degrees in custody) will play a notable role in solving some of the challenges we face in our communities and in the wider world.

3

Pioneers and politics: Open University journeys in Long Kesh during the years of conflict 1972–75

Philip O'Sullivan and Gabi Kent

Introduction: unusual beginnings and the scope of this story

This chapter outlines the events which sparked the educational journeys of hundreds of loyalist and republican Open University (OU) students who were prisoners in British and Irish prisons during the conflict in and about Northern Ireland. While other prisons were also important sites of study, our story centres around the legacy of OU teaching at a particular place and time, namely at the Maze and Long Kesh prison near Belfast in Northern Ireland at the height of the conflict. This story is a testament and witness to the pioneering vision of educationalists and students whose paths crossed in the fight for the right to higher education and prefigures how these stories form part of the wider narrative of the conflict and eventual peace process in Northern Ireland.

This story starts with the escalation of the conflict in Northern Ireland on 9 August 1971, the resolve of two remarkable women, one a social worker and one an OU staff tutor, a donkey in a field and a disused Second World War US Army base. The importance of and connections between those events will be revealed by the narrative content of this chapter which draws on Time to Think, an oral history project started by OU staff in Belfast in 2010. These oral histories are now housed in a digital archive launched in 2019 (Open University, 2019).[1]

The OU involvement in teaching students who were in prison as a result of the conflict in Northern Ireland began at the height of the conflict in 1972 and ended in 2000, when, under the terms of the

1998 Good Friday Agreement, all political prisoners were released. Our aim is to tell one small but significant part of this story – namely how the OU first became involved in education with loyalist and republican prisoners in Long Kesh. It is worth noting that there is a body of literature on the definition, and use of the term 'political prisoner' and also a comparison with the term 'politically motivated prisoner' (Shirlow and McEvoy, 2008; Shirlow et al, 2010). For the purposes of this chapter the authors just use the terms 'internee' and 'prisoner'.

This account is not intended as a case study to illustrate a theoretical analysis. Nor is it a critical examination of the educational practice or pedagogy of the OU's supported distance learning methodology in a prison environment. The content of the interviews, including many extremely powerful reflections on teaching and learning, inevitably lend themselves to such further examination. Within the constraints of this chapter we limit ourselves to a more descriptive account of how the OU study of those in prison as result of the conflict started, including some key individuals and events of the time. In the conclusion we do suggest some emerging themes from this initial phase, and consider some of the political and educational impacts of these study journeys.

Politics, prison and pioneering women

The most recent phase of the 'Troubles' or conflict in Northern Ireland started in 1968. The OU was founded in 1969 in Milton Keynes, and the following year a regional office of the university opened in Belfast. On 9 August 1971, internment without trial was introduced in Northern Ireland by the British government, leading to the imprisonment without trial of hundreds of people, the vast majority of whom initially were nationalists and republicans. Internment proved a seminal event in the conflict in Northern Ireland and in the creation of a special chapter in the history of the OU. Yet, as much as these wider political, military and criminal justice processes were the structural context, the actions, determination and values of certain individuals at key moments equally shaped this story. The most important individuals in this regard, at the beginning of this story, were two women: a young academic called Jane Nelson and a social worker called Elizabeth (Liz) Kennedy.

Jane Nelson was appointed in 1970 as the first staff tutor (in Science) for the OU in Northern Ireland, and also taught in the Maze and Long Kesh prison from the early 1970s until her retirement in 2001. It was

Jane's receptiveness to a plea for help in the early 1970s which had an impact for students far beyond her own discipline.

With hundreds of people arrested under the new policy of internment, and increasingly short of space to contain the expanding prison population, the Northern Ireland government decided to open up a detention camp known as the Long Kesh Internment Centre, on the site of the disused former RAF Long Kesh airfield. The airfield had first opened in 1941 and, from 1942 to 1946, was the temporary headquarters for the US Army Air Force. More recently the site had been used as a barracks for British soldiers sent to Northern Ireland after the outbreak of civil disorder in August 1969.

From Jane's interview we learn how she was an eyewitness to the development of the site when visiting a friend who lived near the Long Kesh site in the Maze townland area. This friend kept a donkey in some adjacent fields and told her there was "a prison being built beside my donkey". Nissen huts left over since the Second World War were being redeveloped and surrounded by wire fencing and security towers to house the internees. Jane Nelson then recalls a phone call in early 1972:

> A social worker attached to the prison rang me, and her name was Miss Kennedy … She said she'd heard about the OU. She said, 'People interned in Long Kesh are in a terrible state. They don't know anything. They don't know why they're there, they don't know how long they're going to be there, and they have no facilities. They are being kept away, taken away from their homes and being kept in very poor conditions with a lot of people, strangers, they don't know.' … She said 'People are finding it very hard, psychologically and emotionally, to cope with their situation. They have to have an outlet and The Open University can give them one.' (Nelson, 2012)

Elizabeth Kennedy was the Senior Welfare Officer in Long Kesh Internment Camp in 1971. In response to this pivotal telephone call from Elizabeth Kennedy to Jane Nelson, the OU started what its student newspaper *Sesame* referred to in May 1972 as 'the OU's oddest study centre' in the Long Kesh Internment Centre. Following the request from Miss Kennedy, Jane and her two colleagues in the new Belfast regional office, Maurice McNicholl and Bill Lindsay, undertook to help.

At first Jane encountered some resistance and bureaucracy in trying to get internal OU approval. From Jane's 1972 diary we can see that on 8 February 1972 she met with the chair of the admissions committee on prison education to whom she had written saying the people interned in Northern Ireland shouldn't be excluded from OU education. Jane said that the chair was unimpressed and all he asked was who was going to pay the fees. It later became clear that any OU education for the internees would have to be met by voluntary means, not by state funding. When Jane told an old friend in Cork about this funding problem, he contacted Cristoir de Baroid, a socialist republican (also from Cork), who confirmed the committee of a local voluntary organisation called 'Between' would stand the fees. With the promise of funding sorted, Jane and Bill started simultaneous negotiations with the civil service of the Northern Ireland government (based at Stormont) who were legally responsible for the internees, and the OU at its head office in Milton Keynes.

Jane and Bill met the civil servant in charge of internees on 11 February 1972. He explained "that these internees were not prisoners and because they were not prisoners, they had no rights, for example, to education and we couldn't rely on any legislation that provided for exercise of the right to education" (Nelson, 2012). Jane describes being taken aback when informed that internees, as compared to sentenced or remand prisoners, had no statutory right to education. As the civil servant had no authority to help, Jane and Bill then had a crucial meeting four days later on 15 February with the relevant Minister in the Department of the Prime Minister of Northern Ireland, G.B. Newe, who was more sympathetic and willing to help. Jane recalls that his backing was key to "unlocking the door to the idea that we would establish education in the form of Open University courses in Long Kesh" (Nelson, 2012).

At the same time Jane was lobbying the OU to also formally approve teaching at Long Kesh and used her powers of influence to achieve a majority vote at a decisive university committee meeting on 17 February at which the students were officially admitted. Jane's determination to involve both the Northern Ireland government and the university together – to let each authority know the other supported and approved OU education in Long Kesh – succeeded. In an intense period of nine days in February 1972, with Jane and Bill writing letters, lobbying relevant decision makers, and as the result of a series of meetings with both the Northern Ireland government and the OU at Milton Keynes, approval from both parties was achieved. OU education in Long Kesh for the internees would go ahead, facilitated by Liz Kennedy on the inside. By the end of February 1972 the first 10 students were registered and so OU study for internees in Long Kesh began.

Long Kesh expands to more than an internment camp

By 1972 the prison for remand and sentenced prisoners in Belfast, Crumlin Road Gaol, was full to capacity. These were people on remand or sentenced under the Civil Authorities (Special Powers) Act (1922) and subsequent emergency and anti-terrorism legislation. Republican prisoners staged hunger strikes for political status which was effectively conceded by the British government in the form of Special Category Status. This was afforded to both Republican and Loyalist prisoners.

Originally Long Kesh only held republican internees, but due to lack of space elsewhere the first loyalist remand prisoners came in August 1972, and sentenced loyalist and republican prisoners (once sentenced they became Special Category Status prisoners) arrived in December 1972. While initially intended to be a temporary camp for internees, Long Kesh was therefore extended in 1973 to accommodate the influx of these sentenced Republican and Loyalist prisoners. By 1973 it was estimated that "there may have been up to fifteen hundred prisoners and internees held within those confines" (McCullough, 2012).

The sentenced prisoners were likewise housed in a collection of Nissen huts known as compounds – also described by the prisoners as "cages" because of the surrounding tall wire fencing – segregated according to their political and military affiliations. This was in a different area of the Long Kesh site, away from the internees. The geography of the Long Kesh site is important to picture. Each compound or cage contained four large Nissen huts each containing 30 iron prison beds (Smith, 2014) and the compounds and huts were identical to the prisoner of war camps depicted in Second World War films. (This was only 27 years after the end of the Second World War so this was less dramatic than it may appear now some 50 years on.)

> Living in an open army-style Nissen hut with thirty beds in each hut, we had relatively more freedom of association, and of course this allowed prisoners to sit in groups and discuss matters of interest. (McCullough, 2012)

Notably, loyalists and republicans were segregated. The three loyalist paramilitary organisations in the loyalist compounds were the UVF (Ulster Volunteer Force), the Red Hand Commandos (RHC) – though essentially the UVF and RHC were sister organisations with very close ties – and the UDA (Ulster Defence Association). On the republican side were the Provisional IRA (Irish Republican Army) and the Official IRA. Each faction had several compounds – they communicated between them using their own semaphore system, the codes for which they constantly changed to remain secure from the guards in the overlooking watchtowers. In his interview, McCullough recalls that:

> By 1974, each faction had almost complete autonomy within their cage or compound. The factions organised themselves along military lines. Each compound had an appointed Officer Commanding, hut sergeants and volunteers who adhered to a code-of-conduct in which they undertook their daily routines. It was organised, efficient and seemed an obviously easier way to maintain discipline and control for both the prisoners and the prison authorities. (McCullough, 2012)

For the next phase of this history it is crucial to note that this structured organisation of each compound was managed by the prisoners themselves and included an Education Officer. It is to education that the focus now turns.

The struggle for education in the compounds of Long Kesh

By late 1972, OU study was still only available to internees and funded by a voluntary donation. The battle for the right to formal education provision for sentenced prisoners however had yet to be fought. The education of sentenced prisoners, unlike internees, was the domain of the Northern Ireland Office. Here the demand for higher education was led by the various political and military groupings themselves. It is this pioneering role of loyalists and republicans in bringing OU education into the compounds of Long Kesh that we turn to next.

Four students who were among the first group of sentenced prisoners to study with the OU in 1974 and 1975 pick up the story. They are Ronnie McCullough from the UVF/RHC; Noel Quigley from the Provisional IRA; Brendan Mackin from the Official IRA and William 'Plum' Smith also from the UVF/RHC. All four were among the first group of sentenced prisoners moved into Long Kesh from Crumlin Road Gaol in 1973.

Ronnie McCullough left school at 15, gained a City and Guilds certificate in 1971 and was imprisoned in 1972. He was in the first group of loyalists to be transferred to the newly opened UVF/RHC compounds in Long Kesh. Ronnie first studied O-levels and then, in 1974, was in the first group of Special Category prisoners to study with the OU, taking courses in social sciences and the arts. Later Ronnie became Education Officer for the UVF/RHC in Long Kesh and their education representative on the Camp Educational Committee – this was a committee comprised of representatives from all factions in Long Kesh.

Sentenced prisoners already had a system of self-education and political education while in prison. But there was also an understanding of the importance of education and its value both individually and collectively among loyalists and republicans. Ronnie recounts that initially their prisoners held political seminars but, under the guidance of Gusty Spence, the overall UVF/RHC Commander within the camp, "they were directed towards educational classes. Gusty recognised the need for remedial learning and to that end he appointed a faction educational officer whose role would be to assess educational needs and to have those needs requested to the prison authorities" (McCullough, 2012).

All of the groups understood that they were not going to be going anywhere for quite some time. As Ronnie McCullough (2017) put it, the feeling was "we may as well get our heads down and try and improve our lot, try and improve facilities within the camp for the benefit of our people. Uppermost in the fight for improved conditions was education and recreation." This focused people's minds on the importance of the struggle for education.

Brendan Mackin was Officer Commanding of the Official IRA in Long Kesh. He had left school at 14 with no qualifications and was imprisoned in his late teens in Crumlin Road Gaol in 1972. Brendan was one of the Official IRA prisoners on hunger strike in 1972 for political status and one of their negotiators. After the granting of Special Category Status Brendan was moved in 1973 to the newly created Official IRA compound in Long Kesh. In 1974 Brendan was in the first group of Special Category prisoners to study social sciences with the OU. Mackin also realised the importance of education, noting that: 'there was a general acceptance that education was a good way forward' (Mackin, 2011).

Noel Quigley, who was 24 when he was imprisoned in Crumlin Road Gaol in 1972, was one of the Provisional IRA prisoners who was on the hunger strike for political status. In 1973 Noel was among the first group of prisoners to be transferred from Crumlin Road Gaol to the newly created compounds in Long Kesh. Having qualified as a quantity surveyor before prison, Noel was instrumental in setting up the informal education system for the Provisional IRA compounds and was their first Education Officer.

Quigley, in his interview, recalls that the general living conditions had to be sorted first before they turned their focus to the fight for education:

> Education wasn't exactly the first thought, I mean, our first thought was to try and improve our conditions because you don't exactly think about getting smart before you can live in some sort of comfortable conditions and the places we lived in the huts were leaking and you had to move the beds about at night you know, to miss the leaks and things like that, you know. So I mean it wasn't exactly our first thought but our first thought was getting ourselves organised ... and then we had to fight for different rights and conditions and things like that there before we could, before we could look for education. (Quigley, 2011)

William 'Plum' Smith left secondary school in Belfast after passing his O-levels and worked as an apprentice printer. Aged 18, he was imprisoned in 1972 in Crumlin Road and Armagh gaols and was among the first loyalists to be transferred to the newly opened UVF/RHC compounds at Long Kesh. With Ronnie McCullough he took turns as Education Officer for the UVF/RHC compounds where Smith taught English classes for fellow prisoners, gained an O-level in sociology and learned Irish from a republican prisoner in an adjacent compound. Smith was an early advocate for education in the compounds. Initially however, as Smith recalls in his memoirs, the 'authorities were not interested in providing prisoners with any sort of education' (Smith, 2014, p 110).

As McCullough also noted, the infrastructure was not in place for study:

> There was no established educational system, the prison library was really in its infancy and we wished to contribute to get better facilities for ourselves. So, the fight was on thereafter to try and improve the educational facilities. At the beginning it was a hard fight because the Camp Commandant as we called him at that time, I'll not mention any names, but it was that he was quite a hard man and he was quite an intransigent man. (McCullough, 2017)

Independently this account of a struggle was verified by Noel Quigley in his interview:

> [Y]ou had to fight for everything you got you see because they automatically tried to keep control over everything and of course we fought our corner, we had to try and get as much control as we could because you knew you were going to be there for a while, like you know, so you needed as much room to manoeuvre as you could and you were, they had already accepted that we were political prisoners, like you know, so we were entitled to the status that should be accorded to political prisoners. (Quigley, 2011)

Loyalists and republicans were also working together on a strategy to secure access to OU education. Mackin describes how there was a consensus between loyalists and republicans on the importance of introducing formal education:

> We had discussions with the UVF and UDA and they agreed to try and use this as a mechanism for people to take the time to educate themselves you know, both within the political process but also to personally educate as the vast majority in the cages had little or no academic background or little or no qualifications. (Mackin, 2011)

Noel Quigley became involved in negotiations for the OU to come into the compounds for sentenced prisoners. So too did Ronnie McCullough and William 'Plum' Smith. In his memoirs Smith recalls how the struggle for education progressed through a series of hard-won concessions:

> Despite great opposition from the prison authorities, and some prison staff, we eventually negotiated to bring in qualified lecturers to stimulate the men's thinking and also to attempt to set up Open University (OU) correspondence courses in the camp. (Smith, 2014, pp 110–11)

The early work by Jane Nelson and colleagues in securing education for internees also proved pivotal in their struggle. The groups drew on the experiences of internees as they began to lobby the prison authorities for their right to education. As Brendan Mackin explains:

> Some of the internees, I think they had started to do Open University studies and therefore from them ones we used that as the template for us to take that over to the sentenced prisoners ... We learnt from the experiences, the very fact that they had it we were saying we want it. All we were saying when it came to the negotiations with the authorities we were saying 'well really all we are asking is an extension of something that is already here.' (Mackin, 2011)

In 1973 representatives from the various groups requested, through the prison authorities, to meet with the OU. Shortly after his appointment as the first Regional Director of the OU in Northern Ireland, Gordon Macintyre found himself in an extraordinary meeting. In his written account of the period, Gordon describes how attendees included:

> Billy McKee ... Officer Commanding the Provisional IRA in the prison; Gusty Spence, Officer Commanding the UVF/RHC, and the Officers Commanding the Official IRA and the UDA ... No prison officer was present. The four men clearly knew each other, and treated each other, and me, with great courtesy and respect. All the men testified to the need for educational facilities within their ranks, and it seemed in keeping with this rather extraordinary occasion that I undertook to represent them all in passing on their pleas to the Northern Ireland Office.

Macintyre's efforts on behalf of the prisoners, proved to be successful. By the end of the year the Northern Ireland Office agreed that OU courses would be formally offered by the authorities to loyalists and republicans in the compounds of Long Kesh.

In February 1974 the first sentenced prisoners from the UVF/RHC, UDA and Official IRA embarked on OU study, with an option of a foundation course in social sciences and later in humanities. As Noel Quigley testifies, members of the Provisional IRA also studied with the OU in 1974 before withdrawing from education until 1984, a period of relative stability for them in the prison following the Hunger Strikes of 1981 and the escape of 1983. However, for political reasons, they studied separately from the other groups.

Fittingly, Elizabeth Kennedy, who had pioneered the introduction of education for internees in Long Kesh, oversaw this initial intake of loyalist and republican students. In April 1974, she handed over to the prison's first official Education Officer for the compounds of the Maze and Long Kesh Prison, Harry Hughes. (Notably Liz Kennedy became an OU student herself a year later, studying with the OU from 1975 to 1977.)

The legacy of those early pioneers

From a handful of OU students in the compounds in 1972, the numbers quickly grew. Within a decade, 10 per cent of all the loyalist and republican prisoners in the H Blocks (which housed prisoners convicted of 'scheduled' offences related to the Troubles) were studying with the OU and by the end of the peace process in 2000 hundreds of loyalists and republicans had undertaken educational journeys with the OU in British and Irish prisons.

These first two years of formally approved OU study (1974 and 1975) laid the foundations for a 30-year journey in OU education with loyalists and republicans in British and Irish prisons. From this emerged what was a unique model of higher education in which OU students and OU tutors and staff collectively determined the nature of that education. This ranged from the choice of modules on offer, to how study material was disseminated to others within the prisons.

The relationships forged between loyalists and republicans in these early days of study also had a lasting impact and, as many former students testify, played a not insignificant role in nurturing and supporting the peace process. Given that the compounds were separate self-contained areas within Long Kesh housing different political and military groups, people from these different groups who would not normally have an opportunity to mix. Studying with the OU therefore, provided an opportunity for men from these different compounds to meet. Relationships forged in these early days were to prove pivotal in opening up pathways for discussion and building trust during future peace negotiations and beyond. As Brendan Mackin explains:

> I think The Open University study group in many respects allowed people to discuss within a, their own environment, do you understand what I mean ... the very fact that we were studying together, there was, it built up a rapport between ourselves and others you know, so The Open University I think in many respects was probably, played perhaps an unwitting role in being a bit of a catalyst for further discussions to take place in the Camp. (Mackin, 2011)

The significance of both studying higher education courses, and of studying together with republicans was also evident to Smith at the time:

> This initiative was unique and very progressive [compared] to anything that had gone before ... The tutor would have access once per month and study huts that were located in a compound between the two football pitches would be used as joint educational facilities. This was a massive step for loyalists and republicans sitting down in the same room to be taught jointly by a tutor from the OU. (Smith, 2014, pp 112–13)

The pioneering students, who first sat down together in 1974 and 1975 all sought to continue their studies, although the political realities of life inside prison and financial realities outside of prison imposed some constraints.

William 'Plum' Smith was released half way through his university course in 1977 and describes how, once outside, he found there was little practical support for ex-prisoners to continue with their studies. The cost of books and course fees proved prohibitive. Plum was a member of the loyalist delegation for the negotiation of the Good Friday Agreement. In 2012 he worked for EPIC (Ex-Prisoners Interpretative Centre, working with ex-prisoners from a UVF or RHC background).

Brendan Mackin was one of the first students to study social sciences with the OU between 1974 and 1975 and again after his release. In Brendan's own words: "I left school at thirteen and a half and the only academic study I have done in my life has been The Open University studies." Brendan was offered a place in University College Galway and in Ruskin College but couldn't afford to take up these opportunities. Brendan went on to establish the Belfast Unemployed Resource Centre and was instrumental in community development.

Ronnie McCullough studied social sciences and arts with the OU between 1974 and 1976. Upon his release in 1977, he says "I did wish to continue with my studies and attain my degree but the main obstacle was the costs of so doing." Ronnie was part of the loyalist representatives involved in discussions with the British and Irish governments in the years before the Good Friday Agreement.

Noel Quigley was among the first cohort to study social sciences in 1974. He didn't sit his exams that year however, because of the disruption caused by a fire which burned down the Long Kesh Camp.

He was released in 1976 and imprisoned again in the republican wings of the H Block in 1980, where he took part in protests for political status. In 1985 he studied technology with the OU. After his release he worked with the republican political party, Sinn Féin, in North Belfast.

Conclusion

This has been story of pioneers and campaigners who fought for the right to higher education for loyalists and republican prisoners. This confluence of individuals and events led to the formation of relationships that would continue across time and place. In the words of the students, many of the connections forged through OU study became the foundation of negotiation pathways for the future peace process leading up to the Good Friday Agreement. More than this, these early days of the OU in Long Kesh was a unique experiment in how an education model can be co-created by students and staff. It is one which lasted for almost 30 years, with transformative impacts which are still being explored.

Acknowledgements

We are immensely grateful to our colleague and friend Jenny Meegan (Meegan et al, 2019), without whom this article would not have been possible, and to all of the participants in the Time to Think oral history archive project.

Note

[1] Time to Think: Open University journeys in British and Irish prisons during the years of conflict 1972–2000 is a unique oral history archive collection. It contains interviews on the educational journeys of loyalist and republican ex-prisoners, OU staff who tutored in the prisons or were involved in administration of study from the Belfast Office, prison education staff and OU students who worked in the prisons. You can explore our exhibition about Time to Think and excerpts from the collection on the OU digital archive: www.open.ac.uk/library/digital-archive.

References

Mackin, B. (2011) 'Brendan Mackin interview', in Time to Think: Open University journeys in British and Irish prisons during the years of conflict 1972–2000, Open University Ireland and The Open University digital archive.

Meegan, J., O'Sullivan, P. and Kent, G. (2019) 'Time to Think: An introduction' in Time to Think: Open University journeys in British and Irish prisons during the years of conflict 1972–2000, Open University Ireland and The Open University digital archive.

McCullough, R. (2012) 'Ronnie McCullough interview', in Time to Think: Open University journeys in British and Irish prisons during the years of conflict 1972–2000, Open University Ireland and The Open University digital archive.

McCullough, R. (2017) 'Ronnie McCullough interview', in Time to Think: Open University journeys in British and Irish prisons during the years of conflict 1972–2000, Open University Ireland and The Open University digital archive.

Nelson, J. (2012) 'Jane Nelson interview', in Time to Think: Open University journeys in British and Irish prisons during the years of conflict 1972–2000, Open University Ireland and The Open University digital archive.

Open University (2019) Time to Think: Open University digital archive, Milton Keynes: Open University. www.open.ac.uk/library/digital-archive/exhibition/152.

Quigley, N. (2011) 'Noel Quigley interview', in Time to Think: Open University journeys in British and Irish prisons during the years of conflict 1972–2000, Open University Ireland and The Open University digital archive.

Shirlow, P. and McEvoy, K. (2008) *Beyond the wire: Former prisoners and conflict transformation in Northern Ireland*, London: Pluto Press.

Shirlow, P., Tonge, J., McAuley J. and McGlynn, C. (2010) *Abandoning historical conflict? Former political prisoners and reconciliation in Northern Ireland*, Manchester: Manchester University Press.

Smith, W.P, (2014) *Inside man: Loyalists of Long Kesh – The untold story*, Newtownards: Colourpoint.

VIGNETTE 2

Avoiding the mind-numbing vortex of drivel …

Thomas

I had started my Open University (OU) studies prior to my conviction. I had completed the first of six years and had begun my second year just prior to my incarceration.

I was fortunate that the various men I shared a cell with were happy for me to continue my studies. One of them took inspiration from my studying and is currently halfway through his own BA (Hons) undergraduate degree.

To be denied my liberty hit me very hard. I had made a number of suicide attempts, thinking that my life was over. In fact, my time in prison was an opportunity to reassess my life, a time to take stock and see how I could make a meaningful contribution to society, having decided to turn my life around.

After being made redundant from my job, the original reason for starting the course was to improve my chances of securing work. Life with a criminal record is hard enough, anything one can do to augment the chances of employment should be seized with both hands.

Being banged up for long periods means that you have the opportunity to use the time wisely in an attempt to better your prospects when your release comes around – an energy-sapping alternative is to be sucked into the mind-numbing vortex of drivel that is broadcast on the terrestrial channels in the form of daytime tv and soap operas.

Access to the education department to support the learning process seemed to be very hit and miss (one of my TMAs [tutor-marked assessments] sat on someone's desk for ten days as the deadline came and went, but I had handed it in). It was a shame that the 'support' staff and I weren't on the same wavelength with regard to priorities. Why should they care? I'm someone who has committed an offence, and as such deserves to be locked up. Why should they exercise their duty of care, when not to do so, is a far easier option? I found that the enthusiasm of the prison education staff was not always mirrored by that of the wing staff.

For six of the nine months I spent at Brixton I was the Distance Learning Rep on the wing. My role was to encourage my fellow inmates to embark on distance learning courses where possible. The fact that one is able to dip one's toes in the academic pool with an OU foundation course is a brilliant idea and should be encouraged.

Gaining access to study materials was frustrating. One very prevalent problem I encountered was with men who had transferred from one establishment to another. Their study materials didn't always arrive with them. The OU should be informed when prisoners are transferred, but it would appear that this is one of the jobs that often fell between the cracks of (ir)responsibility.

The prison library visits were far too brief and irregular. Access to computers to write up assignments was limited. The positive side of this was that, come the exam, because my TMAs had been drafted, written and re-written by hand, my ability to write for three hours was not adversely impacted. Unlike fellow students who had become 'de-skilled' in handwriting techniques because they had used computers for their TMAs.

By working with the education staff, I was able to augment my stationery supplies to include items such as notepads, the occasional highlighter or different coloured pens – things that I had taken for granted in my life beyond the wall. But utterly invaluable to a prison student.

The variety of modules is greatly restricted for SiSE students (students in secure environments), which I found enormously frustrating as the courses I wanted to do were no longer available to me – for no discernible reason that I could determine, as they were not offence related. However, given the situation, I had to make do with the next best thing and count my blessings that some greatly appreciated form of distraction was available and I could focus my energies on something constructive (albeit not my first choice).

Post-release, the SiSE Support team, headed by Ruth McFarlane, have been utterly magnificent. They have proved to be the epitome of supportive, with improvements made on the non-computer study materials, advice on study-related financial support and coordinating communication between departments and tutors. It is worth noting that while on inside and on probation you should receive the additional study books too (they may be used copies, but it is far better than having to buy them with no regular source of income).

Naturally, while confined attending tutorials was impossible. However, I was able to have face-to-face meetings with my tutors prior to my transfer to Brixton, where my education officer facilitated telephone tutorials when she could. Post-release, I have been able to continue with telephone tutorials whereby the tutor will call me at home for an hour to discuss the module – course work, and TMAs and exam.

During my time 'away', the OU gave me a chance to focus on something positive and immerse my mind in an activity that would benefit my life on the outside when my liberty was restored. Returned to the community, I try to watch as many documentaries about my chosen subject (history) as I can, to bolster the learning process.

To conclude, if you were prevaricating about whether or not to embark on an OU course, my advice would be to opt for a foundation course to see if you like the format. Student Finance companies will help you to fund the course – your Distance Learning Rep and Education Officer should be able to help you to secure the required paperwork. A life with *Jeremy Kyle*, *Judge Rinder* and *EastEnderdale Street* seems a very shallow alternative. My friends and family are very supportive of my academic achievements thus far. I am due to graduate next summer (June 2020) and I will be the first in my family to achieve a degree.

4

A university without walls

Dan Weinbren

> The Open University has, in a real sense, two ancestries. One is technological. The other is ideological – the notion of a people's university for continuing education throughout life, the notion of deschooling and universities without walls.
>
> (Hooper, 1974, p 183)

During its formative years the development of prisoner education at The Open University (henceforth OU) was shaped by prisoners, prison and OU staff, and framed by a government desire to maintain and develop society through broadening prospects for social improvement. OU staff tended to see the university as part of a social democratic commitment to rehabilitation. Their pedagogy encouraged learners to be active in constructing knowledge by reflection on experience. For many prisoners, education was a means of escape, or at least engaging with ideas from beyond the walls.

The first part of this chapter outlines the OU's creation as an element of the support for pluralism, wider opportunities and the belief that humans can and should shape the world which defined the post-war settlement. Directed by overt government audit and intervention, the OU employed industrial-scale teaching and a range of media to showcase scientific efficiency and to promote British-focused culture and western values. Within the context of a Cold War rivalry which stimulated further expansion of welfare provision, the OU normalized the marketisation of social democracy. This understanding of the OU's role informs the focus in Chapters 6 to 14 on the perspectives and understandings of some of those involved in the OU's prison work.

The OU had its roots in part-time education for adults, developed from the 18th century, in the correspondence courses and university extension initiatives of the 19th century, and in the 20th-century sandwich courses, summer schools and educational radio and television broadcasts. These seeds were nurtured in the 1960s when the post-war population bulge led to an increased demand for higher education, greater interest in post-compulsory education and widespread acceptance that expenditure on education was reasonable and likely to aid sound governance.

Leader of HM Opposition, Harold Wilson wrote an introduction to a Labour Party report which argued that 'Britain's economic stagnation is a direct result of its neglect of higher education' (Labour Party study group on higher education chaired by Lord Taylor, 1963) while the Robbins Report on higher education concluded that a 'highly educated population is essential to meet competitive pressures in the modern world' (Robbins, 1963, p 268). Wilson told the 1963 Labour Party conference that a university of the air could enable aspirant learners to contribute to 'the Britain that is going to be forged in the white heat of this revolution' (Wilson, 1963; Dorey, 2015). He stressed that 'we cannot as a nation afford to cut off three quarters or more of our children from virtually any chance of higher education' (Wilson, 1963). Labour's 1964 manifesto called for 'a major change of attitude towards the scientific revolution' and a 'national economic plan with both sides of industry operating in partnership with the Government' (Labour Party, 1964). The OU was to be economically viable through the sale of teaching materials. Students did not receive grants. Many worked and paid both taxes and fees. It benefited from lower fixed costs than other universities as it used off-the-shelf components, notably books, telephones, gramophone records and state broadcasting equipment. OU students used the libraries and buildings of other universities and received teaching materials at home.

Other UK universities which opened in the 1960s saw themselves in the tradition of communities of investigative scholars. Sussex (which received its Royal Charter in 1961) was compared to a wealthy and prestigious Oxford college when it was referred to as Balliol-by-the-Sea. By contrast, the OU was regarded more as 'an industrial revolution in higher education', aiming to create an administrative and teaching workforce using the latest ideas of modern production and industrialisation (Drake, 1972, p 158). Teaching materials were created stage-by-stage, with different batches produced by teams, which included editors and BBC producers as well as academics. There was a division of labour (with short-term, teaching-only contracts and specialist support staff), economies of scale, mass mailouts and the language of 'lines of study', 'units' and 'production', central control of content and automated assessment. This fragmentation of work enabled the OU to promote social goals at low cost.

The OU was not regulated by the University Grants Committee system, which channelled funds from governments to universities. Rather, it was a 'very eccentric institution [being] a university funded directly by the state, and run by a direct grant from the state' (Pratt, 1970, p 375). Jennie Lee, the minister tasked with creating the OU, took a personal interest and ensured 'that little bastard that I have hugged to my bosom and cherished, that all the others have tried to kill off, will thrive' (Hollis, 1998, p 321). The OU was a product of the 'great reappraisal' of the 1960s, when governments sought to create a 'developmental state' as a means of revitalising the economy (Brittan, 1964, pp 204–45). There was support for scientific intellectuals with technocratic expertise and an enthusiasm for rational planning (Savage, 2011). Modernisation was promoted as a response to Britain's perceived decline and 'Wilson and his team displayed great skill in presenting growth, modernisation and social justice as part of a seamless internationalist, socialist, whole' (Block, 2006, p 349). 'Resembling a school or university campus' HMP Blundeston, opened in 1963, reflected the shift in attitudes 'from detention and retribution towards training and rehabilitation' (Jewkes and Johnston, 2007, p 188). The Criminal Justice Act 1967 aimed to streamline court procedures and to modernise the penal system. The 1968 report on the civil service by Lord Fulton revealed how the machinery of state would be restructured on scientific lines. The 1969 White Paper, *In place of strife* aimed to end 'unscientific' workplace practices and to promote greater sharing of control; in the same year the government presided over the opening of Longbridge, the biggest car plant in Europe.

The OU was one of many state projects of the 1960s which sought to promote high art and higher education. The publicly owned Royal Festival Hall in London was extended and refurbished and a second concert hall and an art gallery were added. Arts Council of Great Britain funding increased by 45 per cent in 1966 and a further 26 per cent in 1967, raising it to £7.2 million (Fisher, 2019). The BBC television series *Civilisation: A personal view by Kenneth Clark*, the benchmark for educational broadcasting of the era, focused on western art, architecture and philosophy. It echoed Senator William Benton's series Great Books of the Western World, which he hoped would enlighten citizens and act as a bulwark against communism. The 1966 White Paper, which set out the role the OU was to play, made clear that it was to 'advance technological studies', make a 'vital contribution to the education and cultural development' and that its 'main aim is to improve the educational, cultural and professional standards of the country as a whole' (*A university of the air*, 1966, para.

8). The state's role could be wide-reaching and ambitious; there 'was the pervasive influence of communal ideologies and state intervention' (Glendinning, 2003, p 277). These developments framed the decision to support OU learners in prison.

The OU would employ scientific, industrial means not only to disseminate culture but also to support the creation of economically productive citizens. It was an element of the Keynesian compact. The OU was, Wilson (1963) said, to 'cater for a wide variety of potential students [including] technologists who perhaps left school at sixteen'. Reflecting on why he had accepted prisoners as students, Walter Perry, the OU's first vice-chancellor, argued that the OU was 'providing an opportunity of retraining that may prove to be of inestimable value in reclaiming them as active and useful citizens on their release' (Perry, 1976, p 174). Personal accounts by prisoners underline the point. David, from HMP Long Lartin, studied with the OU and concluded 'no longer do I think of myself as only able to do menial jobs' (in Open University, 2018, p 5). Forster's 1976 study revealed that there was recognition that employment prospects might not be improved through study. 'As an ex-con is difficult to employ anyhow, an ex-con with a degree is practically impossible' said one; and 'I'm doing an Open University degree' said another, adding 'Not a scrap of use when I get out' (Forster, 1976, pp 17, 22). However, a more recent study concluded that learning in prison could raise hopes and aspirations for learning and employment upon release (Pike and Hopkins, 2019).

The OU built on the experiences of other countries, including the USSR's model of using radio, television and correspondence for propaganda and education (King, 1963, p 182, 185). This impressed Wilson and his US-backer, William Benton (Benton, 1966; MacArthur, 1974). The latter saw the OU as a means of countering the achievements of communism, arguing that 'the cold war between the open and closed societies is likely to be won in the world's classrooms, libraries, and college and university laboratories' (Benton, 1960). Benton advised Wilson on a 'television university' and introduced him to Geoffrey Crowther, Vice-Chair of the *Encyclopaedia Britannica* editorial board (which Benton owned). Crowther became the first chancellor of the OU. Asa Briggs, who would also become an OU chancellor, edited a ready reference version of the *Encyclopaedia Britannica*. The OU's first vice-chancellor, Perry felt that Benton contributed to the decision to found the OU and considered purchasing 280 sets of the 27 volume *Encyclopaedia Britannica* in order to equip OU study centres (Perry, 1973, p 30; Weinbren, 2014, pp 35–6). It was these contexts that informed the historian Eric Hobsbawm's (1990: 21) pithy statement that, 'Whatever Stalin did to the Russians, he was good for the common people of the West.' They reflect Benton's Cold War strategy of reliance not on the threat of conflict but on the building of higher education for social and economic development. The approach was also manifest in the appointment to the OU's first council of Norman MacKenzie. He worked in propaganda and for the secret intelligence service, MI6, in eastern Europe (Purcell, 2015). Subsequently, the government directed the OU to buttress open learning institutions in Thailand, the Netherlands, the Republic of Suriname and the Federal Republic of Nigeria. It sent teams to Iran, Venezuela, Pakistan and Israel. In this sense, the OU operated as an arm of the state.

Wilson sought 'to provide an opportunity for those, who, for one reason or another, have not been able to take advantage of higher education' (Wilson, 1964, p 27). The Labour Secretary of State for Education, 1965–67, Anthony Crosland, felt that education was the 'main engine in the creation of a more just society' (Crosland, 1982, p 69). Studying was a route to peaceful social progress through personal development. In common with the seven new campus universities built in England in the 1960s, the first stated objective of the OU's 1969 Royal Charter was to advance and disseminate learning and knowledge. In addition, the OU was, 'to promote the educational well-being of the community generally' (Open University, nd). In 1993 OU Professor Stuart Hall noted that the OU was 'filled with good social democrats. Everybody there believes in the redistribution of educational opportunities and seeks to remedy the exclusiveness of British education' (Hall, 1993, p 15). He added that 'it would have been funny to come to the OU and not to be committed to redistributing educational opportunities'.[1]

This approach was reinforced by the OU's teaching strategy. Available to students from January 1971, the OU taught adults, on a part-time basis, regardless of their prior qualifications, largely through correspondence and, to a lesser extent, through broadcasting and group tutorials held in local study centres and during residential weeks, arranged on hired campuses. Central staff prepared the teaching materials, which initially were mainly in the form of books, television programmes and radio broadcasts. Students could study a wide range of courses for an 'Open' degree. Each course was staffed by specialist course tutors. Part-time tutors, resident all over the country, taught and assessed groups in their area, often employing the OU's preferred pedagogy of collaborative engagement. Some tutors were also counsellors, offering advice on course choices, study skills and a range of other issues. These councillors remained with the student throughout their studies. Tutor-counsellors were managed by senior counsellors.

Tabulawa noted that 'democratic tendencies' and learner-centred pedagogical practices are intertwined (2003, pp 7, 10). The OU encouraged student self-help groups and by 1974 there were over a thousand of these (Sewart, 1975). In his 1976 study of prisoner students William Forster concluded that 'One of the most valuable things I saw was the 'self-help' group which was a mixture of inmates and non-inmates meeting regularly in a prison' (1976, p 26). The specialist press called the OU the 'great liberal experiment' and a 'cosy scheme that shows the Socialists at their most endearing but impractical worst' (*The Times Education Supplement*, 1966; *The Times Higher Educational Supplement*, 1971). When OU Vice-Chancellor Sir John Daniel sought to emphasise the values of the OU he cited the case of the graduate who said with exasperation that ever since he studied with the OU he has been unable to see less than six sides to any question (Lunneborg, 1997). Daniel (1998) concluded: 'That is what our founders meant by openness to ideas. That is a wonderful contribution that the OU is making to a free, democratic and civilised society.'

Although it was not designed to support the learning of prisoners, the OU's structure meant that whenever and wherever a prisoner moved to another prison, there could be support. Sometimes this meant long distances to travel. One tutor who lived in Milton Keynes supported a student in prison in HMP Acklington, Northumberland (Regan, 2003, p 5). OU teaching materials were largely suitable for isolated part-time adult learners and OU staff were often motivated by a belief in the positive impact of education on recidivism. In 1970, starting with two prisons for men, the Home Office offered to make OU courses available to prisoners to pay fees and provide facilities. This system was amended in 2012 when students serving sentences with fewer than six years left were permitted to access student loans. In 1971 6 prisoners in HMP Albany and 16 in HMP Wakefield started their OU studies. By the end of the presentations that year two had gained credits with distinction, 15 gained credits, four failed and one had dropped out. Thirteen students continued their studies in 1972 and they were joined by 27 more students, including 8 from HMP Gartree. The scheme was extended beyond England with a further prisoner in Belfast and two in Scotland (Perry, 1972). The prisoners pass rate in 1974 was 45 per cent as many withdrew before they reached the examination. Those who sat the examinations had what the vice-chancellor, Walter Perry, called 'reasonably good' results (Perry, 1976, p 173). In 1974 the first prisoner graduated. By 1975 there were 109 students at 11 establishments and by 1976 142 prisoners in 14 establishments studying 197 subjects (Forster, 1976, p 7). Expansion has been uneven but by 2018 there were 1,444 OU students in secure environments.

It was OU staff based in the regional and Celtic nation offices who negotiated initiatives with prisons in their area. OU students in prison could not attend the residential schools or tutorials but at least one prisoner was permitted to attend a mainstream residential school. The School Director said "I decided to keep it to myself, and let him have a week as a normal student" (personal communication, 29 April 2019).[2] In 1976 Bob Davies, a senior counsellor, arranged a version of a summer school in a prison and also for students from outside the prison to join those inside in tutorials. There was a five-day programme to mimic the residential school attended by other students studying the same course. Donald Burrows went in to play the piano in the chapel as part of the course's music element (*Open Forum*, 1976). Student Sue Astbury was not a prisoner but was unable to attend the conventional summer school. In 1978 she attended a prison version (*Open Forum*, 1978). In HMP Frankland and HMP Durham, "we organised informal summer schools 'in both prisons and each prison had its own counsellors allocated'", recalled Assistant Regional Director Peter Regan (personal communication to author, 28 Feb. 2019). At Frankland the Acting Governor felt this should be repeated (D.J. Cornwall, personal communication to Peter Regan, 30 November 1994). It was 'for many years a prison with an excellent record for OU study' (Regan, 2003, p 4).

The OU also taught about 6,000 British citizens in mainland Western Europe (*The Times Higher Education Supplement*, 2002). The logistics of arranging OU teaching was largely the responsibility of the 12, later 13, offices. Peter Regan recalled that "we needed no input from Walton Hall [the OU's Milton Keynes headquarters]. Regions were autonomous." He emphasised that "Walton Hall had little involvement [...] We collaborated with administrators at Milton Keynes, rather than following their instructions" and, in particular, "we didn't take many orders from Walton Hall; they didn't intervene in our European operations" (personal communication, 28 February 2019). This division may have led to a reduced sense of responsibility from Walton Hall. Counsellor Vicki Goodwin pointed out that "secure units were always complex and difficult" and "I felt that [the OU] senior management never really wanted to know" (personal communication, 27 February 2019). Moreover, Forster's study concluded that 'the essential weakness of the present system is its local, sporadic, nature'. He called for a 'national relationship' (Forster, 1976, p 30). The OU was not routinely informed when prisoners were moved to other prisons. This could often result in a reduction in support or access to study facilities (B. Stevenson, personal communication, 9 March 2019; R. Peoples, personal communication, 11 March 2019). Eventually the Scottish Office agreed that, in Scotland only, students should not be moved from prison to prison without notice being given to the OU, and that they should have a place and time to study and access to tutors. Counsellor Judith George noted that while this "created a more productive environment [...] the Prison Service institutionally did not and probably does not value education highly, and we always had to keep a firm hand on the conditions of the scheme" (personal communication, 11 March 2019). Katla Helgason started to study at the OU in 1971, became a tutor and later Assistant Director in Scotland. She developed the Scottish Prison Scheme and felt that tutors "had to be very proactive and very positive".[3]

Locks on doors and metal bars on windows, and the focus on punishment, correction and rehabilitation indicate that there are many ways in which prisons are different to the world beyond the gates. In prisons there is surveillance and little trust. This is how one prisoner described it to his tutor:

> In prison there is rarely another inmate following the same course and visits from a tutor can be infrequent and sometimes impossible. There is noise, arbitrary interruption, tension and sometimes the threat of violence [...] The student in prison can face prejudice, jealousy and ridicule in an environment which is often hostile to intellectual activity. (Regan, 1996)

If a student needs to be employed to register for an OU module, for example, as a teacher or in social work, then access to the module is unlikely to be allowed or the module may not be made available to students in prisons. Students convicted of sex offences against children were unlikely to be permitted to study a module which features children among its topics.

Initially VHF radios were not permitted in prisons, although subsequently in some prisons it was agreed that OU students could be permitted own their own VHF radio sets in order to receive broadcasts.

Most forms of media are regarded with suspicion by prison authorities as they undermine the aim of removing a person from society. Sometimes CDs, DVDs and calculators have been banned. Telephone calls are monitored and restricted. This is however, 'a vibrant economy in illicit and thus unmonitored, mobile phones' (Earle, 2011, p 27). Internet access for students in prison is limited, although a Virtual Campus is now accessible from public prisons (Tickle, 2012). Although students' Home Experiment Kits, which contained chemicals, were often banned, Jack Singleton, who presented a radio magazine series for OU students, recalled conducting an interview "with someone in a top security mental hospital who had killed someone with an axe and he got to the stage where he was allowed to do the Biological Bases of Behavior [module], in which you have a kit which includes a scalpel" (*Open Forum*, 1976).

Teaching in prisons in England and Wales relied on the support of the Home Office, later the Ministry of Justice, and individual prison staff (Regan, 2003, p 1). Particular wing management styles had an impact on student's ability to study (Regan, 2003, p 10). OU tutor Anne Langley, recalled the secure unit at HMP Whitemoor which, was, for tutors, "quite a frustrating business – getting in and out took a very long time and if there was a lock-down the session would be cancelled without notice" (personal communication, 27 February 2019). The OU Regional Centre for mainland Europe, excluding Ireland, was in Newcastle and the Assistant Director in that location recalled a British prisoner held in a prison in Madrid who wrote regarding a forthcoming OU visit: "if they say I'm not here, which has been known to happen, please do your best to insist" (personal communication to P. Regan, 20 April 1995). OU Tutor Counsellor Pete Cannell said that at HMP Shotts "the prison officers were fairly hostile and made things difficult for visiting tutors on occasions" (personal communication, 12 March 2019). Prison officers could be resentful (Weinbren, 2018, p 51). One tutor noted 'the generally negative and uncooperative attitude of prison officers' (Watts, 2010, p 59). In general, there was often an 'anti-intellectual atmosphere' in prisons (Simpson, 2002a, p 158; Irwin, 2008, p 519). Most OU teaching materials were delivered through correspondence, yet no prisoner was able to receive mail or send mail freely. There was reliance on intermediaries and often delays to the arrival (Regan, 1996).

OU Senior Counsellor Richard Peoples, recalled that students:

> said that finding time for quiet study was often a problem. They could opt for education during the day instead of

working in the prison workshops (and thus giving up the chance of earning), but this did not provide enough time and trying to study in their cells in the evenings before 'lights out' was often difficult because of noise and other interruptions. (Personal communication, 11 March 2019)

Although Peter Regan noted, of the prisons of north-east England, that 'most classrooms in prisons bear comparison with those in an average Further Education college', sometimes teaching took place in a room not designed for that purpose (Regan, 2003). Tutors recall teaching in cells. Often the door was open and a prison officer was outside (Irwin, 2008, p 520; Watts, 2010, p 60; M. Paris, personal communication to O. Simpson, 12 March 2019). However, when tutor Valerie Pedlar taught 19th-century literature to a man in Ashworth high security psychiatric hospital she was left alone with him. She nervously taught *Mansfield Park* and recalled that when the student explained that "he couldn't wait to get to *Wuthering Heights*, and me thinking he looked rather like Heathcliff and hoping he wouldn't act like him!" (personal communication, 27 February 2019). Teaching at HMP Wormwood Scrubs 'took place in a kind of goldfish bowl room' while elsewhere a dining room was utilised (Regan, 2003, p 14; Youle, personal communication, 27 February 2019).

Personal accounts also refer to support for learners from within prisons. Tutor Tony Kelly said prison education staff 'were always positive and they were helpful' (Regan, 2003, p 13). Senior Counsellor Pete Cannell improved relationships by constructing a creative writing course for the Scottish Prisoner Officers Association (personal communication, 12 March 2019). Senior Counsellor Chris Youle recalls having a "good, fairly close, relationship on behalf of the London Region, with the Education Department at HMP Wormwood Scrubs prison". He was permitted to take a student, accompanied by a prison officer, to the London Region office in order to use a computer and was allowed to bring a car full of materials for a Course Choice meeting into the prison (personal communication, 27 February 2019). Tutor Counsellor Richard Peoples recalled that HMP Whitemoor "had a very enthusiastic education officer who encouraged OU study for prisoners who were deemed to benefit from it" (personal communication, 11 March 2019). HMP Maidstone permitted a student to accompany a tutor for four days for a version of a residential school and allowed prisoners to watch video recordings of television programmes and to listen to cassette recordings of radio programmes.

OU students do not start their studies assuming that a university education is a birthright determined by their class position, previous educational qualifications or age. Graduation, being awarded a degree certificate, is not another step on an apparently seamless, individual intellectual journey from school to degree. It is achieved after years of hard work, commitment, and support. Whether they take place in prestigious public buildings or prisons, award ceremonies are valued by students and their teachers (Simpson, 2006, p 11). Norman Woods, a Regional Director, fondly recalled prison graduation ceremonies: "You used to put on your glad rags and go and hand them their diploma and certificate, whatever. And their families used to come in. You know, it was quite good. And the prison would provide some cakes and cup of tea."[4] At HMP Whitemoor the graduand and other OU students (and those applying) were allowed to attend ceremonies held in the chapel. Richard Peoples recalled:

> we wore robes, had a procession with music etc. in order to try to simulate a normal degree ceremony. The last one I attended was at Whitemoor, when the graduand told me that he had been in prison for 18 years, that he could not read or write when he first went in and that he had been in trouble for fighting and other offences many times before he started OU but had now 'calmed down'. (Personal communication, 11 March 2019)

Peter Regan wrote that 'it was affecting to see a man detained for decades in tears as we read out a list of his academic achievements, a man serving time for serious terrorist offences' (personal communication, 28 February 2019). In 1982 OU's North Region took responsibility for students in Benelux. In 1994 it added responsibilities for students in Switzerland, Austria, Slovenia and the EU. Senior Counsellor Liz Manning, the country manager for Germany, Austria, Switzerland and France, arranged for a tutor to travel from Vienna to a remote prison in Austria to tutor 'Michael'. On graduation, permission was granted for 'Michael' to travel to Vienna to receive his degree certificate from Liz: "I made a speech to an audience of our office staff, a former fellow prisoner, the British Consul General and his [Michael's] social worker. We then went out for lunch before he returned to prison" (personal communication, 28 February 2019). Ron's graduation in a prison chapel was attended by staff, prisoners (Ron had taught many of them) the chaplain, the governor and Ron's parents. Counsellor Ormond Simpson, wearing his gown, gave a speech. Ron, in a gown borrowed from a tutor, said that this was the first time that he had been a credit to his parents and burst into tears (Simpson, 2002b, p 38, 2006, p 10). The OU has taken pride in the success of its students in prisons. The keynote speaker, to mark its fortieth birthday in 2009, was former bank robber Bobby Cummines OBE (Open University, 2009). In February 2019 the OU's Chancellor, Martha Lane Fox, tweeted about the 'amazing inmates and staff' when she presided over an award ceremony in a prison. She added: 'I'm so impressed by dedication of our students even in the most complex and difficult situations ... Two women fought for the budget to get computers for 5 years – and with that changed their own + peers ability to study' (Lane Fox, 2019). A degree certificate is not only a symbol of the possibility of personal redemption through education, it is also a sign of success for a wider community. Supporting adult learners in prison has been a collaborative effort involving a range of prison and university staff. There have been positive impacts on those outside the prisons. An OU student in HMP Barlinnie said that his relationship with his wife and children improved as a direct result of his having studied P912, The Pre-school Child, a module designed for prisoners. Prisoner James Crosby explained that 'studying in prison for me is a collective effort' and cited help from his family who provided him with information based on their 'lengthy searches of the internet' (Open University, 2009, p 6).

OU students, in prison or not, need to be self-reliant, to create new spaces for themselves where they can imagine themselves as part of a community of scholars and can think and feel outside their existing normative and conceptual frameworks. This work of carving out space is described by one prisoner who said that he applied to study at the OU 'so that for just a few hours a week I could get away from the obscenities, the prison gossip, the scheming' (Forster, 1976, p 24). One OU broadcast concluded that "when you become an [OU] undergraduate you become a member of that university and it gives you a sense of belonging to something else other than the prison community". The OU offered "some sense of a lifeline to the world outside" and "a completely different dimension" (*Open Forum*, 1976). 'When I'm working,' reflected one student prisoner, 'I know that I'm doing what others outside are doing, and most likely doing it just as well.' Another spoke of studying as 'a lifeline – it reaches outside. I'm a member of the University and that means that I'm still am member of the human race' (Forster, 1976, p 21).

The notion of places where two different worlds mesh or collide was employed in the 1970s by founder of the French-based Prison Information Group, Michel Foucault. He categorised a prison as a 'place which lies outside all places and yet is localizable', a heterotopia. Isolated and penetrable, with its own rules it also conformed to the wider social order. These were places where people could juxtapose 'in a single real space, several spaces, several sites which are themselves incompatible' (Foucault, 1986). These features of profoundly intersecting realities are commonly recognised by OU staff and prisoner students. Studying, engagement with OU texts, took people in prison to these 'other places' in which existing arrangements of their lives in prison could be 'represented, contested and inverted'. Such places, by altering the mundane, provided an escape but one which involved no physical movement (Foucault, 1986). Forster's 1976 analysis of studying in prison included interviews with 53 student prisoners. He concluded that to enter a prison is to 'enter another world', that 'the concentration required [for study] removes the student from prison for a while', and that many saw studying as an 'escape from routine'. He quoted a prison officer's view that 'it doesn't help them to adjust to prison at all – it just helps them to pretend they're not here' (Forster, 1976, pp 12, 15, 22, 31). A former Irish Republican prisoner in the Maze/Long Kesh prisons of Northern Ireland recalled how students disassociated their studies from the rest of the prison regime by calling the classroom by its Irish name, '*seomra rang*' (McAtackney, 2006). Recent efforts to re-label the prison as 'a campus of offender learners' or a 'secure college' may be critically illuminated by Foucault's idea of a problematic and productive juxtaposition of competing worlds trying to occupy a single space (Irwin, 2008, p 523).

High theory and hard prison grind can meet in relatively mundane penal experiences. During one OU exam a prisoner had to be guarded by an officer with a dog. When there was a shift change the next officer arrived with another dog. The animals fought. Prison staff rushed to the scene. The OU invigilator recalled 'alarms went off, prison officers appeared from all over the place and there was general turmoil'. Afterwards, the student merely said 'I just kept on writing. I wasn't going to miss my chance of the exam' (Simpson, 2006, p 13).

For many, however, moving into and remaining in the alternative space was not always straightforward. 'Andrew' recalled: 'You can treat it like you're in a university [...] I didn't feel like a student most of the time. Occasionally when I'm here [independent learning room] I do, but you are reminded very quickly on the wing that you're in prison!' (Pike and Hopkins, 2019, p 13). Student prisoner Jed noted that 'I sort of dissociate myself with prison [...] I'm like at a crossroads. I've got one foot in and one foot out of my previous life' (Pike and Hopkins, 2019, p 14).

Tutor Tracy Irwin noticed that 'prisoners would often come to the classroom in disturbed or distressed state after a difficult visit or following bad news from outside' (Irwin, 2008, p 517). Tutor Jackie Watts explained:

> During my three years as a higher education tutor in prison I was never once able to move straight into a teaching role at the start of the session. This was because before the student could move into the student 'self' to be fully engaged in the learning situation, it was necessary for [the student] to actively, if only temporarily, leave and 'unlock' the prisoner 'self'. (Watts, 2010, p 62)

Having taught her non-prisoner OU students about the justifications for killing people, Liz Manning took the topic up with an OU student prisoner in HMP Durham who had been found guilty of murder. While the situation "must have been extremely stressful", Liz recalled that "our conversation was no different from the one I had with my main groups" (personal communication, 28 February 2019). Other prisoners found sociology and psychology difficult to study as they encouraged critical awareness of their environment. One sociology student in prison said:

> Attitudes, roles and structures are so easy to see in here and so unchanging and I had nothing else to think about. I spent weeks feeling as though I was behind a glass window, just watching it all. I could hardly speak to people. (Forster, 1976, p 25)

Study in prison held up a mirror to institutions and, as Foucault noted, in a mirror there is a virtual space that opens up behind the surface:

> The mirror functions as a heterotopia in the sense that it makes this place I occupy at the moment when I look at myself in the glass both utterly real, connected with the entire space surrounding it and utterly unreal. (Foucault, 1986)

Studying the immediate situation, albeit in a relatively abstract fashion, left some prisoners less able to cope on their return to their non-academic surroundings.

The desire to escape to a different space is one that features in narratives inside and outside prison walls. For those outside prison the OU could also aid transportation from the everyday and, just as in prison, students outside sometimes faced hostility. One student recalled her husband's reaction when he discovered that she was studying with the OU by finding her books: 'He threw them all down the rubbish chute (we live on the 7th floor)' (Atkins and Beard, 2010, p 26). In Willy Russell's popular play (later film) *Educating Rita*, the eponymous heroine initially has difficulty studying with the OU as she cannot open the door to her tutor's office. By the end she has left her husband, who burnt her books, and claimed the space as her own. Director and actor David Heley noted, regarding a tour of the play to a prison, that 'many of the prisoners said how they recognised themselves within the play's action and meaning'.[5] When students in prison and elsewhere have built spaces of alternative ordering as a defence against isolation, marginalisation and lack of confidence it is because, within a few years of its creation, the OU had constructed an ethos and relatively robust pedagogic support systems for its learners.

Conclusion

While all UK universities relied on public funding for survival, the OU, during its formative years, had closer and more numerous ties to central government than most. It exemplified government commitments to securing social peace and stability, to the efficiency associated with large-scale production and to enabling the market, as well as the public sector, to thrive. It also drew support from private institutions in the USA which delivered cultural elements of the Cold War (Berghahn, 2001; Czernecki, 2013). Since that period there has been a shift from government towards governance. Funding has been linked to auditing and a discourse of efficiency. There has been a development of quasi-markets that attempt to blend and blur the distinction between self-regulation and state regulation (Le Grand and Bartlett, 1993). The roles played by the state have changed (Rhodes, 1994). Some of those alterations were prefigured in the OU (Weinbren, 2012, 2014). Universities are expected to focus less on educating citizens for democratic engagement and more on functioning as an industry (Kezar, 2004, pp 430, 433). There have been parallel changes within the prison sector. The OU was well-positioned to ease the development of universities bidding for funds for student teaching and for the replacement of grants with student loans. It was because, as Pimlott (1993, p 515) notes, it 'took the ideals of social equality and equality of opportunity more seriously than any other part of the British education system' that the OU was able to render as normal an industrial model of teaching and the further commodification of knowledge. These values were translated by staff at the personal, social, levels where the learning occurred. In secure environments OU tutors and counsellors embodied the university's foundation values as a social democratic counterpoint to communism, while also drawing on modern industrial-scale technology to disseminate enlightened cultural values.

Notes

1 Unpublished interview with Stuart Hall conducted by Hilary Young in 2009.
2 E-mails to the author as part of ongoing archival and historical research about the OU.
3 Unpublished interview with Katla Helgason conducted by Hilary Young in 2009. Transcript is held in the OU Archives and forms part of the OU Oral History Project collection.
4 Unpublished interview with Norman Woods conducted by Hilary Young in 2009. Transcript is held in the OU Archives and forms part of the OU Oral History Project collection.
5 Pitchy Breath Theatre, www3.open.ac.uk/near-ypu/south-east/p3.asp.

References

A university of the air, Cmnd 2992 (1966) London: HMSO.

Atkins P. and Beard, J. (2010) Learning with practitioners. Rationale: frameworks: learning, Milton Keynes: The Open University.

Benton, W. (1960) 'The Cold War and the liberal arts', Speech, 5 June, University of Chicago, Special Collections Research Center, Box 522, File 17, University of Chicago Library.

Benton, W. (1966) Letter 1966 to C.A. Thompson, Acting Consul General in the British Consulate in New York, 24 February, University of Chicago, Special Collections Research Center, OU archive WP1/1/1, University of Chicago Library.

Berghahn, V. (2001) America and the intellectual cold wars in Europe, Princeton, NJ: Princeton University Press.

Block, A. (2006) 'Harold Wilson, Labour and the machinery of government', Contemporary British History, 20(3): 343–62.

Brittan, S. (1964) The Treasury under the Tories 1951–1964, Harmondsworth: Penguin.

Crosland, S. (1982) Tony Crosland, London: Jonathan Cape.

Czernecki, I. (2013) 'An intellectual offensive: the Ford Foundation and the destalinization of the Polish social sciences', Cold War History, 13(3): 289–310.

Daniel, J. (1998) 'Has The Open University lived up to the ideals of its founders?', Jean Posthuma Memorial Lecture, Association of Open University Graduates AGM, 28 November.

Dorey, P. (2015) '"Well, Harold insists on having it!": the political struggle to establish The Open University, 1965–67', *Contemporary British History*, 29(2): 241–72.

Drake, M. (1972) 'The Open University concept', *Studies: An Irish Quarterly Review*, 61(242): 155–8.

Earle, R. (2011) 'Prison and university: a tale of two institutions', *Papers from the British Criminology Conference*, 11 (3–6 July): 20–37.

Fisher, R. (2019) 'United Kingdom. Historical perspective: cultural policies and instruments', in Europarat / ERICarts (ed.) *Compendium of cultural policies and trends*, 20th edn, www.culturalpolicies.net.

Forster, W. (1976) 'The higher education of prisoners', Vaughan Paper 21, Department of Adult Education, University of Leicester.

Foucault, M. (1986) 'Of other spaces', trans. J. Miskowiec, *Diacritics*, 16(spring): 22–7, http://web.mit.edu/allanmc/www/foucault1.pdf.

Glendinning, M. (2003) 'Teamwork or masterwork? The design and reception of the Royal Festival Hall', *Architectural History*, 46: 277–319.

Hall, S. (1993) 'Thatcherism today', *New Statesman and Society*, 26 November: 14–17.

Hobsbawm, E.J. (1990) 'Goodbye to all that', *Marxism Today*, October: 18–23.

Hollis, P. (1998) *Jennie Lee*, Oxford: Oxford University Press.

Hooper, R. (1974) 'New media in the OU: an international perspective', in J. Tunstall (ed.) *The Open University Opens*, London: Routledge.

Irwin, T. (2008) 'The "inside story": practitioner perspectives on teaching in prison', *The Howard Journal of Criminal Justice*, 47(5): 512–28.

Jewkes, Y. and Johnston, H. (2007) 'The evolution of prison architecture', in Y. Jewkes (ed.) *Handbook on prisons*, Cullompton, Devon: Willan Publishing, pp 174–96.

Kezar, A. (2004) 'Obtaining integrity? Reviewing and examining the charter between higher education and society', *Review of Higher Education*, 27(4): 429–59.

King, A. (1963) 'Higher education, professional manpower and the state: reflections on education and professional employment in the USSR', *Minerva*, 1(2): 182–90.

Labour Party (1964) *Let's go with Labour for the New Britain: The Labour Party's manifesto for the 1964 general election*, London: Labour Party.

Labour Party study group on higher education chaired by Lord Taylor (1963) *The years of crisis: The report of the Labour Party's study group on higher education*, London: Labour Party.

Lane Fox, M. (2019) Tweet @Marthalanefox, 20 February, https://twitter.com/Marthalanefox/status/1098242304559726592.

Le Grand, J. and Bartlett, W. (eds) (1993) *Quasi-markets and social policy*, Basingstoke: Palgrave Macmillan.

Lunneborg, P. (1997) *OU men: Work through lifelong learning*, Cambridge: Lutterworth.

MacArthur, B. (1974) 'An interim history of The Open University', in J. Tunstall (ed.) *The Open University opens*, London: Routledge, pp 3–17.

McAtackney, L. (2006) 'The negotiation of identity at shared sites: Long Kesh/Maze Prison site, Northern Ireland', paper presented at the 10th International Seminar of Forum UNESCO – University and Heritage: 'Cultural Landscapes in the 21st Century', Newcastle-upon-Tyne, 11–16 April 2005 (revised July 2006), p 3.

Open Forum (1976) BBC Radio 2, 10 July.

Open Forum (1978) BBC Radio 2, 12 August.

Open University (nd) Open University Charter. www.open.ac.uk/about/main/sites/www.open.ac.uk.about.main/files/files/ecms/web-content/Charter.pdf.

Open University (2009) *Inside News: The Open University Newsletter for Secure Environments*, March.

Open University (2018) *Steps to success*, Milton Keynes: The Open University.

Perry, W. (1972) *Report of the Vice-Chancellor to the Council, 1971*, Milton Keynes: The Open University.

Perry, W. (1973) *Report of the Vice-Chancellor to the council, 1972*, Milton Keynes: The Open University.

Perry, W. (1976) *Open University: A personal account by the first Vice-Chancellor*, Milton Keynes: The Open University.

Pike, A. and Hopkins, S. (2019) '"Education is transformational": positive identity through prison-based higher education in England and Wales', *International Journal of Bias, Identity and Diversities in Education*, 4(1), http://oro.open.ac.uk/51754/3/51754.pdf.

Pimlott, B. (1993) *Harold Wilson*, London: HarperCollins.

Pratt, J. (1970) 'Gone to lunch: a critical look at The Open University', *Education + Training*, 12(10): 374–75.

Purcell, H. (2015) *A very private celebrity: The nine lives of John Freeman*, London: Biteback Publishing.

Regan, P. (1996) 'Opening opportunities for students at a disadvantage', presentation of positive practices in the field of lifelong learning, Athens.

Regan, P. (2003) *The Open University in the North: Widening participation in prisons, 2002. An evaluation*, Newcastle: Open University.

Rhodes, R.A.W. (1994) 'The hollowing out of the state: the changing nature of public service in Britain', *Political Quarterly*, 65(2): 138–51.

Robbins, L. (1963) *Higher education: Report of the committee appointed by the Prime Minister under the chairmanship of Lord Robbins*, Cmnd 2154, London: HMSO.

Savage, M. (2011) *Identities and social change in Britain since 1940: The politics of method*, Oxford: Oxford University Press.

Sewart, D. (1975) 'Some observations on the formation of study group', *Teaching at a Distance*, 2: 2–6.

Simpson, O. (2002a) *Supporting students in online open and distance learning*, 2nd edn, London: Routledge.

Simpson, O. (2002b) 'Doing it hard', in G. Crosling and G. Webb (eds) *Supporting student learning: Case studies, experience and practice*, London: Kogan Page, pp 34–40.

Simpson, O. (2006) 'Mapping the work of The Open University in prisons', Education paper, circulated by National Institute of Adult Continuing.

Tabulawa, R. (2003) 'International aid agencies, learner-centred pedagogy and political democratisation: a critique', *Comparative Education*, 39(1): 7–26.

The Times Educational Supplement (1966) 4 March.

The Times Higher Education Supplement (1971) 3 December.

The Times Higher Education Supplement (2002) 'OU title fails to convince', 27 September.

Tickle, L. (2012) 'Distance learning breaches prison walls', *Guardian*, 20 February, www.theguardian.com/education/2012/feb/20/distance-learning-for-prisoners [accessed 21 August 2019].

Watts, J.H. (2010) 'Teaching a distance higher education curriculum behind bars: challenges and opportunities', *Open Learning: the journal of open, distance and e-Learning*, 25(1): 57–64.

Weinbren, D. (2012) '"Filled with good social democrats": The Open University and the development of the knowledge economy, 1969–1989', *Journal of the World University Forum*, 5(2): 99–112.

Weinbren, D. (2014) *The Open University: A history*, Manchester: Manchester University Press.

Weinbren, D. (2018) 'Prisoner students: building bridges, breaching walls', in J. Burkett (ed.) *Students in twentieth-century Britain and Ireland*, London: Palgrave Macmillan, pp 45–75.

Wilson, H. (1963) *Labour's plan for science: Reprint of speech by the Rt. Hon. Harold Wilson, MP, leader of the Labour party at the annual conference Scarborough, Tuesday, 1 October*, London: Labour Party.

Wilson, H. (1964) *Purpose in politics: Selected speeches by Rt. Hon. Harold Wilson*, London: Weidenfeld and Nicolson.

VIGNETTE 3

Starting a new chapter

Mr C.T. Morgans

I am 71 years of age and I was convicted in 2009. I find very little for me in the day-to-day life of an inmate but I have always had an interest in the world about me and I discovered the OU prospectus in the library. It seemed to be a Godsend, both a means of keeping busy and as a way of gaining some sort of higher education that I missed out on before. The process of enrolling was somewhat fraught in that the education department of the prison I was in had personnel that had no interest in higher learning. The whole remit was to cater for people to come up to 11+ standards, not that they had any interest in helping those who could not read at all.

I looked through the prospectus and rather than go for a specific degree course, I decided to instead to opt for an Open degree, which gave me the freedom to explore as my fancy took me, so I took an Openings Course in Law. I found the discipline required was totally different from that I remembered from my schooling, but with the support and guidance of both my tutor and my fellow inmates, I managed to do my first TMA (tutor-marked assignment). When I got it back from my tutor with their comments, I felt that I was truly beginning a new chapter of my life. I will not kid you, it was not easy, at times I felt that I was fighting the prison and the Ministry of Justice to get the computer time to enable me to do the work, but now I am on the closing straight, the battles I have fought fade into insignificance. There is one thing you should know – you will only be allowed to take one 60 point module per year, so if we ignore all the other things which will interfere with your studies, it will take a minimum of six years to gain your chosen degree (I have been doing mine since 2010 with about 18 months to go). It will not be easy, but nothing worthwhile ever is.

Keep in mind the end goal, nothing else matters. I have found that there is a vast range of people in the prison who may be ready to help you, the very least they will do is give you their support. My own family thought, and still thinks, I am mad to put myself through all the stress of gaining a degree, but they have always been supportive. If you are over middle age, you probably will not get to use your degree, as the public seem to have a bias about employing ex-cons, but by doing the work to gain a degree, you will prove to them that you are trying to put your old life behind you and make a fresh start, and that may make the difference between getting and not getting employment. The very least that will happen is that you will gain a fresh insight into your own capacity to move on and start again.

Unlike 'normal' education, you are responsible for your studies. How and when you study is up to you. There is no teacher checking to make sure that you complete the assignments on time and that you are doing all the research that is required. I know that this is a daunting prospect, but it gets easier as time goes on. Remember that you are doing all this work because you want to, you are doing it for you and only for you, invest in yourself and enjoy the ride. You are starting the next phase of your life, one that will make a huge difference to the way you look at problems and problem solving. By doing an OU course, you are showing the world that even in some really difficult situations, you have the ability to focus on the job in hand. That skill alone may get you the job you are after.

5

Open universities, close prisons: critical arguments for the future

Rod Earle and James Mehigan

Preamble: a moment of conference

When I started to attend criminology conferences nearly twenty years ago, I was treated to a rare moment of unintentional humour and collective self-awareness. In a large lecture theatre at the University of Portsmouth a rising academic star was presenting a paper on the penal climate in the Netherlands, renowned for its humane, parsimonious approach to incarceration. As Dr Francis Pakes put up a slide illustrating a newly built Dutch prison cell, chuckles could be heard rippling round the auditorium as academics recognised the cell's facilities and dimensions as almost completely identical to the university's student accommodation they had just vacated to attend the presentation. Like their rooms, the cell had an en-suite shower and toilet, a fitted single bed, work bench, wardrobe and storage facilities. Although delegates' funny bones were tickled as they shared with each other the irony of their willingness to swap their conference accommodation for a prison cell, I felt an edge to this levity. Alongside these images a memory lurked; the cell I had been in some twenty years earlier in HMP Norwich had no sanitation and a battered steel bunk bed was crammed next to a single bed so as to accommodate three men in a cell designed nearly a hundred years earlier for a single prisoner.

The comparison entertaining the conference delegates was not lost on me but the apparent ease of the appraisal was troubling, the nerve it tickled also burned. It felt personally anchored in a serious criminological question, the one posed by Michel Foucault in the 1970s: 'Is it surprising that prisons resemble factories, schools, barracks, hospitals, which all resemble prisons?' (Foucault, 1979, p 228) Now, the relentless march of penal progress has advanced to include universities in this list of resemblances. And we find it more amusing than alarming.

In this chapter, James and I seek to extend the critical tradition of The Open University (OU) approach to questions of crime, punishment and social order by exploring the wider ramifications of imprisonment. We also seek to contextualise the OU's contributions to higher education in prisons and contribute to wider critical discussions about what universities are for (Collini, 2012; Connell, 2019; Dawson, 2019). If the appearance of modern prisons is now starting to resemble that of retail warehouses that themselves resemble call centres that resemble university residence halls, the questions that troubled Foucault may be as relevant for the 2020s as they were for the 1980s.

Days of hope: the end of prisons or the end of dreams?

Not so long ago, in the middle of the 20th century, it seemed to many prison experts that the future for prisons was short and shrinking. This optimism arose from a confident belief that crime rates could be reduced because they were causally linked with forms of social deprivation and/or pathology that had their origins in offenders' lives in their community. They could thus be 'cured' by suitable treatment in, or of, that community. Looking forward in the 1940s, Hermann Mannheim, the UK's most eminent criminologist, suggested: 'The days of the prison as a method for the mass treatment of law breakers are largely over' (cited in Tonry, 2004, p 3). In the early 1960s, the prevailing post-war optimism prompted another professor, Norval Morris (1965, p 12), towards prediction: 'It is confidently predicted that before the end of the century the prison in its present form will become extinct.'

Looking back from the end of the second decade of the 21st century it is clear they could hardly have been more wrong. The number of prisons has grown and the number of people sent to prison has vastly increased. This has been a global trend (Coyle et al, 2016) and one in which the UK has been a prominent leader, although no country on earth has managed to keep pace with the United States when it comes to incarceration. Within the three criminal justice jurisdictions of the UK, England and Wales is the largest and has the highest rate of incarceration. From a prison population of just below 20,000 people at the beginning of the 20th century the number of people in prison has risen by over 400 per cent to more than 83,000 people by 2018 (House of Commons, 2018). In 1968 there were only 168 people serving 10 years or more in custody. Now there are more than 18,500 (Prison Reform Trust, 2019).

For criminologists the only consolation is that as prisons have swelled and multiplied, so has the discipline of criminology. From being a relatively marginal sociological specialism for most of the post-war period in the UK, it is now the second most popular social science option for undergraduates. Only psychology attracts more students. Indeed, the OU itself has followed the trend, launching its criminology degree in 2018. And criminologists are still trying to unwrap the enigma of the extraordinary growth of imprisonment and the enduring public fascination with its ugly charms, so at odds with the confident predictions. In 1970, Laurie Taylor's astute assessment seems to have been more 'on the money' than those of Mannheim or Morris: 'As a group, criminologists look to have a comfortable future ... the demand for criminology seems assured' (Taylor, 1969, pp 115–16).

The optimism of criminologists in the middle of the 20th century reflects the fact that the idea of imprisonment as the primary response to crime and the default mode of punishment had not, at that stage, become so entrenched, widespread and popular. Imprisonment, as the comments from Mannheim and Morris suggest, was then regarded as an impermanent, probably inadequate response to crime. It is important to recognise that the onset of the rapid growth of imprisonment in England and Wales is relatively recent, rather than a timeless truth of crime and punishment. While the post-war rise in imprisonment roughly corresponds to increases in crime during the same period, declining crime levels since the late 1990s have not been matched by declining imprisonment. The fact that the reverse has occurred, and prison populations just keep rising, is commonly linked to the combative remarks of a Conservative Home Secretary, Michael Howard. In 1993 he spelt out his belief that 'prison works' and his intention to revive his party's reputation for being the party of law and order and hence 'tough on crime'. The emergence of New Labour under the leadership of Tony Blair took up the 'tough-on-crime' gauntlet thrown down by the Conservatives with the sublimely unimaginative 'tough on crime, tough on the causes of crime' couplet. Thus was launched a party political bidding war on crime and punishment throughout the 1990s, resulting in a relentless upturn in the prison population.

However, for critical criminologists the comparatively recent surge in the size of the imprisoned population is only part of a problem that has much deeper roots and a far stronger hold on the public imagination. This is what we turn to next.

Why are prisons a bad idea? Meet Michel Foucault ...

According to the French social theorist and philosopher, Michel Foucault (1991 [1979], p 232): '[Prison] is the detestable solution which one seems unable to do without.' Emerging in the late 18th century, the 'theory of prison' was nothing if not ambitious. It sought to realise the virtue, intrinsic or incipient, of the prisoner. In this respect the scale and energy of the vision for prisons dwarfs the modest scope of its current ambitions to 'manage risky offenders'.

The original theory of prison, according to Foucault, was that it would:

> assume responsibility for all aspects of the individual, his physical training, his aptitude to work, his everyday conduct, his moral attitude, his state of mind; the prison, much more than the school, the workshop or the army ... is omni-disciplinary. (Foucault, 1979, p 235)

This ambition is still just about recognisable as the general idea of prison lurking somewhere in the public mind. The prison is a vision of social control. Stan Cohen (1985, p 287), the celebrated sociologist, recognised it as a 'notion of such imaginative intensity' that it has never been reducible to the 'brute facts' about imprisonment that criminologist can harvest with such ease and regularity. The prison does something so much more than attempt to manage crime, and it is a serious error, argues Foucault, to think of it principally in terms of crime and punishment. Crime is part of the story, but far from the whole story. Any sustained or detailed study of the prison reveals it to be an institution that, more than almost any other, exposes the 'very moral fabric of society' (Cohen, 1985, p 288). Its architecture, its regimes and its ambitions all declare its intentions to shape the character of the person by locating them in a particularly controlled physical setting. In this the prison projects a classic modernist 'grand design'.

The terrible travesty of prison that anyone who has actually been inside one quickly realises, is that it falls so far short of this design, so often and so predictably. Take, for example, the idea of the prison officer combining 'not exactly judges, or teachers, or foremen, or non-commissioned officers, or parents, but something of all of these things' (Foucault, 1979, p 294). This is an absurd idea that lurks beneath the remarks of every government minister who has ever passed comment on the state of the nation's prisons, from Gladstone in the 19th century to Gauke in 2019. It is nothing short of ludicrous. It is so far from the actuality it would be funny if it wasn't so tragic. It feeds the impossible dream of prison as a place of gently administered correctional guidance delivered by virtuous public servants to grateful and submissive felons who will disappear on release to lives of quiet invisibility. The prison wants to produce a 'docile body', as Foucault refers to men in prison rather facelessly.

White ideas, wrong places

The flattering self-image of the reforming, rehabilitative prison is profoundly colonial in origin. It was established through the course of one English century in which the chaotic tumult of Newgate prison in 1750 was transformed into "the orderly solitude of the Model Prison at Pentonville of 1840" (Cohen, 1985, p 289). Its origins correspond so closely with the white man's dream of civil order, endlessly rehearsed through prison regimes across the empire, that they cannot be completely suppressed. The dream–image transforms the avaricious imperial project of exploitation and extraction to one of cultivation and domestication in which the imagined 'natives' (prisoners) are simple, mostly pre-literate, but potentially good, or at least redeemable. They are tractable, malleable raw material that can be rendered, if properly treated, into model citizens.

The convict settlements and new penal institutions of America, Australia and Tasmania were the testing ground and prisons became the hard frontier of this expanding vision of how the world should be (Anderson, 2018). This dream-image of docile compliance, manageable and teachable prisoners, is the prison's most persistently cherished utopian delusion. It is a vision whose presence dips and weaves through the peaks and troughs of prisons' tangled and contested history. For the most part, sustaining the positive rhetoric around imprisonment and public faith in its potentials has involved ignoring the actual voices of prisoners, their subjective accounts of imprisonment. The marginal position of prisoners' accounts of imprisonment has fostered cold indifference to their predicaments and reinforced their remoteness from human community (Earle, 2018, 2019).

The early Victorian zeal for reforming the individual prisoner both coincided with, and then gave way to, a less idealistic pragmatism that tended towards more conventionally punishing practice, characterised thus by Bill Forsyth (2005): 'bleak, pessimistic, purposefully inflicted severity with a very poor diet, severe hard labour and all amelioration of regime won under a system of marks awarded for conformity, with intensive and rigid enforcement of the rules'. This is the kind of penal austerity that loiters with malicious intent behind the policy regime of the same name deliberately promoted by the UK Coalition government of 2010 as a response to the global banking crisis of 2008, and subsequently sustained by its successor Conservative government in 2015. It is a reminder of the functional, curated ignorance[1] at work in thinking about prisons as if they are exclusively concerned with crime issues rather than broader issues of control in the prevailing social hierarchy.

It is also no accident that in the colonies of the 19th and early 20th centuries those members of the indigenous populations who found themselves imprisoned were largely excluded from the reforms that gradually tempered the extreme physical brutality of penal regimes. These reforms emphasised austere penal regimes which sought to prioritise the civilising, rehabilitative functions of imprisonment. Because of racial differentials in the way these reforms were implemented they were manufacturing not just a new kind of punishment but also a certain kind of whiteness. Chris Cunneen (2011) shows how particularly brutal physical chastisements and tortuously violent punishments were maintained for black, indigenous and Indian prisoners throughout the colonies as they were withdrawn from use on white prisoners. The racial differentials in punishments are consistent with, and functional to, the racism that accompanied and sustained colonial expansion, a racism based in the formulation of a durable white supremacy (that is, belief in the 'white race') and the logics of extermination (Lindqvist, 2018) in which black lives were more disposable than salvageable. White lives, however abject and degraded by imprisonment and class structures, had rehabilitative potential, a place in human society. The pervasive power of whiteness secured these meagre but differentially consequential dividends for white prisoners at the expense of black lives (du Bois, 1903).

Zookeepers of deviance create a petting zoo: the seductions of reform

White prison criminologists, in particular, can run the risk of embodying, more unintentionally than intentionally, a stance identified by Alvin Gouldner (1968:104) that:

> expresses the satisfaction of the Great White Hunter who has bravely risked the perils of the urban jungle to bring back an exotic specimen. It expresses the Romanticism of

the zoo curator who preeningly displays his rare specimens. And like the zookeeper, he wishes to protect his collection: he does not want spectators to throw rocks at the animals behind the bars. But neither is he eager to tear down the bars and let the animals go. The attitude of these zookeepers of deviance is to create a comfortable and humane Indian Reservation, a protected space within which these colourful specimens may be exhibited, unmolested and unchanged.

The delusions of penal practice, its 'false, lurid promise' (Forsyth, 2005, np), are secured not by evidence of success (there is precious little of that) but by denial and its ever-expanding, always unfinished business. There is a terrible shame in punishing that must be disavowed (Cohen, 2001). Foucault (1979, p 10) again: 'It is ugly to be punishable, but there is no glory in punishing. Hence the double system of protection that justice has set up between itself and the punishment it imposes.' No one but the most deranged of psychopaths really relishes causing pain. Especially not the slow asphyxiation of vital signs that long imprisonment implies. If punishment was once done in the name of 'the King' as a spectacularly brutal display of sovereign power, those days are long gone (Hallsworth and Lea, 2012), if only to be much relished in the *Game of thrones* television series.

What follows from the disavowal of the pains prisons deliver is the habit of thinking that the prison is primarily a correctional device with benign intentions. Its aim is to correct, cure or rehabilitate individual prisoners. And refining this mission to reform the prisoner, to within an inch of his life if need be, is what prisons are continually trying to do better. Except that prison persistently fails to deliver on this promise to reliably render up the model prisoner/citizen. If you get sent to prison, the likelihood is that you will go back there, especially if you are an economically marginal young man. The clichéd image of the revolving prison door is an empirical reality rather than a political scandal. As Wayne Morrison (1996, p 116) points out, the 'contemporary western prison, exists in a ... social order which does not require a high level of manual labour ... The simple fact is that those who are currently sent to prison are largely unwanted outside the prison wall and have no skills which are in demand.'

Critical criminologists frequently point to Foucault's observation that prisons are persistently and permanently trying to 'raise their game'. Their quest for the perfect regime that repairs broken, damaged or delinquent men is as endless as it is elusive, tantalisingly just beyond its reach but graspable with a few more resources, a few more reforms, a few more years (Scott, 2013; Drake, 2018). The crisis of imprisonment is not a recent crisis but is built into its penal DNA, its source code. It is the unending nature of the quest that serves the purpose, not the dubious results. Modern prisons have always been in urgent need of reform and thrive on such a semi-permanent state of semi-crisis. Their reform becomes their *raison d'être*:

> One should recall that the movement for reforming the prisons ... is not a recent phenomenon. It does not even seem to have originated in a recognition of failure. Prison reform is virtually contemporary with the prison itself: it constitutes, as it were, its programme. (Foucault, 1991 [1979], p 234)

The Irish playwright and author, Samuel Beckett, distils Foucault's dismal formula in his mournful evocation of modernism's habitual optimism: 'Ever tried. Ever failed. No matter. Try again. Fail again. Fail better' (Beckett, 1983/2009). Prisons, unlike many institutions of government, thrive on failure and seem to be immune from the pervasive nostalgia that infuses contemporary political visions (Gilroy, 2004). For prisons there is no real desire to go back, no use in calling up the glories of an imagined past to comfort the present and postpone the future. Its always forward to the next best prison regime, just around the corner. What's promising is what's next not what works.

Radical critics of imprisonment have tried to expose the dangers of approaching the question of imprisonment from the position of crime because doing so means there is no escape from prison's self-sustaining grip on the concept. Prison-centric reform has very little critical traction and tends to fuel expansion. It is important to situate discussion of imprisonment within its wider social context so as to challenge the popular belief in the necessity of prison as the principal response to crime. It is equally important to contest the prevailing definitions of crime and dislodge their hold over the demarcation of socially harmful behaviour (Cooper and Whyte, 2017; Boukli and Kotzé, 2018; Tombs, 2018, 2019; Downes, 2019, forthcoming). Presenting penal institutions as a logical response to 'crime' may pay political dividends to opportunist politicians, it may maintain the justification for an overpaid and overdressed judiciary, but it cannot offer even a half-baked promise of analytical progress.

The slow demise of the post-war aspiration to make rehabilitation the defining principle of the justice system, and the contemporary reluctance to recognise it as incompatible with punishment, is part of a wider deflation in some of the foundational themes of the modern, colonial era. The prevailing mood in the colonial metropole has become infused with melancholic fatalism (Gilroy, 2004). Faith in politics, belief in ideologies, confidence in the power of governments to ameliorate social ills or trust in the collective power of people to change their lives and prospects by political action, has receded from a high point in the middle of the 20th century. Morbid symptoms of crisis in the hegemonic order take shape in the form of populist identifications with nostalgic, backward-facing visions. It is no wonder that the internet records a recent spike in the frequency of online references to Antonio Gramsci's famous observation on the cyclical crises that characterise capitalism: 'the old is dying and the new cannot be born; in this interregnum a great variety of morbid symptoms appear' (cited in Achcar, 2017).

Prisons are a paradigmatic example of the grip of the pessimistic TINA doctrine that 'there is no alternative'.[2] But perversely, rather than shrinking as have other public institutions associated with big governmental ambitions, prisons have expanded as interest in alternatives has withered. Prisons have come to represent common sense; they are seen as immutable matters of fact; indisputable. Thinking otherwise is dismissed as simple and naïve at best, irrational and idiotic at worst. Just as Mark Fisher (2009) argues that it has become easier to imagine the end of the world than the end of capitalism, imagining a world without prisons, or the need for them, has become almost unthinkable, beyond the realm of serious or sensible discussion. The TINA doctrine eternalises all its assumptions to present them as unchanging, timeless truths. Which is why universities, as places to think differently – and especially a place like the OU – are so important. Because, almost alone among its peers, the OU is an alternative.

What's wrong with universities and why the OU is a good idea

Prisons and universities might be thought of as representing two contrasting ideals of order and civilisation. Crudely put, prisons represent a disciplined, authoritarian hierarchy while universities evoke images of a liberal meritocracy. Universities can be sources of wonder and curiosity (Connell, 2019); prisons are usually places of closure and dread. While it is relatively easy, if not particularly popular, to criticise prisons, universities tend get a gentler critical ride, and no one argues for their abolition as some do for prisons. Universities, at one level or another, have been seen as places to think (Cohen, 2004), but they have also operated historically as guardians of privilege and property; mostly men's, mostly white people's, and mostly of those in the middle and upper classes. In Europe they emerged out of the craft guild system of the Middle Ages where 'Masters' and 'Doctors' hoarded exclusive knowledge as trade secrets. They became, in the late 19th and early 20th centuries, 'finishing schools' where the sons (and more lately, daughters) of the ruling class formed alliances, friendships and networks to equip them with the skills and contacts to govern (Haiven, 2014).

As Dan Weinbren mentions in Chapter 4, the expansion of higher education in the years after 1945 quickly acquired Cold War dimensions as the twin forces of Keynesianism and Sovietism vied for hearts and minds that might sustain the historic triumph over fascism in the Second World War. The OU emerged from the imaginative spaces and possibilities that opened up in the post-war years, part of the democratic, egalitarian surge that the defeat of fascism released (Fisher, 2009). In the UK, Keynesian economic policies and the accompanying principles of social democracy ensured the state's financial resources were directed towards universities by subsidising the costs of higher education. Funding would have general uplifting outcomes that would encourage more effective contributions to a growing, dynamic economy. In the Soviet Union, Stalinist state control guaranteed high levels of resourcing that ensured wider access to an expanding university sector but allowed little room for intellectual freedom or contestation of ideas. Both models, although in very different contexts, shared the view that state-led extension of higher education produced direct and indirect benefits for economic growth.

In the late 1970s the post-war balance between market economies of the West and the state-managed economies of the East shifted powerfully towards the West (Dawson, 2019). The Keynesian compromises and compacts between organised labour and capital gave way to what has become known as neoliberalism. State-led economic planning and structural safety nets were to become history while newly 'liberalised' and 'unfettered' markets would make the future. Universities have not just been pulled into the slipstream of this economic restructuring, they have been complicit in it. There has been little evidence of sustained resistance and most are fully aligned to its ethos of competition and privatisation (Collini, 2012; Haiven, 2014; O'Sullivan, 2016; Connell, 2019). Universities have embraced new epistemological hierarchies stressing the utility of so-called STEM subjects (science, technology, engineering and maths) at the expense of 'the humanities' (arts, history, languages and social science), once the traditional bedrock of the university sector. Universities have tended more and more towards 'competitive schooling' rather than open intellectual inquiry. They are increasingly driven by prestige based on spurious ranking systems that promote the 'credentialization' and 'testification' of academic performance (O'Sullivan, 2016; Connell, 2019).

In these threatening neoliberal and increasingly populist times it is tempting to lapse into lazy nostalgias that romanticise the old liberal university as if it had never been complicit in cementing the epistemic hegemony of the West over the rest of the world through much of the 18th, 19th and 20th centuries. In the process, western universities have played an active role in the dismissal of non-western institutions of higher education and non-western ways of knowing the world. The Italian University of Bologna is widely acknowledged as the 'first university' even though it was preceded by more than a century by the establishment of the University of Al-Quaraouiyine in Morocco and Al-Azhar University in Egypt (Dawson, 2019). Al-Azhar's roots in Egypt's Islamic cultures, in particular, offers a long tradition of combining forms of knowledge about, and understanding of, the world that are increasingly threatened (Connell, 2019).

As students have diversified from the white, upper- and middle-class male norm that characterised much of their history, they have frequently protested against the status quo. Inspired by student-led struggles 'within, against and beyond' universities in South Africa in 2015 and 2016, protests against the whiteness of UK universities and their curricula have emerged. Campaigns such as UCL's (University College London) Why is My Curriculum White? (and Why Isn't My Professor Black?) and Rhodes Must Fall at Oxford,[3] combine with critical pedagogical interventions to forcefully pressure universities for substantive change (Joseph-Salisbury, 2018). Statistical data documenting more minority ethnic than white academics on temporary contracts, fewer in senior roles, with fewer minority ethnic students attending Russell Group institutions, and their lower attainment in degree performance have emphasised intersecting concerns about inequality and racism in higher education (Tate and Bagguley, 2017). When the Royal Historical Society publishes a report (RHS, 2018) that reveals history in UK universities to be an overwhelmingly white discipline, where 93.7 per cent of history staff are white, and the history curriculum to be dominated by white scholars and white perspectives, the conventional narrative that British universities are colour-blind meritocracies is clearly flawed.

Universities are no more islands of virtuous liberalism than they are passive agents of the economy or idle bystanders to the triumphant march of neoliberalism with its low-wage economy and widening inequality (Picketty, 2017). Using only slightly different terminology, Bousquet (2008, p 44) insists 'late capitalism doesn't just happen to the university; the university makes late capitalism happen'.

Opportunity knocks: inside and out

As universities struggle to adapt to the conditions they have helped to bring about, the search for alternatives becomes more urgent. The same can be said for the development of university education in prison. The growth of imprisonment and the expansion in the number of penal institutions has generated opportunities for universities that they have seized. While the OU led the way with higher education in prisons in the 1970s, many other universities across the UK are now engaging in outreach work and teaching within the prison walls themselves.

This is in part down to the growth of the Inside-Out prisoner education movement, which began in the United States and has spread far beyond its borders. This type of programme brings non-prisoner students at higher education institutions into prison classrooms to receive part of their tuition alongside prisoners (Pompa, 2013). There are now significant numbers of universities in the UK (including the OU's Law School) that engage in a version of this kind of teaching.

The strength of the process is that it allows students to break down their preconceptions of each other. The prison student can begin to understand, and de-mystify, the lives and perspectives of the full-time student and the full-time student can begin to understand the experience and perspective of their incarcerated classmate (see Tynan, 2019 and Nichols et al, 2019). These approaches to higher education in prison do not lead directly to a degree or diploma for the student in the same way that OU study does. However, they may help give confidence to a prisoner intimidated by or unfamiliar with the very notion of studying for a degree. Graduates of Inside-Out and similar programmes have gone on to successfully complete degrees both while incarcerated and upon release. There can be no doubt that there are benefits to these sorts of programmes.

However, these programmes, and higher education in prison generally, raise difficult questions of universities as co-producers of the expanding prison-industrial complex and the neoliberal agenda that survives so symbiotically with it (Wacquant, 2001). Inspirational as it may be to attend classes with professors and students from universities, what is the value of that tuition if the university will almost certainly not select you to continue your studies and graduate from the institution because of your criminal record? Or saddle you with a debt you may never be able to repay? What is in it for a student who wants to gain a degree (for all the myriad reasons set out by contributors to this book), when they are unlikely to get a meaningful amount of formal academic credit for their studies? Many running these types of Inside-Out programme agonise about these questions even as they present them. Some worry about the possibility of encouraging freedom of thought and expression with prison officers in their classroom, or of the 'outside' students' role. What, after all, is really in it for them? Is it a transformative experience, or just a novel teaching environment offering a bit more stimulation than a university classroom and a new marketing opportunity for aggressive institutional strategists? The risk of such programmes becoming little more than voyeuristic penal tourism around the 'Indian Reservations' referred to by Gouldner, with educative add-ons, is always present but less frequently critically interrogated. These may well be risks that can be managed by committed teachers, students and prison staff, but is it really the case that everyone wins as universities expand into an expanding penal estate? There is something of a politics of virtue driving this work in which virtuous motivations and intentions are taken to be sufficient justification for such projects.

The mutual expansion of higher education and imprisonment raises some difficult questions about the place of higher education in the carceral environment. As students, prison administrators and the voluntary sector champion education and its reformative capacity for those prisoners who find themselves in the position to benefit from it, it becomes easier to ignore the pains of imprisonment (Scott, 2012) and the less visible, concussive damage that prison does to so many. These are extensive, real, long-lasting and deeply felt traumas which are widely documented in penal sociology but rarely escape the academic ghetto. For many critical scholars and penal abolitionists, the prison is the ultimate symbol of a failed system of criminal justice, a system that should be scrapped as part of a wider and more systematic struggle for social justice. Such aims do not fit easily with notions of the prison as a 'rehabilitative' institution whose ambitions cannot extend beyond returning people to their place in an unjust society.

For penal abolitionists who, like us, are committed to prison education, this raises a question of conscience; is it conscionable to be providing services that make the carceral project marginally less unpalatable when in fact it is the whole carceral project that needs to be taken down? By reducing the pain, and generating much-needed examples of 'desistance' or 'rehabilitation' are we giving support to those who argue that 'prison works' or that it can at least occasionally work?

This discomfort with working on a relatively minor problem while ignoring, or perhaps even reinforcing the bigger, more harmful process is a familiar political dilemma that can be seen in other areas of activism. For the Israeli human rights defender Jessica Montell, this tension has long been present for those campaigning against the occupation of Palestine. Some activists argue that by providing basic services, such as drinking fountains, at otherwise inhospitable locations, such as military checkpoints where long queues are commonplace and predictable, they are enabling and supporting the occupation:

> Rather than removing the illegal checkpoints, the argument goes, we have merely succeeded in ameliorating the suffering there, and in doing so, perhaps entrenched the checkpoints further. There are many human rights activists who believe that Israel's occupation is even stronger than ever and that the human rights community constitutes another organ of the occupation, pointing to the fact that, in spite of, or perhaps partly because of, our work, the occupation is even stronger than ever. We essentially make the intolerable tolerable and therefore permanent. (Montell, 2018, p 53)

Ultimately Montell rejects this strategy of declining to provide humanitarian aid and refuses to accept that there is a singular, correct approach to the struggle for human rights. This may be a useful way to look at the tension between the story of further education in prison and the struggle for penal abolitionism. The OU prison education story is one of reform, while the penal abolitionist story is much closer to a revolutionary change in society. However, we believe there can be room for both. The revolutionary, hoping to end the occupation of Palestinian territories or the prison-industrial complex, should not be afraid to, or lack the compassion to, support those who are living through the pains of each of these oppressive, long-standing and entrenched practices.

Many of the contributors to this book describe the challenges they (or their students) have had with accessing learning materials, speaking to tutors, or completing their studies in other ways. The importance of prison staff in facilitating basic access to materials (or more recently online materials, see McFarlane and Pike, Chapter 2) cannot be overstated. Education, particularly higher education, can allow the prison student to take more control, exert some power, of at least some part of themselves on their own terms. It offers them agency and greater capacities for self-determination. This may fall short of the revolution aspired to by the ardent penal abolitionist, but in can still be consistent with Paulo Freire's revolutionary philosophy of education as liberation. Freire (1970, p 51) argues for a process of 'conscientisation', in which people approach education 'not as recipients, but as knowing subjects' who become more aware of 'the socio-cultural reality which shapes their lives and of their capacity to transform that reality'. Many of the prison students who have contributed to this book indicate that Freire's vision infuses much of their higher education in prison. In personal, if not structural terms, it is revolutionary, transformative and empowering.

The driving force behind the OU for the last 50 years has been a radically democratising, egalitarian vision; to allow knowledge and education to be obtained by anyone, regardless of their lack of formal qualifications; to be 'open to people, open to places, open to methods and open to ideas'. That quiet revolution in access to higher education has been a remarkable achievement, but to include prisoners, in the face of public indifference to their predicaments was perhaps an even greater one.

Know better blues: open universities, close prisons

In 1967, when Laurie Taylor and Stan Cohen began their sociology classes with prisoners in HMP Durham, they were regarded as hostile radicals by the government, prison authorities and probably some prisoners (Cohen and Taylor, 1972, 1976). As Fielding and Fielding (2000, p 672) point out, 'they were being oppressed by the Home Office, which regulated their research and ultimately prevented their follow-up study'. Theirs was a politically motivated sociological intervention with a general repudiation of the prison system as its objective. They predicted that most prison research would do little 'to disturb the political and legal structure' (Cohen and Taylor, 1972, p 207). Much has changed since then. Prisons now welcome academics with open arms and fears of radicalisation settle on Muslim clerics and neo-fascist activists rather than sociologists.

When HMP Berwyn in north Wales was opened, to much fanfare, in 2017, it was heralded as bringing a whole new set of ideas to British prisons. The conventional boxy modern architecture was jazzed up with strips of colour to break the dull uniform grey of concrete and steel. With its stripes of red, blue, green and yellow people said it might be mistaken for a school from the outside. You couldn't see the bars on the windows unless you looked closely. And it wasn't just the buildings that would be different. Inside, prisoners would be called by their names rather than by their numbers. They would be referred to as men rather than prisoners. They would have phones and laptops linked up to a secure internal network emulating web-based communication systems. There would be showers in their rooms, and rooms is what they would be called, not cells. The *Daily Mail* called it 'the cushiest jail in Britain'. Holding 2,100 men, it would also be one of the largest prisons in Europe, and, with a visionary new governor, one of the best – the future of prisons is how it was promoted to the media. In 2019, just two years after it opened, it was in deep crisis. Many of the promised facilities had failed to materialise and as a result it was half empty. Assaults on staff were higher than in other prisons. Violence was rife and 'use of force' incidents by staff on prisoners were higher than the sector average. Life for prisoners was not all bad, but it was a far cry from what had been promised. Visiting her partner a year after he had been transferred there from another prison, 'Sally Smith' told reporters from the *Financial Times* "They sold him the dream. They said it's a new prison to help people, but it's terrible" (O'Connor and O'Murchu, 2019).

This kind of story, reported in some detail in the *Financial Times* in 2019, can be found again and again in any history of modern imprisonment. Its resemblance to the story of Soledad Prison in the USA is striking. Soledad was opened in 1946 as the post-war progressive optimism cited by Mannheim and Morris began to build. Soledad was to be the flagship of the new generation of therapeutic, rehabilitative prisons. It was 'a collage of floral walkways, baseball diamonds, gymnasiums, movie theatres, classrooms and private cells' (Yee, 1973, p 10). Twenty-five years later, in 1971, Soledad prison officers were found to be setting up, and betting on, fights between black prisoners and white nationalist prisoners. It was the prison where George Jackson was accused of killing a prison officer as a reaction to such activity, an accusation that led to his murder by prison guards later the same year in San Quentin prison. In *Blood in my eye*, Jackson's account of his adoption of the Black liberation politics championed by the Black Panther movement, there is a memorable observation that eludes many criminologists: 'The ultimate expression of law is not order – it's prison' (Jackson, 1971, p 29). As America addressed the politics of black liberation by seemingly replacing its war on poverty with a war on drugs, the US prison estate, and particularly the number of its black inhabitants, mushroomed.

New prisons like Soledad and Berwyn will keep being built and keep promising to do their best. Critical criminologists know better. Reforming prison seems to be a lot more realistic than radically changing society, but prison-centric reform rarely does much more than make more prisons more possible. The more prisons are built that resemble schools or universities, and the more academics find themselves accommodated there, the more worried we should be because as prisons grow, freedom shrinks.

For both of us, celebrating the 50th anniversary of the OU demands fidelity to its traditions of critical social science. The quiet revolution was accomplished not by cautious acquiescence to the status quo, but from radical, daring and imaginative leaps of faith. What many sceptics insisted was impractical if not impossible was demanded and made real. Mike Fitzgerald was one of the OU's original cohort of critical academics who joined the OU in 1975. A founder member of the activist organisation Preservation of the Rights of Prisoners (PROP), he persuaded Stuart Hall (one of the UK's most internationally celebrated sociologists) and other critical sociologists to join the OU and was a passionate advocate for widening access to higher education. Writing in a 1975 Review Symposium on Changing the Penal System he urged activists and academics to differentiate between positive and negative reforms. Drawing on the radical originator of penal abolitionism, Thomas Mathiesen (1974), he cautioned against investing in positive reforms that 'improve or build up the system so that it functions more effectively' but fail to impact on the underpinning ideology. By contrast, he advocated negative reforms that 'remove greater or smaller parts on which the prison system in general is more or less dependent' (Fitzgerald, 1975, p 94). Such reforms constrain expansion and diminish penal options. In the Netherlands, where reform has tended more towards this approach by addressing general social conditions rather than penal specifics, new prisons (like those that entertained the delegates at the Portsmouth conference) stand empty and others have closed. Over the next 50 years original, radical and daring visions are vital if critical scholars at the OU are going to continue to challenge the sweet-toothed preference for positive reforms that deliver penal obesity on the back of a short-lived sugar-rush of optimism.

Notes

1   See the emerging critical literature on agnotology – the study of how ignorance is manufactured, distributed and sustained as a counterpoint to knowledge (Proctor and Schiebinger, 2008).

2   The TINA principle is commonly associated with Margaret Thatcher's advocacy of it, but it was first expounded by her hero and economic inspiration, Milton Friedman (1979): '[T]he record of history is absolutely crystal clear. That there is no alternative way, so far discovered, of improving the lot of the ordinary people that can hold a candle to the productive activities that are unleashed by a free enterprise system.'

3   See www.nus.org.uk/en/news/why-is-my-curriculum-white and https://rmfoxford.wordpress.com.

References

Achcar, G. (2017) 'Morbid symptoms: what did Gramsci mean and how does it apply to our times?', *International Socialist Review* 108, https://isreview.org/issue/108/morbid-symptoms.

Anderson, C. (2018) *A global history of convicts and penal colonies*, London: Bloomsbury

Beckett, S. (1983/2009) *Worstward Ho*. London: Faber and Faber.

Boukli, A. and Kotzé, J. (eds) (2018) *Zemiology: Reconnecting crime and social harm*, Basingstoke: Palgrave Macmillan.

Bousquet, M. (2008) *How the university works: Higher education and the low-wage nation*, New York: New York University Press.

Cohen, P. (2004) 'A place to think? Some reflections on the idea of the university in the age of the "knowledge economy"', *New Formations* 53(1): 12–27.

Cohen, S. (1985) 'Review of *The fabrication of virtue: English prison architecture, 1750–1840*', *British Journal of Criminology* 25(3): 288–90.

Cohen, S. (2001) *States of denial: Knowing about atrocities and suffering*, Cambridge: Polity Press.

Cohen, S. and Taylor, L. (1972) *Psychological survival: The effects of long-term imprisonment*, London: Allen Lane.

Cohen, S. and Taylor, L. (1976) *Escape attempts: The theory and practice of resistance to everyday life*, London: Allen Lane.

Collini, S. (2012) *What are universities for?*, Harmondsworth: Penguin.

Connell, R. (2019) *The good university: What universities actually do and why it's time for radical change*, London: Zed Press.

Cooper, V. and Whyte, D. (eds) (2017) *The violence of austerity*, London: Pluto Press.

Coyle, A., Fair, H., Jacobson, J. and Walmsey, R. (2016) *Imprisonment worldwide: The current situation and an alternative future*, Bristol: Policy Press.

Cunneen, C. (2011) 'Postcolonial perspectives for criminology', in M. Bosworth and C. Hoyle (eds) *What is criminology?*, Oxford: Oxford University Press.

Dawson, M. (2019) 'Rehumanising the university for an alternative future: decolonisation, alternative epistemologies and cognitive justice', *Identities: Global Studies in Culture and Power*, doi: 10.1080/1070289X.2019.1611072.

Downes, J. (2019, forthcoming) 'Re-imagining an end to gendered violence: pre-figuring the worlds we want', in E. Hart, J. Greener and R. Moth (eds) *Resist the punitive state: Grassroots struggles across welfare, housing, education and prisons*, London: Pluto Press.

Drake, D. (2018) 'Prisons and state building: promoting 'the fiasco of the prison' in a global context', *International Journal for Crime, Justice and Social Democracy*, 7(4): 1–15.

Du Bois, W.E.B. (1903) *The souls of black folk*, Harmondsworth: Penguin.

Earle, R. (2018) 'Convict criminology in England: developments and dilemmas', *British Journal of Criminology*, 58(6): 1499–516.

Earle, R. (2019) 'Narrative convictions, conviction narratives: the prospects of convict criminology', in L. Presser and J. Fleetwood (eds) *Handbook of narrative criminology*, Basingstoke: Palgrave.

Fielding, N. and Fielding, J. (2000) 'Resistance and adaptation to criminal identity: using secondary analysis to evaluate classic studies of crime and deviance', *Sociology*, 34(4): 671–89.

Fisher, M. (2009) *Capitalist realism: Is there no alternative?* London: Zero Books.

Fitzgerald, M. (1975) 'The strategies of radical prisoners' groups', Review Symposium on the Penal System, *British Journal of Criminology*, 15(1): 92–4.

Forsyth, W. (2005) 'Review of *English society and the prison: Time, culture and politics in the development of the modern prison, 1850–1920*, by Alyson Brown', Reviews in History, www.history.ac.uk/reviews/review/443.

Foucault, M. (1991 [1979]) *Discipline and punish: The birth of the prison*, Harmondsworth: Penguin.

Freire, P. (1970) *Cultural action for freedom*, Harmondsworth: Penguin.

Friedman, M. (1979) Appearing on the Phil Donahue show, www.youtube.com/ watch?v=RWsx1X8PV_A (1:00–1:38).

Gilroy, P. (2004) *After empire: Melancholia or convivial culture*, Abingdon: Routledge.

Gouldner, A. (1968) 'The sociologist as partisan: sociology and the welfare state', *The American Sociologist*, 3(2): 103–16, available at https://www.jstor.org/stable/27701326.

Haiven, M. (2014) *Crises of imagination, crises of power: Capitalism, creativity and the commons*, London: Zed Press.

Hallsworth, S. and Lea, J. (2012) 'Reconnecting the king with his head: the fall and resurrection of the state in criminological theory', *Crime, Media, Culture: An International Journal*, 8(2): 185–95.

House of Commons (2018) 'UK prison population statistics briefing paper', CBP-04334, https://researchbriefings.files.parliament.uk/documents/SN04334/SN04334.pdf.

Jackson, G. (1971/1990) *Blood in my eye*, New York: Black Classic Press.

Joseph-Salisbury, R. (2018) 'Institutionalised whiteness, racial microaggressions and Black bodies out of place in Higher Education', Critical Pedagogies Group Annual Lecture 2018, University of Westminster, 24 May.

Lindqvist, S. (2018) *'Exterminate all the brutes'*, London: Granta.

Mathiesen, T (1974) *The politics of abolition*, New York: John Wiley & Sons.

Montell, J. (2018) 'The drinking fountain at the checkpoint', in E. Murray and J. Mehigan (eds) *Defending hope: Dispatches from the front lines in Palestine and Israel*, Dublin: Veritas, pp 47–66.

Morris, N. (1965) 'Prison in evolution', *Federal Probation*, 29: 12.

Morrison, W. (1996) 'Modernity, imprisonment, and social solidarity', in R. Matthews and P. Francis (eds) *Prisons 2000*, London: Palgrave Macmillan, pp 94–120.

Nichols, H., Young, S. and Behan, C. (2019) 'Editorial: Critical reflections on higher education in prison', *Journal of Prison Education and Reentry*, 6(1): 1–5.

O'Connor, S. and O'Murchu, C. (2019) 'What went wrong at Britain's prison of the future?', *Financial Times*, 7 March. www.ft.com/content/e8454c86-3f9d-11e9-9bee-efab61506f44.

O'Sullivan, M. (2016) *Academic barbarism, universities and inequality*, Basingstoke: Palgrave.

Picketty, T. (2017) *Capital in the 21st century*, Boston, MA: Harvard University Press.

Pompa, L. (2013) 'Drawing forth, finding voice, making change: inside-out learning as transformative pedagogy', in S. Davis and B. Roswell (eds), *Turning teaching inside out: A pedagogy of transformation for community-based education*, New York: Palgrave Macmillan, pp 13–26.

Prison Reform Trust (2019) *Prison: the facts – Bromley Briefings Summer 2019*, London: Prison Reform Trust.

Proctor, R. and Schiebinger, L. (eds) (2008) *Agnotology: The making and unmaking of ignorance*, Stanford: Stanford University Press.

RHS (Royal Historical Society) (2018) *Race, ethnicity and equality in UK history: A report and resource for change*. London: Royal Historical Society.

Scott, D. (2012) 'Sympathy for the devil: human rights and empathic construction of suffering', *Criminal Justice Matters*, 88(1): 8–9.

Scott, D. (ed.) (2013) *Why prison?* Cambridge: Cambridge University Press.

Tate, S.A. and Bagguley, P. (2017) 'Building the anti-racist university: next steps', *Race Ethnicity and Education*, 20(3): 89–99.

Taylor, L. (1969) 'Criminologist and criminal', *Anarchy*, 98 (April): 114–21, www.thesparrowsnest.org.uk/collections/public_archive/7126.pdf

Tombs, S. (2018) 'For pragmatism and politics: crime, social harm and zemiology', in A. (Paraskevi) Boukli and J. Kotzé (eds) *Zemiology: Reconnecting crime and social harm*, Basingstoke: Palgrave Macmillan, pp 11–31.

Tombs, S. (2019) 'Grenfell: the unfolding dimensions of social harm', *Justice, Power and Resistance*, 3(1) (in press).

Tonry, M. (2004) *The future of imprisonment*, Oxford: Oxford University Press.

Tynan, R. (2019) '"It's about whose voices matter": Reflections on insider/outsider status in prison classrooms', *Journal of Prison Education and Reentry*, 6(1): 121–26.

Wacquant, L. (2001) 'Deadly symbiosis: When ghetto and prison meet and mesh', *Punishment and Society*, 3(1): 95–133.

Yee, M. (1973) *The melancholy history of Soledad prison: In which a utopian scheme turns bedlam*, New York: HarperCollins.

Out of the abysmal

'Eris'

Only a prisoner (and possibly a prison officer) can truly understand the sheer tedium of prison life. Without considerable effort, the fact is every day is Groundhog Day – depressingly identical to the last and the next. The majority of each day is spent in what is, to all intents and purposes, a large toilet – which is often without a lid so life is lived, and meals consumed, next to an open sewer. Being trans I'm lucky in that I never have to share my cell/toilet with another prisoner but even so the uniformity of the environment is bleak, with any attempt to personalise your living space frowned upon and treated as a disciplinary offence.

It was to puncture this tedium that I decided to provide a more varied structure to my time by studying with The Open University. My subject choice was based on reviewing a selection of module materials kept in the prison library (from previous students and transferred from regional centres when these were closed by the OU) which convinced me that while level 1 modules would be useful for those with little experience of study and essay writing, they would be insufficiently challenging for me. Fortunately, the PPE (Politics, Philosophy and Economics) degree allowed me to study a single level 1 module followed by three level 2 modules and two level 3 modules. If the OU needs to make any changes, then this is the one I would encourage, a greater variety of subjects available with only a single level 1 module.

While prison management is almost universally abysmal, I have been in the fortunate position of studying at three prisons with well-managed distance learning functions. This is particularly the case with my current prison where the level of support and commitment to OU students from the education department is outstanding – unfortunately it has to be because the general management is even worse than most prisons. For example, it took over ten months to obtain the pen and cartridges I wanted to write my exam. (I prefer using a 'proper' ink pen to biros and am a tiny bit OCD about this) and that only happened after I threatened legal action. The response was to minute a statement in the prison council (a body of lickspittle prisoners that provides an invisibly thin veneer of accountability of management to prisoners) that a procedure for obtaining study materials existed. Interestingly, this worked because obtaining more cartridges for my third year of study took only (sic) six months! Mind you, no one else has managed to get it to work and I only obtained the academic year diaries I had sent in by a friend by writing to my MP (it appears that Grayling's book ban* lives on, lightly disguised with the allegation that books and diaries might be soaked in some psychoactive substance ... like education and knowledge perhaps?).

The great thing about studying at this particular prison is that the number of OU students means that we can interact and support each other. It is much easier to spot your own faults when you are reviewing someone else's TMA (tutor-marked assessment) and realise you make exactly the same errors you are pointing out to them. It's quite surprising just how uncritical we can be of faults in our own work. This, of course, is where the support from OU tutors comes in – whether by tutorial visits to the prison or telephone tutorials they have been wonderfully supportive and argumentative, making me think clearly and justify the positions I have taken. I suppose on reflection, I might have read more post-structural philosophy than was strictly necessary and I ought to apologise for that!

Thanks should also go to the county library services of Nottinghamshire, Staffordshire and Cambridgeshire who have provided access to endless useful books through their support of the prison libraries. Indeed the library here (supported by Cambridgeshire) has acquired so many new philosophy and politics texts over and above those I requested (which were more often than not purchased) that I've struggled to read them all and irritated a number of tutors by quoting from works they then have to check!

In an innovation this year, the Open University Students Association (OUSA) has introduced a research support facility for level 3 students that has proved absolutely brilliant. It has allowed me to ask the OU support manager here to print queries from Google Scholar that I can select from and send to OUSA knowing that the selected articles will be printed and sent to me in a week or so.

As I write this, I am 10 days from release. OK I have one TMA and an EMA (end-of-module assessment) to complete and post next week and an exam to sit a month after release, but I'm already signed up for the final level 3 module (Key Questions in Philosophy, starting October) that will complete my degree and provide a comforting element of continuity between prison and my first year out.

---

* In 2012, as the government's Justice Secretary, Christopher Grayling, banned prisoners from receiving books from relatives or friends. Challenged in the court by The Howard League for penal Reform, the ban was ruled unlawful in December 2015.

6

The light to fight the shadows: on education as liberation

Kris MacPherson

Realising one of your childhood aspirations is a strange feeling. Ever since I was a kid, one of my ambitions was to write a book. Reading books has always been a massive part of my life, regardless of whether I was engaged in offending behaviour or not. I would always tell people that I wanted to enter a shop like Waterstones and find something I had written on the shelves to experience the sense of achievement I am sure it would bring. Therefore, I feel privileged as well as excited to be given the opportunity to contribute to the book *Degrees of freedom*, conceived to celebrate the 50th anniversary of The Open University (OU).

Funnily enough, I had always wanted to go to university and study for a degree too. However, bad decision-making signposted me towards a life of offending and incarceration. It wasn't until I had been handed down a custodial term of 16 years in 2003 that I realised my life was at a monumental crossroads. At that time, I was 21 years old and knew that the prospect of an eternity of crime and prison – perhaps even premature death – hung over my head like the Sword of Damocles. Unfortunately, this was my third stint behind bars and I was well aware that all of my 'legal lives' were used up. If I was going to transcend the ruins of my life, it was now or never. In this way, I recognised that the way I chose to use my time in custody would likely define how I would live the rest of my days.

Interestingly, Cusson and Pinsonneault (1986, p 57) found that several factors precipitated the cessation of offending behaviour in a qualitative study of former bank robbers: 'shock (such as being wounded in a bank raid); growing tired of doing time in prison; becoming aware of the possibility of longer prison terms; and a reassessment of what is important to the individual'. In retrospect, I can see how these processes paralleled my own situation. While I had put my 'injuries' to the back of my mind, it wasn't until I had time to reflect on my lifestyle that it dawned on me that I was lucky to be alive. That being said, I realised my injuries were not only physical but mental, emotional and spiritual as well. This revealing analysis of my personal reality braided with a 'growing tired[ness]' of serving time and 'increasing sentence lengths', leading me to 'question what is important' in life (McNeill et al, 2012).

Post-sentencing, I was transferred from HMP Barlinnie to HMP Shotts. Frankly, I was a little apprehensive about going there. After all, a major violent incident had occurred in the institution only a year before my arrival, which didn't auger well for staying out of trouble, at least in my own opinion. In this way, it felt like I was walking into the lion's den of the Scottish penal system, perhaps correlating with King and McDermott's (1995) notions of the 'depth' and 'weight' of imprisonment as well as Freeman and Seymour's (2010) 'tightness' (both cited in Crewe, 2011).

Respectively, 'depth' and 'weight' are terms academics use to describe the extent of prisonisation – the way someone experiences the effects of imprisonment – and the 'oppressiveness and distance from release' (Crewe, 2011: 521). On the other hand, 'tightness' refers to generic feelings of tension and anxiety brought on by the uncertainty of the prison environment. Therefore, I knew I would have to be 'on the ball', to use a carceral colloquialism, while searching for something constructive to fill my days. Upon admission to HMP Shotts, I went straight to the Education Department and discovered that inmates could study with the OU provided they passed the prerequisite courses.

Twin peaks or grave error?

When I heard that the Scottish Prison Service (SPS) subsidised prisoners' OU degrees, I knew I had found my next mountain to climb. In other words, I chose to scale the academic mountain to achieve a degree while simultaneously climbing the penal peak to complete my sentence. I didn't even know if I could succeed in meeting the scholarly standards but was prepared to do anything to excavate myself from the metaphorical grave I had dug for myself over the course of my 'offending years'. In this manner, I had clearly reassessed 'what is important' to me, a process described in the academic literature as being central to desistance (McNeill et al, 2012). Initially, I started my OU odyssey pursuing a BSc. (Hons) Psychology but shifted to a BSc. (Hons) Criminology with Psychological Studies, graduating in 2017. Not only was criminology a more logical fit due to my life experiences, but I also achieved a 'Distinction' grade in the subject while receiving average scores in psychology. Learning alone was, at times, difficult but quitting never entered my head. In the beginning, I was sceptical about whether a degree would benefit me in the community. After all, I had a criminal record instead of an employment history. However, my desire to finally break the cycle of crime and incarceration through education burned inside me like Dante's *Inferno*.

Nevertheless, if prison is usually a 'very expensive way of making essentially "good" people who [have] done "bad" things "worse"' (Daniels, 2013, p 303) or, worryingly, reinforces criminal relationships and contacts (McNeill and Weaver, 2010), how is it feasible to construct a pro-social identity in a carceral setting? Regardless of my desire to 'go straight', it wasn't until I stumbled across the desistance literature (see McNeill and Weaver, 2010 and McNeill, 2014 for examples) that I realised I had gradually begun to deconstruct my pro-criminal identity. I did so by refraining from accumulating 'criminal capital' in prison, which refers to the social interactions that reinforce and sustain criminal behaviour and identities (Bayer et al, 2009, cited in Drago and Galbiati, 2012), and building a new narrative centred on academic studies. In this way, I utilised education in order to catalyse desistance, referred to as a 'hook-for-change' (Giordano et al, 2002).

Indeed, desistance is described as the cessation of illegal behaviour for those living criminal lifestyles (McNeill et al, 2012). However, Kirkwood and McNeill (2015) later postulate that desistance not only involves the termination of offending but also the successful reintegration of 'offenders', achieved through conformity with social and legal norms. Intriguingly, scholars believe the process is driven by different phases of transformation. For example, Maruna and Farrall (2004, cited in McNeill and Schinkel, 2015) suggest the notions of 'primary desistance' and 'secondary desistance' to describe the cessation of criminal behaviour and a shift in identity respectively. On the other hand, McNeill (2016) offers the idea of 'tertiary desistance' to explain the sense of belonging that depends upon civic and social inclusion of the person re-entering society from custody. In this way, the opportunity to catalyse, nurture and sustain the desistance process is arguably an integral dynamic in the rehabilitation journey.

If the *raison d'être* of incarceration is (punishment and) rehabilitation, couldn't it be postulated that desistance is the *raison d'être* of rehabilitation? For example, how could someone be classified as reformed if they hadn't already desisted from crime? More to the point, do Scottish prisons promote desistance or do they undermine it? Intriguingly, it seemed the more I studied the desistance literature, the more I could use my unusual position to help others answer such pressing questions from the inside/out rather than outside/in approach of conventional academics. After all, as the great theorist of the liberatory powers of education, Paulo Freire, might have put it:

> who [understands] the effects of [incarceration] more than the [incarcerated]? Who can better understand the necessity of [desistance/rehabilitation]? They will not gain this [desistance/rehabilitation] by chance but through the praxis of their quest for it, through their recognition of the necessity to fight for it. (Freire, 2005 [1975], p 45)

Indeed, my deep immersion as an imprisoned person is exactly the kind of experience that eludes most prison administrators and researchers. They can only 'observe from the outside' while I navigate 'penal realities' from the inside, to paraphrase Shammas (2014). As Macedo's (2001, p 19) account of Freire's dialogic methods further tells us, 'If students are not able to transform their lived experiences into knowledge and to use the already acquired knowledge as a process to unveil new knowledge, they will never be able to participate rigorously in a dialogue as a process of learning and knowing.' Therefore, I gradually arrived at the conclusion that I could utilise my position to my own academic advantage by shining a light on the Scottish prison system through the lens of 'convict criminology', described as examination of crimino-penological issues through the prism of first-hand experiences (Earle, 2018). In this way, I feel I am using a 'bad' situation to do 'good'.

Slipping through the net or off the path?

Although I have used academic study in prison to catalyse desistance and shape my own 'anthropocentric' path towards rehabilitation (Rotman, 1986, cited in Behan, 2014), life wasn't always so optimistic. In fact, there came a point when my drive towards transformation suffered a crisis of confidence when I was recalled to custody in 2011 after a year-and-a-half of freedom. Worryingly, re-entering prison briefly resuscitated the pro-criminal philosophy I had battled hard to banish throughout my previous years inside. While I stoically longed to renounce my offending lifestyle, I wondered if it was already way beyond my control. People like me couldn't change and if they could, so what? Who would employ someone like me? Who would give me a second *look* never mind a second *chance*? In this way, it seemed the only people who would 'accept' me were themselves involved in the criminal subculture.

This kind of fatalistic mindset was exacerbated by the media exposure of high-profile political, banking and corporate scandals (for examples, see: Klein, 2007; Kotz, 2009; Mishkin, 2011; Vulliamy, 2011; Dooley, 2014; Mell et al, 2015; Global Witness, 2015) that I used to justify the seemingly modest, relative nature of my illegalities. Interestingly, Wacquant (2010a, p 205) argues along the same lines that:

> The widening of the penal dragnet under neoliberalism has been remarkably discriminating: in spite of conspicuous bursts of corporate crime (epitomized by the Savings & Loans scandal of the 1980s and the folding of Enron a decade later), it has affected essentially the denizens of the lower regions of social and physical space.

At that time, it appeared to be 'acceptable' for middle- and upper-class people to perpetrate illegal behaviour while lower-class individuals seemed overly punished for doing the same. I wonder if this seemingly unbalanced treatment of the poor fortifies criminal identities and behaviour? This may correlate with the claim that 'Many convicts bring with them a commitment to a subculture which is not stripped from them, and in fact, prepares them for life in prison, and that many convicts orient their behaviour towards the larger criminal world, of which prison is a part' (Irwin and Cressey, 1962, cited in Novis, 2013, p 40).

Little did I know that being recalled to custody would present the ultimate test in my faith of 'going straight'. Worryingly, it seemed as though I was a cog in a 'risk renaissance' upon arrival in HMP Low Moss, a recently constructed institution that felt like the first step into the 'Malopticon'. Derived from Jeremy Bentham's penal design for an all-seeing 'Panopticon', a 'Malopticon' is described as 'a penal apparatus or process through which the subject is seen badly, is seen *as* bad and projected and represented as bad' (McNeill, 2018, p 3, emphasis in original). To compound matters, I was faced with the customary depth, weight and tightness of the prison fused with the new 'pessimistic, deficit focus of risk-orientated management strategies' (Burnett and Maruna, 2006, p 101). It almost destroyed the pro-social identity I had strived hard to build through years of carceral education.

In this way, I seriously considered throwing in the 'desistance towel' and embracing the life of crime I had created thus far, for better or worse. This may reinforce claims made by Uggen et al (2004) that 'criminal re-labelling may fracture a "fragile, pro-social identity"' (cited in Burnett and Maruna, 2006, p 100). Furthermore, other academics allude to the ramifications of being labelled as a 'high-risk offender'. For instance, Farrall et al (2010, p 561) assert that:

> Categorization as high-risk and as an offender is likely to be inimical to these processes of individual change. An effective policy on reducing crime rates needs to concentrate on precisely these high-risk offenders (who have been offending most frequently) with the aim of constructively helping some to reduce or cease offending – rather than categorizing them as hopeless.

While wrestling with all of this darkness in the 'securocracy' of HMP Low Moss, I religiously attended the education centre and bonded with the teachers. Strangely, the polar contrasts between the prison residential areas and the education centre almost felt like a manifestation of the two warring polarities battling for control of my heart and soul. The more we got to know each other, the more I felt able to confide in the teachers. Trusting others isn't easy for me because I always feel the need to remain vigilant. In fact, I expect almost everyone I meet to betray or hurt me in some way, thanks to life experiences.

However, the selfless belief, concern and genuine humanity shown me by the teachers slowly thawed the ice that encased my heart during a critical period when I believed I was hurtling towards the edge of a penal cliff. Indeed, they cared more about *who I am* and *where I am going* rather than *who I was* and *where I have been* in the past. This may bolster claims by McNeill and Weaver (2010) that individuals may be inspired to change by someone else believing in their potential to do so. Undeniably, the teachers functioned as a 'life-support machine' for my battered and bruised pro-social identity. In this way, it seemed they nurtured my assets while the prison 'securocrats' magnified my risks and deficits. Paradoxically, it could be argued that the carceral environment reinforced my criminal identity while, at the same time, the teachers fortified the burgeoning pro-social side. In this spiritual tug-of-war, the light trumped the darkness.

In the final year of my degree, I studied the OU module DD301 Crime and Justice and was engrossed with the breadth and depth of the criminology it presented. Excitingly, I had to conduct a piece of research on a topic of my choosing and, perhaps predictably, opted to write about rehabilitation in Scottish prisons (or lack thereof!). I devoured reams of journal articles and academic research to develop a sense of the different arguments while honing my analytical abilities.

Almost by accident (or fate), I discovered a particular text (McNeill and Weaver, 2010) that acted as an epiphany and became my key-in-the-door to the desistance literature.

In fact, McNeill and Weaver's (2010) paper functioned as a theoretical manifestation of my entire struggle to 'go straight' and helped many puzzling facets of this enigmatic journey make sense. Indeed, I was so impressed by this article's comprehension of the struggles vis-à-vis 'going straight' that I literally felt compelled to write to Fergus McNeill at the University of Glasgow to inform him of the impact this document had on me. To my surprise, Fergus replied and offered to visit me in prison. His altruistic support has helped me continue reinforcing the academic-based identity on the foundations laid by my previous teachers. In this way, I feel that higher learning with the OU has changed (and *is* changing) my life.

Nevertheless, the significance of learning on individual development is well-documented. Intriguingly, Friedrich Nietzsche states, 'Real education is a liberation. It removes the weeds and rubbish and vermin that attack the delicate shoots of the plant. Real education is the light warmth and tender rain' (Nietzsche, 2013 [1874], cited in Armstrong, 2013, p 13). In addition, Behan (2014) has referenced numerous studies on the transformative potential of education in prison (see Reuss, 1999; Brookfield, 1987; Rotman, 1986; Hughes, 2009 and Davis, 2003, all cited in Behan, 2014). Yet how could I utilise my own educational journey to extricate myself from my carceral coffin?

Making good with criminology

Initially, Fergus allowed me to use his Discovering Desistance blog, with the blessing of the prison hierarchy at HMP Kilmarnock, to post articles discussing penal rehabilitation and desistance (see MacPherson, 2017a, 2017b, 2017c for examples). Interestingly, it could be argued these posts helped establish a modicum of 'academic capital'. In this way, I was able to lay the groundwork for the academic lifestyle I hope to inhabit after I am released in September 2019. In fact, I feel that I am beginning to shed my 'condemnation script' (Maruna, 2001, cited in Schinkel, 2015), which alludes to the notion that criminalised individuals believe themselves to be consigned to their fate as offenders. In my view, this condemnation narrative is a significant theme experienced by others in custody. How does one nurture and sustain transformation in such hopeless conditions?

Crucially, Ripple et al (1964) suggest pursuing change involves three factors: *motivation* to transform; the *capacity* to behave differently and the benefit of *opportunities* to reinforce desistance (cited in McNeill and Weaver, 2010, emphasis in original). Thankfully, the teachers at HMP Low Moss instilled in me the motivation to catalyse transformation by allowing me to utilise education as a vehicle to build a new character that was unsuited to a criminal existence. This may parallel claims by Giordano et al (2002) that alternative pro-social identities are incompatible with offending lifestyles. By demonstrating the *motivation* and *capacity* to change, the teachers provided *opportunities* to enable matriculation post-release by arranging interviews with Glasgow and Strathclyde universities under the 'Widening Participation Scheme', a programme enabling marginalised groups to access higher education.

However, I could not take advantage of these life-changing opportunities unless the parole board released me. Frustratingly, they had consistently refused to do so based on their perceptions of risk and recidivism. This appears to parallel the notion of 'selective incapacitation', which sees 'offenders' incarcerated based on their perceived risk to society and likelihood of re-offending (Cavadino and Dignan, 1997; Scott and Flynn, 2014). Such Kafkaesque parole tribunals made me feel like I was going through the court process and being tried over and over, correlating with Foucault's (1977 [1975]) notion of being 'judged all over again'. Although the annual parole rejections dented my confidence, this negativity was outweighed by academic opportunities that have come my way post-graduation, such as writing blog posts, publishing journal articles and composing book chapters.

Interestingly, one could suggest that achieving a criminology degree, coupled with the gradual construction of a new identity, parallels Maruna's 'redemption script' (Maruna, 2001, cited in Schinkel, 2015). The redemption script contains three characteristics: (1) confidence about one's ability to overcome barriers; (2) enthusiasm about contributing to causes greater than the individual; and (3) belief in one's 'good self' (Maruna, 2001, cited in Schinkel, 2015). It could be argued that I have overcome obstacles created by parole rejections through academic contributions (a cause greater than myself) while maintaining belief in my 'good self' throughout these negative processes. In this manner, one could postulate that I have turned a dire situation of recidivism and prison to my advantage by using my OU degree as a 'passport to rehabilitation'.

In fact, Ford and Schroeder (2010, cited in Runell, 2017, p 3) claim that 'The perceived or actual acquisition of social capital through educational attainment (re)attaches individuals to conventional values and aspirations'. Moreover, Lockwood et al (2012, cited in Runell, 2017) suggest that participation in academic study is linked with a decreased propensity for re-offending. Ironically, this does not appear to be taken into account in the Scottish penal context, at least in my own experience. Perhaps those who pursue OU degrees in custody are examples of individuals assuming responsibility for their own rehabilitation? Although the value of studying in prison is noted for its transformative potential (Behan, 2014; Prisoners' Education Trust, 2016; Warner, 2018), the sad fact is that those who engage in academic learning in custody are a small minority.

Worryingly, no prisoner I have spoken to about desistance theory had heard of it beforehand. This is worrying because the SPS's (2014, p 22) *Corporate plan 2014–2017* claims to 'embed a desistance-based approach at the heart of purposeful activity' while no such implementation has occurred. Furthermore, the *Annual delivery plan 2018–2019* (SPS, 2018) contains no mention of desistance or utilising asset-based approaches to implement purposeful activity. As a serving inmate, I can confidently state that purposeful activity contains nothing desistance-related. Tellingly, McNeill (2016, p 208) points out how 'the routine activities of life in prison, even if rendered "purposeful", are detached from the desistance-supporting routines that need to be established in the community'. Although I have used education in prison to carve my own path towards desistance, is it possible to initiate the process for those less academically inclined?

Evocatively, the SPS reported that 80 per cent of prisoners were unemployed prior to custody, while, at the same time, finding it eight times more difficult to find work (Scottish Government, 2015). Moreover, the Scottish government (2015) further states that a criminal record is a major impediment to finding employment. Also, the Ministry of Justice (2018) claims that 75 per cent of businesses in the UK would not consider employing someone with criminal convictions. Thus, one could argue that not only will 75 per cent of British employers not provide work for those with a conviction, they won't even *consider* such a proposition. Therefore, wouldn't it be logical to nurture and sustain connections between prisons and employers if the overwhelming majority of prisoners in Scotland were unemployed prior to custody? Wouldn't this enable and support desistance?

In fact, some scholars (Sapouna et al, 2015 and Shapland et al, 2018, cited in Piacentini et al, 2018) propose building work-based links between prisons and communities, which could promote desistance in prisoners. I suspect this would be more successful in combating recidivism and supporting desistance in Scotland. Troublingly,

Wacquant (2010b) argues how those re-entering society from prison in the US return to communities with high rates of poverty and offending. Isn't this setting them up to fail? Doesn't this simply feed the ravenous criminal justice system, allowing crime to flourish in communities? I ask myself these questions daily in the run-up to my own release.

While I am looking forward to liberation in September 2019, I am apprehensive about re-entering society. The fact is that I am where I am only because I managed to engineer a path towards a pro-social future through lots of reflexive analysis and hard studying with the OU. This, in turn, led to others noticing my 'assets' and offering to help me post-release. I wasn't proselytised by behaviour modification programmes or prison psychologists. In fact, I could argue that I changed because I *actively sought* transformation. I didn't wait for someone to hand it to me; I realised that I had to do something about my chaotic life and took necessary steps to catalyse change. If it wasn't for the fact that the OU enables prisoners across the UK to study for degrees, there's no telling where my life would be right now.

But what about others with shorter sentences who don't have the benefit of the OU programmes? Encouragingly, the advent of an organisation, Release Scotland (BBC News, 2018), could see more 'offenders' lead productive lives through gainful employment. However, it seems there is another way for 'offenders' to 'make good'. For instance, scholars have offered the notion of the 'wounded healer' (Le Bel et al, 2015) to describe an individual revising a deviant past to aid in the rehabilitation process of other 'offenders'. Although I feel it pretentious to describe myself as a 'wounded healer', I hope that in the future other prisoners will utilise education with the OU as the light to fight their own shadows, just as I have done. As Ernest Hemingway says, 'There is nothing noble in being superior to your fellow man; true nobility is being superior to your former self" (Li, 2016, p 163).

Acknowledgements

I'd like to take this opportunity to thank the following people: my previous teachers, Sarah McKee, Anna MacKenzie, Ruth Facchini, Nikki Cameron, Eoghann MacColl and David McCusker (all of you inspired me to renounce my old identity when I nearly embraced it – I love all of you!); Fergus McNeill at Glasgow University and Fiona McKenzie at Centrestage (massive thanks for enabling the construction of my academic identity and laying the foundation for my re-entry into society – I feel like we are on the cusp of an amazing journey); a huge thanks to The Open University for enabling prisoners to achieve new beginnings and build different narratives while still in custody; and last but not least, my 'trophy son', Kristopher Anthony MacPherson (I love you more than words could ever describe and hope you become the person I should have been).

References

Armstrong, J. (2013) *Life lessons from Nietzsche*, London: Pan Macmillan.

BBC News (2018) 'New body aims to get ex-prisoners back into work', 22 May. www.bbc.co.uk/news/uk-scotland-glasgow-west-44196724.

Behan, C. (2014) 'Learning to escape: prison education, rehabilitation and the potential for transformation', *Journal of Prison Education and Re-entry*, 1(1): 20–31.

Burnett, R. and Maruna, S. (2006) 'The kindness of prisoners: strengths-based resettlement in theory and in action', *Criminology & Criminal Justice*, 6(1): 83–106.

Cavadino, M. and Dignan, J. (1997) *The penal system: An introduction*, 2nd edn, London: SAGE.

Crewe, B. (2011) 'Depth, weight and tightness: revisiting the pains of imprisonment', *Punishment & Society*, 13(5): 509–29.

Cusson, M. and Pinsonneault, P. (1986) 'The decision to give up crime', in D.B. Cornish, and R.V. Clarke (eds) *The reasoning criminal*, New York: Springer-Verlag.

Daniels, G. (2013) 'Restorative justice: changing the paradigm', *Probation Journal*, 60(3): 302–15.

Dooley, K. (2014) 'The LIBOR scandal', *Review of Banking & Financial Law*, 32: 2–12.

Drago, F. and Galbiati, R. (2012) 'Indirect effects of a policy altering criminal behavior: evidence from the Italian prison experiment', *American Journal of Applied Economics*, 4(2): 199–218.

Earle, R. (2018) 'Convict criminology in England: developments and dilemmas', *British Journal of Criminology*, 58(6): 1499–516.

Farrall, S., Bottoms, A. and Shapland, J. (2010) 'Social structures and desistance from crime', *European Journal of Criminology*, 7(6): 546–70.

Foucault, M. (1977 [1975]) *Discipline and punish: The birth of the prison*, trans. A. Sheridan, London: Penguin/Allen Lane.

Freire, P. (2005 [1975]) *Pedagogy of the oppressed*, 30th anniversary edn, trans. M. Bergman Ramos, New York and London: Continuum Books.

Giordano, P.C., Cernkovich, S.A. and Rudolph, J.L. (2002) 'Gender, crime and desistance: toward a theory of cognitive transformation', *American Journal of Sociology*, 107(4): 990–1064.

Global Witness (2015) *Banks and dirty money: How the financial system enables state looting at a devastating human cost*, London: Global Witness.

Kirkwood, S. and McNeill, F. (2015) 'Integration and reintegration: comparing pathways to citizenship through asylum and criminal justice', *Criminology and Criminal Justice*, 15(5): 511–26.

Klein, M. (2007) *The shock doctrine: The rise of disaster capitalism*, London: Penguin/Allen Lane.

Kotz, D.M. (2009) 'The financial and economic crisis of 2008: A systemic crisis of neoliberal capitalism', *Review of Radical Political Economics*, 41(3): 305–17.

Le Bel, T.P., Richie, M.J. and Maruna, S. (2015) 'Helping others as a response to reconcile a criminal past: the role of the "wounded healer" in prison re-entry programs', *Criminal Justice and Behavior*, 42(1): 108–20.

Li, C. (2016) *Chinese politics in the Xi Jinping era*, Washington, DC: Brookings Institution Press.

Macedo, D. (2001) 'Introduction', in P. Freire (2001 [1975]) *Pedagogy of the oppressed*, 30th anniversary edn, trans. M. Bergman Ramos, New York and London: Continuum Books.

MacPherson, K. (2017a) 'Desistance: an inside view', blog. http://blogs.iriss.org.uk/discoveringdesistance/2017/07/26/desistance-an-inside-view/.

MacPherson, K. (2017b) 'Rehabilitation through education? An apotheosis of a hook-for-change', blog: http://blogs.iriss.org.uk/discoveringdesistance/2017/08/11/rehabilitation-through-education-an-apotheosis-of-a-hook-for-change/.

MacPherson, K. (2017c) 'Governmentalities, tertiary desistance and the responsibilisation deficit', blog. http://blogs.iriss.org.uk/discoveringdesistance/2017/09/15/governmentalities-tertiary-desistance-and-the-responsibilisation-deficit/.

McNeill, F. (2014) 'Punishment as rehabilitation', in G. Bruinsma and D. Weisburd (eds) *Encyclopedia of criminology and criminal justice*, New York: Springer, pp 4195–206.

McNeill, F. (2016) 'Desistance and criminal justice in Scotland', in H. Croall, G. Mooney and M. Munro (eds) *Crime, justice and society in Scotland*, London: Routledge.

McNeill, F. (2018) 'Mass supervision, misrecognition and the "malopticon"', *Punishment & Society*, 21(2): 207–30.

McNeill, F. and Weaver, B. (2010) *Changing lives? Desistance research and offender management*, Glasgow: Scottish Centre for Crime and Justice Research. www.sccjr.ac.uk/documents/Report%202010_03%20-%20Changing%20Lives.pdf.

McNeill, F. and Schinkel, M. (2015) 'Prisons and desistance', in Y. Jewkes and J. Bennett (eds) *Handbook on prisons*, Portland, OR: Willan Publishing.

McNeill, F., Farrall, S., Lightowler, C. and Maruna, S. (2012) *How and why people stop offending: Discovering desistance*, Glasgow: Institute for Research and Innovation in Social Services. http://eprints.gla. ac.uk/79860/.

Mell, A., Radford, S. and Thévoz, S.A. (2015) *Is there a market for peerages? Can donations buy you a peerage? A study in the link between party political funding and peerage nominations, 2005–2014*, Department of Economics Discussion Paper Series, Oxford: Oxford University.

Ministry of Justice (2018) *Employing prisoners and ex-offenders*, London: Ministry of Justice.

Mishkin, F. (2011) 'Over the cliff: from the subprime to the global financial crisis', *Journal of Economic Perspectives*, 25(1): 49–70.

Novis, R. (2013) *Hard times: Exploring the complex structures and activities of Brazilian prison gangs*, PhD thesis, London School of Economics and Political Science.

Piacentini, L., Weaver, B. and Jardine, C. (2018) *Employment and employability in Scottish prisons: A research briefing paper*, Glasgow: Scottish Centre for Crime and Justice Research. www.sccjr. ac.uk/wp-content/uploads/2018/02/Research_Briefing_Prisons_ Employability.pdf.

Prisoners' Education Trust (2016) *What is prison education for? A theory of change exploring the value of learning in prison*. London: Prisoners' Education Trust.

Runell, L.L. (2017) 'Identifying desistance pathways in a higher education program for formerly incarcerated individuals', *International Journal of Offender Therapy and Comparative Criminology*, 61(8): 894– 918. doi: 10.1177/0306624X15608374.

Schinkel, M. (2015) 'Hook for change or shaky peg? Imprisonment, narratives and desistance', *European Journal of Probation*, 7(1): 5–20.

Scott, D. and Flynn, N. (2014) *Prisons and punishment: The essentials*, London: Sage.

Scottish Government (2015) Rehabilitation of Offenders Act 1974, 20 May. www.gov.scot/Publications/2015/05/5592/2.

Shammas, V.L. (2014) 'The pains of freedom: assessing the ambiguity of Scandinavian penal exceptionalism on Norway's prison island', *Punishment & Society*, 16(1): 104–23.

SPS (Scottish Prison Service) (2014) *Corporate plan: 2014–2017*, Edinburgh: Scottish Government.

SPS (Scottish Prison Service) (2018) *Annual delivery plan: 2018–2019*, Edinburgh: Scottish Government.

Vulliamy, E. (2011) 'How a big US bank laundered billions from Mexico's murderous drug gangs', *The Guardian*, 3 April.

Wacquant, L. (2010a) 'Crafting the neoliberal state: workfare, prisonfare and social insecurity', *Sociological Forum*, 25(2): 197–220.

Wacquant, L. (2010b) 'Prisoner re-entry as myth and ceremony', *Dialectical Anthropology*, 34: 605–20.

Warner, K. (2018) 'Every possible learning opportunity: the capacity of education in prison to challenge dehumanisation and liberate "the whole person"', *Advancing Corrections* 6: 30–43.

7

From despair to hope

Margaret Gough

Leaving school and learning class

There was nothing in my early life that was particularly unusual or challenging. We didn't have a lot of money, but my parents made sure that their large family ate well, were clean and safe, and did their best to see that we had a good education. I always had a rebellious nature and was often in the middle of any trouble going on, but I knew that my Mom and Dad loved me. I can't blame my background for what happened later in life. My Dad hadn't been able to have much of an education and he was determined that he would provide this for his children as far as he could. As a result, some of us passed our 11 plus and went to a good single-gender grammar school. However, we were not as well off economically as others in the school and I felt out of place there and quickly got a deserved reputation for bad behaviour and poor attendance.

On reflection, it seems that the implicit pedagogic actions and assumptions of the school created conditions that enabled the middle-class children to be more likely to succeed. Bourdieu's (1986) concept of habitus suggests that individuals of similar social classes share similar dispositions which have the potential to influence our actions, construct our social world and shape our movement through it. The dominant habitus of the students from this middle-class school culture was confidence in their ability, and that going to university was a normal part of life. I did not share these feelings. I stopped going to school during my O-level year, much to my Mom's distress, and didn't even turn up for all my exams but somehow managed to pass three O-levels. More recent research by Reay (2015, 2017) analyses how the class system alienates a high percentage of working-class students. She links the concept of habitus with the psychosocial and asserts that when individuals perceive they are viewed as inferior it diminishes their ability and damages their confidence and self-advocacy.

Eventually, I gained enough qualifications to get a place in college. At last I had some choice in what I was doing and achieved a qualification in the care sector. The practical elements in this line of work appealed to me more than the academic side but having found a niche where I felt motivated and also wanting to increase my earning potential, I began to move upwards in my career and gained a professional qualification in this field. I progressed in my career and was happy with this part of my life, but I had less success in my personal life.

I met someone at work and we married but, despite having two lovely children together, the relationship failed soon after my eldest had started primary school. Unfortunately, I repeated this pattern with the next relationship, including having two more wonderful children. Each relationship was abusive; the second one much more so. Domestic violence at this time was not perceived as being as serious as it is now. I remember on one of several visits to the hospital A&E department for a severe injury, being told by the doctor – as he was stitching my wound – to examine how I was annoying my partner to prevent a repeat incidence. This second relationship broke down when my last child was still a baby, the other still a toddler. Life was difficult, working full time with four children, but I was extremely lucky to have a supportive family who were always there to help out and care for my children, so I could work. I adored my children and they were the centre of my world. Financially, I earned enough money to give all of us a fairly good life, but other aspects of my personal life did not reflect this at all.

I could not find the right person to make me feel valued, respected and loved, and I struggled to find a life partner or true friends. As a result, my personal life came to involve some disastrous life choices which led to my arrest and subsequent conviction. I realise that my story so far is not unique; there are many single women trying to keep a career going while raising children and some make poor decisions which cause them to cross the line with the law. No doubt their lives are also turned upside down by an arrest; but what came next is where my story starts to become exceptional.

Trouble in the air

I had been asked by a man I knew to collect two women from Gatwick airport. I remember saying goodbye to my children who were going to school and letting them know I would see them in the evening. My youngest son was in his final year at primary school and his brother, was looking smart in his new school uniform, as he had just started secondary school. My eldest two were still teenagers. However, I would never return to that home, or indeed any home for many years, as I was arrested by customs and charged with importation of 4.8 kilos of cocaine which the young women had brought with them.

I spent the following few nights in a police cell before being sent to prison on remand, awaiting my trial. This was to be my life for several years. At first, I was completely shell-shocked, but once I realised this was happening to me, I tried to keep hopeful during the months waiting for my trial. I hoped I would be found not guilty but if I wasn't, my solicitors had told me to expect six to eight years. This length of time was hard to comprehend and so I focused on doing everything I could to be acquitted. I had a clean record and young children at home and believed that this would have a positive influence on my future despite the awful position I was now in.

In the remand prison, once I got over the initial disbelief and feelings of devastation, I began working on the detox wing. Research data (Prison Reform Trust, 2015) highlights that 58 per cent of women surveyed said they had used Class A drugs in the four weeks prior to custody but many try to hide or downplay their substance misuse for fear losing their children. Many of these women arrived with clear addiction problems, unable to hide their addictions. Many were also pregnant or had children and were grieving the loss of their families into the care system. While it was clear that many were unable to take care of their children without appropriate help and support, I appreciated how they felt in their current situation and had sympathy for them.

In contrast, I at least knew that my children were being well cared for by close relatives and I had weekly visits from them. Many of the women I spoke to described difficult, chaotic and abusive backgrounds, leading to self-medication with drugs and alcohol. Frequently, I heard women talking about the care system they had been brought up in and it was clear that this cycle was being repeated. In reality, 31 per cent of women prisoners have spent time in care as children (Prison Reform Trust, 2015) and these women are far more likely to reconvicted within one year of release from custody (Ministry of Justice, 2012). All too frequently, I saw the women come in and detox and go out looking healthier and smiling, only to return to detox again.

Research highlights that 48 per cent of women are reconvicted within one year of leaving prison. This rises to 61 per cent for sentences of less than 12 months and to 78 per cent for women who have served more than 11 previous custodial sentences (Ministry of Justice, 2016). After a while, I moved and worked on a wing with women with severe mental health problems who were waiting to go to secure hospitals. Researchers have discovered and quantified what was evident to me from the inside: that women in custody have very poor physical psychological and social health. They are five times more likely to have mental health problems than women in the general population, 78 per cent exhibiting some level of psychological disturbance compared with a figure of 15 per cent for the general adult female population (Plugge et al, 2006). Further research states that, despite reforms to improve health services for prisoners generally, major health disadvantages and inequalities of women offenders present a specific and complex challenge (Plugge et al, 2011).

Trials and tribulations

Working on the prison wing helped to pass my time while I was held in the remand prison for approximately a year. I felt good about being able to help the other women but longed to go home, and at this point gave little thought to a long-term future inside prison walls. However, matters did not go to plan at all. The first trial resulted in a hung jury. I was hopeful for the subsequent re-trial, only to be stunned by the guilty verdict. I returned to my cell now knowing that I would not be going home yet. However, the biggest shock was yet to come – my sentence. Hearing the judge say '15 years' was, I think, the worst moment of my life. I can hardly remember anything else that was said, only that the words '15 years' kept on resounding in my head. I think the judge talked about this amount of time being a deterrent. I was utterly devastated. I had children and already felt that I had let them down by being arrested and imprisoned. Also, I could not put my mother through any more as she had worked hard to raise a large family and I had let her down again. She was by then an invalid and I knew that she worried a lot about me. I was put on suicide watch when I returned to the prison for a while afterwards although taking my own life was not an option.

Despite the fact that I would be in prison for many years, I was transferred within a few weeks to a semi-open prison. This gives some idea of how unexpected the judgment and length of sentence was and confirms that the prison authorities did not see me as a serious risk. I was definitely going to appeal but I knew this would take some time. I needed a strategy to cope with living where I was; to help me simply get to the end of each day through the years stretching ahead of me. Prisoners are expected to fill their day with meaningful activity, and once I had accustomed myself to this new environment, I decided to attend education classes. It was much quieter there and the staff were easier to get on with than in some sections of the prison. Furthermore, the students I met there were, like myself, trying to make the best of their situation. I started attending any available classes that I could, and, within a few months, I had worked my way through all the qualifications available in this prison Education Department. I even passed a Maths GCSE with an excellent grade, as concepts such as equations and algebra made sense. This subject had seemed to be totally beyond me at school.

While in the prison Education Department I noticed that many prisoners have very basic education needs. Research data (Creese, 2016) highlights that only 46 per cent of newly assessed prisoners have level 1 and level 2 literacy skills, compared to 85 per cent of the general population. In relation to numeracy skills, 39.8 per cent of prisoners assessed had the equivalent level of numeracy skills compared with 50 per cent of the general population. I was able to provide some support to the other prisoners, which kept me busy and, to some extent, stopped me dwelling on my circumstances. Once I had completed everything the Education Department offered, I knew I needed to find a prison job. I thought that working within the Education Department would be a good choice for me. I applied for a job there and was successful. This work involved going into the classrooms and supporting students in basic literacy, numeracy and IT skills. Additionally, twice a week a tutor came in to help prisoners apply for distance learning programmes, I used to help them there as well. It was through this work that I found out that some prisoners were applying for Open University (OU) courses, and I began to wonder for the first time if that could be possible for me.

Entering The Open University

All my life I had thought that degrees were for clever people, not for someone like me, but I thought that I had nothing to lose by attempting a free introductory course. Perhaps it would give me more of a challenge than some of the classes I had done so far? When the course began, thinking about the content of the course proved to be very good for my mental health as mulling over what I was missing as my family grew up made me feel desolate. I completed the two assignments quickly and passed them with excellent tutor feedback. From there I thought, where next? I thought about a level 4 course but doubted my ability to succeed. Nevertheless, I decided to give further studies a try – despite still believing that studying at degree level would prove beyond me. Once again it gave me a focus and it meant that

I had something to occupy the time spent in my cell each evening. The first unit with the OU was not free and so I knew I needed to find the money for this. I applied to some charities for funding and was fortunate enough to be able to ask my family to put together the remaining money.

The first course I did at level 4 was K100, Working in Health and Social Care. This began in March and I remember the feeling of anticipation on receiving the boxes with the course content. I started reading the books, assignments and all the supporting paperwork, and everything seemed to be clear and straightforward. In fact, I found the books interesting and easy to read. It fascinated me how the world was not as straightforward as I had previously thought. The course introduced me to concepts such as inequalities in health and the problems certain sections of the community have in accessing health and social care. I came to realise that attributing blame was not the answer to these problems. Obviously, my time spent in prison and the people and things I had observed reinforced these concepts. There was no clear right or wrong, good and bad but always another way of looking at issues. It took me a while to work out the Harvard referencing system and how to approach paraphrasing but every time I handed in an assignment I looked forward to doing the next one. I had usually started to read around the next assignment topic before I received my tutor feedback and marks. In fact, I was usually ready to write as soon as this was received, although I studied the tutor's comments carefully and used this to help me refine how I worked on completing future assignments. The feedback was always useful and supportive, much of it relating more to my use – or misuse – of academic skills rather than my arguments. I finished the course with fairly good grades. The fact that I was achieving something motivated me to continue studying and this made my circumstances less dire than they would otherwise have been. Grades, at that time, were not so important; at least I was passing and learning about new and interesting things and my time was passing.

Best foot forward

The time came for my appeal to be heard and I was relieved to have my sentence reduced. However, it was only by three years; not as much as I had hoped. In many ways this was quite bitter-sweet, as I realised that I had no choice now but to think ahead for the longer term. I was nearly two years into my sentence and would have to serve at least four more years before I had any chance of freedom.

While in this semi-open prison, I had seen other offenders go out on ROTL (release on temporary licence) and I knew this was something I must aim for. At the time, this was possible for prisoners in open or semi-open prisons after they had reached 50 per cent of their served sentence, subject to excellent behaviour.

Although my family brought my children to visit me every week, I wanted to see them out of this prison environment and be a mom to them again. As I worked in the Education Department, I also realised that I could also get ROTL for studying in local colleges and universities. I decided I was going to work hard and aim to go to college, or perhaps even university, the following year. Devoting so much time to studying had proved useful in maintaining my record of good behaviour but before long, not wanting to risk losing access to the studies became in itself another reason for not putting a foot wrong.

Immediately, after my appeal, I applied for another OU unit as I needed to look forward and not dwell on what and where I was. This time I chose to study a level 5 unit, U205, Health and Disease, which started in October, leaving a small overlap with K100. The books were more challenging but I liked the fact that the teaching material gave me more opportunity to exercise my newfound skills in critical thinking, referencing and academic writing. I was getting through the coursework quickly and subsequently applied for another level 5 unit, K203, Working for Health, which started the following February. There was more of an overlap here, but I did not mind the work as I had a goal to achieve. I continued to work as expected in the prison and looked forward to visits from my family but, apart from that, I studied and completed assignments as fast as I could. To my good fortune, while in the Education Department another university sent a flyer for a free level 4 distance learning course in interpersonal skills. Once again, I applied for this and received the teaching materials.

Hope, ambition and achievement

Spending nearly all of my free time studying and finding success in my studies reawakened my ambitious nature. At one point in my sentence, any idea of having any kind of ambition had seemed futile. Surviving to the end of each day had, at first, seemed to be the only goal worth pursuing. Now I began to have hope that my life would not always be so bleak. The feedback I was getting was generally positive and the grades reflected this. The lowest mark I had was 56 per cent and I remember this was due to weak academic skills such as introducing something new into the conclusion. However, many of my assignment grades were over 70 per cent and one was 85 per cent.

My situation meant that I did not have the same facilities as many other OU students: the internet, for instance, was out of bounds and I could only use module books sent by the OU. However, these books were well written and had enough in them for me to give balanced arguments. I was also very fortunate to find a tutor who was willing to go above and beyond the role of her job. She applied to see me in prison and actually came to give me personal feedback. This one-to-one tutorial was very important to me; not only did it boost my confidence in my academic abilities but it also made me feel that I was being accepted as a normal student. I asked her about how she thought I was getting on and she said I was doing excellently, mentioning the very critical and detailed approach I took to my work which she rarely saw from other students on this course. An example of this that she cited was in the most recent assignment of mine that she had marked but I had not yet had returned. Apparently, I was the only student to mention the importance of micro-nutrients in healthy development.

My tutor inspired me to believe that my contributions were as valid and valued as any other student. Hearing her say to my face that I had very good analytical skills and that I showed a depth of understanding and reasoning was a huge motivation to continue to study and learn. I passed both the level 5 units with a grade 2 pass and the other level 4 unit with a distinction. I managed to complete all these 180 credits by September, halfway through my sentence. This meant I had completed 240 credits in total, the equivalent to a foundation degree. I applied to a local university to get a place on a 'top-up degree.' This was direct level 6 entry and I was delighted to be accepted but this was dependent on getting the necessary permission from the prison authorities.

Movement, progression and release

The first temporary licence I was granted gave me leave to spend time with my family away from the prison environment. That was the most important privilege for me; being able to spend time with my children in a normal setting without constantly being watched by prison officers. I knew why they watched us but the relief of being away from their gaze and not worrying about standing up or moving my arms was great. Shortly afterwards, I was also allowed to apply for a special licence to attend a university. This was a huge bonus, even if a little nerve wracking. By October of that year I was actually going out to attend lectures as a university student to study.

Despite my recent success in studying, I was anxious about going out to a university as I assumed that it would be more difficult – I still couldn't see myself as a clever person! I worried too about fitting in. Not only was I a mature student but I was living in a prison. People joke about poor standards in student accommodation but I had the reality of an actual cell to go back to. This was obviously a great improvement on never leaving the prison grounds but it wasn't easy. Being out on licence meant that I had to meet certain conditions. Being late back was a genuine fear and I made sure at the end of my classes that I returned to the prison on time as I could not afford to lose this privilege. I was regularly searched and at times some prison officers would suggest sarcastically that it was not like I was in prison but I just smiled and kept quiet. Teaching staff were very supportive and did all they could for me, while keeping my secret safe. In addition to being able to attend lectures, I could now go to the library and get additional books, as well as having access to explore the internet and print off articles and take them back to the prison with me.

Returning home to live with my two younger sons was my greatest desire. They were both now in secondary school and doing well under my sister's care and I was able to spend time with them. However, it was not the same as looking after them and being part of their daily lives. I knew that they would be either leaving school or in the sixth form by the time I came out. The older two were already living independently by then. Although I realised that I was fortunate compared to many women, given that only half of the women who had previously lived with, or were in contact with, their children prior to imprisonment had received a visit since going to prison (Prison Reform Trust, 2015), I was acutely aware of what I was missing. Consequently, I gave thought to what I would do with my qualifications when I was finally released.

Having supported other prisoners previously in the Education Department, I thought that teaching, if I could get an adult teaching qualification, was potentially a career for me on release. I knew that under the Rehabilitation of Offenders Act 1974, my 12-year conviction would never be spent but I hoped to be allowed to teach adults. I made an appointment and spoke to the education manager and offered my time to teach other inmates if they would support me in getting a teaching qualification. I decided I would teach a level 2 Health and Social Care course as I felt confident because I had gained a deeper knowledge and understanding of this subject from my OU studies. I requested another licence and once again it was approved.

First class honours

Having received praise and encouragement from the OU tutor who came to see me in prison for my comprehensive and astute analytical and critical skills, I worked hard in the classroom-based study as well. The lecturers were always positive if I made a contribution in class or in seminars, and I received very good written feedback from my assignments. I was motivated and worked hard to perfect my academic skills and writing style and so I regularly received grades over 70 per cent.

In June I handed in my final dissertation and was awaiting my final degree classification, although I was not sure how this was worked out. I knew I would pass as I not failed anything, I only hoped to be able to carry on studying. I had served nearly a full four years in prison and I had two years left, subject to me getting parole, of course. I had thought about slowing down my studies, but I decided that I wanted to complete my OU degree as well. This meant that by day I attended classes on campus and in the evening I continued studying with the OU. I spent a lot of time looking through the OU catalogue, deciding what looked interesting and preferably assessed by coursework rather than an exam. The first level 6 course I did was K301, Promoting Health: Skills and Perspectives. This was studied while I was doing my BA (Hons) and I achieved high grades in both – a distinction for this unit and, to my surprise, I gained a first class BA (Hons).

I decided I would apply for a Master's degree and then I would apply for a licence that would allow me to work outside of the prison. I would then have qualifications and some money saved for my release. I asked one of the university lecturers to provide me with a reference. His reference was excellent, saying how impressed he was with my maturity and the depth of my work. This reference was an essential factor in my being accepted to do a Master's degree. I also managed to complete a Postgraduate Certificate in Education (PGCE), enabling me to work in further or higher education after I was released.

I continued my OU studies and decided I would choose from a combination that gave me a BSc. (Hons). However, choosing the remaining level 6 course was difficult as I wanted it to be a named degree in Health Studies but this restricted the modules I could choose. The health modules I needed to choose expected me to be working in health care and for me to reflect on my work experience in assignments, which I could not do. I also realised that working in health care was something I would probably not be able to do, due to my conviction. However, I had learned such a lot, so I did not mind.

I finally chose to study D317, Social Psychology: Personal Lives, Social Worlds, which I passed with a high grade 2. There was, once again, a cross-over with completing the assignments in the existing module and starting the new one.

I was by now going out to work, mostly kitchen work, but I received a wage which I could save for my release. I applied for one more OU course because, in addition to wanting something to occupy me in the evening and on days off, I also wanted to ensure that I had studied all of the required credits without accrediting prior learning. I realised my degree would not be 'named degree' so the final unit I chose was something completely different, U210, The English Language: Past Present and Future. I had therefore passed 370 credits before I gained my parole and was released to go home. Once again, to my surprise, I was awarded another first class honours degree.

Out of the dark times

My progress in higher education gave me hope for the future during my time in prison. When I was finally freed, I was able to begin a career within adult education and teaching. I became a respected member of an academic world that had seemed beyond me before my arrest. This was only possible due to the opportunities presented by the OU to prison inmates. This kept me going through some very dark times. Prior to my imprisonment, I had worked and had never expected others to take care of me, and I did not want to live off benefits when I came out. Although I appreciated that some people have no choice, I knew I was and am a person with potential, ability and drive, and I am forever grateful to the OU's role in sustaining and affirming this despite all the odds.

It would be good if this was a completely happy ending and the positive influence of the OU was sufficient to help ex-convicts put their past behind them and give something back to society. Unfortunately, in my case, as in the case of so many others, prejudice is still around and, despite trying to put the past behind me it has not always been possible to do so, due to the challenges and barriers that can keep on occurring.

References

Bourdieu, P. (1986) 'The forms of capital', in J. Richardson (ed.) *Handbook of theory and research for the sociology of education*, Westport, CT: Greenwood, pp 241–58.

Creese, B. (2016) 'An assessment of the English and Maths skills levels of prisoners in England', *London Review of Education*, 14(3): 13–30.

Ministry of Justice (2012) *Prisoners' childhood and family backgrounds*, London: Ministry of Justice.

Ministry of Justice (2016) *Women and the criminal justice system*, London: Ministry of Justice.

Plugge, E., Douglas, N. and Fitzpatrick, R. (2006) *The health of women in prison*, Oxford: Department of Public Health, University of Oxford.

Plugge, E., Douglas, N. and Fitzpatrick, R. (2011) 'Changes in health-related quality of life following imprisonment in 92 women in England: a three-month follow-up study', *International Journal for Equity in Health*, 10, Article 21.

Prison Reform Trust (2015) *Why focus on reducing women's imprisonment?* www.prisonreformtrust.org.uk/Portals/0/Documents/why%20focus%20on%20reducing%20women's%20imprisonment%20BL.pdf.

Reay, D. (2015) 'Habitus and the psychosocial: Bourdieu with feelings', *Cambridge Journal of Education*, 45(1): 9–23.

Reay, D. (2017) *Miseducation: Inequality, education and the working classes*, Bristol: Policy Press.

VIGNETTE 5

Making my commitment

Razib Quraishi

Excuse me are you a prisoner? This is a hilarious question I am often asked as I walk to and from my prison wing to the education block. I never thought that just by developing my knowledge through studying with The Open University, my outwardly expressive demeanour would suggest to others that I am someone of a professional disposition. I can relate this to an early experience when I was challenged for walking with a limp, implying I held a bad attitude.

I grew up with little schooling due to a number of mental and learning difficulties and had little regard for studying, but often in high school I would hang out with university students in Croydon library to avoid getting into trouble with the law. In 2009, after being sentenced to an indeterminate sentence for public protection, I began to reshape my life and self-worth through studying. Today I am considering postgraduate studies and use my diagnosis of dyslexia, dyscalculia, and ADHD as a source of strength to carry on through my current Open University undergraduate studies.

I was sat in my cell in HMP Pentonville New Year's Eve watching the Thames fireworks display both live outside my cell window and on the telly, and after welcoming in 2010 I made myself a commitment. I often thought I would one day start my own charity and decided to start by making plans about what I want to achieve, what I would need to help achieve these goals and how I could put myself in a position to realise my potential of turning my life around permanently.

Since my teens I had become an alcoholic and developed drug dependencies. These disorders contributed towards my former habits of not holding onto, or rather not appreciating, the greater things in life. So, the idea of developing any permanent stability in my life was very daunting. The Open University has helped me find a little bit of independent structure while being in a prison and having to spend my time around the regime's clock.

I started an Access module after completing my level 2 literacy and maths. Maths was long. I had to work up from entry level 1, which is Key Stage 3, up to Key Stage 5, which is equivalent to GCSEs. So I started my Access module in 2010 with Y161, Introducing Environment, as by then, with all of my notes, limited research and past experiences I had developed a conscience towards environmental ethics.

The Access course had allowed me to find belief in myself that I could apply my focus towards gaining university qualifications. I would be untrue to myself if I said that it was easy. In fact I cannot remember a public sector prison I have been resident at during a module, or even registering for a module, where I have not had to use the complaints procedure.

The cynical and negative criminal mind might claim that prisoners are not encouraged to pursue further education through The Open University due to classist discrimination. I would reiterate that my difficulties in pursuing my studies have been in public sector prisons. Had I not been returned to Category B HMP Lowdham Grange (private sector), my studies would have ended with the Access module. I enrolled in an Open degree starting in October 2012, and every successive year have continued with the purpose of achieving an Open University BSc/BA (Honours). Just as events dictate politics, the early experiences of my life continue to do the same. I know I should not continue certain habits that I still do, and one is not to negate people when they suggest that I am very articulate and intelligent. My former automatic response used to be to explain all my learning difficulties. But nowadays, I thank them and remind them that I am studying with The Open University successfully despite my learning difficulties.

I am proud to state that because I dedicated my time to gaining knowledge in areas of interest and to get a qualification I am a learned person. I will remain indebted to The Open University that they allowed my to position myself in stabilising solid foundations for my dream future. I read an incredible quote from a book by T.E. Lawrence which I wish to share with you and close this personal statement.

All men dream but not equally. Those who dream by night in the dusty recesses of their mind wake to the day to find that it was vanity. But the dreamers of the day are dangerous men for they may act their dreams with eyes wide open to make it possible. (From *The seven pillars of wisdom**)

If we could protest in a liberal free democratic society then I would shout at the top of my lungs, what do we want? Social justice! When do we want it? As soon as we've figured out what it is!

---

* Lawrence, T.E. (1991) *The seven pillars of wisdom: a triumph*, Harmondsworth: Penguin.

8

Straight up! From HMP to PhD

Stephen Akpabio-Klementowski

Over a decade ago, my life was completely different. I was involved in the drugs scene in London and had fully embraced a criminal lifestyle. At the time, I saw it as a means of earning a living and felt there were no viable alternatives to the path that lay in front of me. I had a drugs habit, sold drugs and was indifferent to the consequences of my actions. In retrospect, my worldview was flawed, immature for my years and I lacked much in terms of having a moral compass. My attitude was negative, one of contempt for the law and that contempt was fashioned out of my negative encounters with it. I saw the law as a tool used by the powerful to oppress the poor and socially marginalised.

Leaving school without any formal qualifications and other personal factors such depression, a lack of ambition or belief in my own abilities resulted in low expectations. Growing up in poverty on a council estate in London, I was accustomed to 'looking after' myself from an early age. I found school boring and constraining and, having already learnt to read and write, I wrongly believed these were the only skills that mattered. By the time of my father's sudden and unexpected death in a road accident at the age of 53, I had become disillusioned with life. Although I was not particularly close to my parents, mainly because they disapproved of my anti-social behaviour, losing my dad at the age of 17 was a big deal for me. It meant that there was nobody to keep me in check and I promptly left home 'officially'. However, the chances of securing meaningful and gainful employment were low, even though I had experience of working in low-paid manual jobs with few, if any, future prospects. To me, they all represented a dead-end.

On the other hand, dealing in illegal drugs paid immediate benefits, despite the obvious risks involved. Motivated by greed and the potential material rewards involved, I prioritised making large sums of money over everything else in my life, including my wife and daughter. The desire to provide for the day-to-day needs of my young family was intense and I was determined to achieve it at any cost and by any means available to me. This somewhat irrational and ridiculous drive came at great personal cost, ducking and diving in order to avoid arrest, relying on my wits in dealings with some pretty unsavoury characters and having to constantly fabricate lies in order to conceal the true source of my income from family and friends. In addition, any application I made for work, no matter how low paid or unskilled, would involve lying about my educational background and work experience. In the circumstances, it was no surprise that selling drugs seemed more rewarding to this young man.

My luck ran out in 2002 and the long arm of the law caught up with me in a big way. Convicted for the importation of Class A drugs and sentenced to 16 years in prison, I was facing a long time in custody. At the time, my mindset was of the negative sort, wrongly believing that I faced a lifetime of crime, imprisonment and misery. According to classic penal theory, the purposes of punishment can be categorised into two major groups: social defence (crime prevention) and retribution (punishment) (see Mathiesen, 2000). The merit of using punishment as a means of crime prevention is questionable, given the ever-rising prison population in England and Wales. On the other hand, theories of retribution make clear that punishment is first and foremost to fulfil the demands of justice (Cohen and Taylor, 1972; Mathiesen, 2000). The efficacy of such an approach is only a secondary consideration. Kant famously gave expression to this sentiment in claiming that 'justice must be maintained for its own sake', because 'if justice succumbs, the existence of man on earth no longer has any value'. It is a sentiment which still finds widespread support today and was apparent to me from the moment of arrest through to incarceration. This was going to be about punishment and it would be painful.

The impact of my conviction on my wife, our three-month-old daughter, and our wider families was devastating. Knowing I had messed up in the most dramatic way possible, my guilt allowed me to readily accept the sentence imposed by the court. The fact was that I was now a broken man, disreputable, incarcerated, lonely, homeless and penniless. The feeling of anxiety and trepidation about what lay ahead for me was all consuming and resulted in regular panic attacks. By the time I arrived in custody, it is fair to say that the process from arrest to conviction had already begun to take its toll. Physically and psychologically speaking, I was completely exhausted. There was simply so much to take in and, while I had some idea of what to expect in prison, such as the loss of my liberty on a physical level, nothing adequately prepared me for the brutal reality of the situation to come.

My wife and I had been married for less than two years and she had just given birth to our first child. It is impossible to overestimate the feeling of devastation due to the circumstances that she found herself in. Bringing up a child single-handedly is not easy and, as noted by Cohen and Taylor (1972), marriage and relationship break-ups are a common casualty of long-term imprisonment. Thus, the decision by my wife to support me during the darkest period in my life was a salient factor in my determination and ability to cope with my situation. It also provided the motivation to do something 'new', something really positive with myself in order to improve my future prospects and give us hope as a family for the future. But it was not obvious to me what to do and how to bring this change about. What I did know was that I owed her everything, even though I had nothing at this point in my life to offer.

In the 1970s, Nils Christie defined the modern prison as 'A physical structure creating high internal visibility with possibilities for some absolute restrictions in movements where the stay is decided by other persons independent of the wishes of those staying there because those staying there are to blame with the purpose of creating pain' (Christie, 2013 [1977], p 183). Unfortunately, in the four decades or so since this observation was made, not much has changed. Prisons are physically imposing and forebidding structures which can lead to a sense of intimidation and vulnerability, even for those with strong personal characteristics who could stand up for themselves.

The government's own figures put the current prison population in England and Wales at over 82,000 (Ministry of Justice, 2018) and one impact of this dramatic increase in the numbers of prisoners is overcrowding. Prison overcrowding puts pressure on the system in many ways and can contribute to issues around order, safety and the ability of officers to positively engage with those in their care. This issue of overcrowding is also linked with the threat of and actual use of violence to maintain order by prison officers or to settle personal disputes between prisoners which is a feature of any prison.

According to the latest figures from the Ministry of Justice (2018), the number of assaults in prisons in England and Wales has reached a record high. There were some 33,803 attacks by prisoners in the year to the end of September 2018, a 20 per cent increase on the previous year. Furthermore, the figures include a record 10,085 assaults on prison staff which represents a 29 per cent increase. Of the total number of assaults 3,949 (12 per cent) were serious, up 6 per cent from the previous year. Indeed, the figures, published by the Ministry of Justice, also revealed a 10 per cent increase to 325 deaths in prison custody in the 12 months to December 2018, 24,138 prisoner-on-prisoner assaults, up 18 per cent in the same period and four killings in jail last year (2018). Unfortunately, many prisons in England and

Wales continue to see surging levels of violence, drug use and self-harm in recent years.

Psychologically, the initial impact of long-term imprisonment almost defies description. Gresham M. Sykes' classic 1958 text, *The society of captives: A study of a maximum-security prison* on the 'pains of imprisonment' comes close. According to Sykes, 'the deprivation of liberty', through confinement in an institution and being forcibly separated from family and kin, over time facilitate the loss of connections to free society outside the prison walls, leading to loneliness and boredom. Individual egos are threatened both by their moral rejection from legitimate society through this forced separation and by the many forms of degradation and humiliation that incarceration produces, such as full-body strip search, wearing of uniform and the reading by others of personal or intimate communications. Furthermore, 'the deprivation of goods and services' forces prisoners to live in what Sykes describes as 'a harshly Spartan environment which prisoners define as painfully depriving'. In addition, 'the deprivation of heterosexual relationships', which involves 'involuntary celibacy' and which, Sykes argued, is a form of 'figurative castration', is both physically and psychologically serious. Sykes goes on to talk about 'the deprivation of autonomy', meaning the ways in which prisoners are denied self-determination, or the ability to make choices with respect to basic individual preferences or the work that they do. In agreeing with Sykes, it is noted that these forms of 'irritating, pointless gesture[s] of authoritarianism' are compounded by the prison authorities' deliberate withholding of information and refusal to explain their decisions. Finally, Sykes notes 'the deprivations of security' through the forced and prolonged relationships with violent or aggressive men, along with being in the constant companionship of thieves, rapists, murderers, are less than ideal. Prisoners are also at risk of sexual abuse and, taken together, these issues make prisoners acutely anxious, because the need to stand up to threats against them is a test of their 'manhood' (Sykes, 1958). This sociological 'window' provides a rich glimpse into the nature of prison culture and Goffman (1968) built on it through his influential account of the 'mortification' of self which the long-term prisoner has to endure as his privacy is trashed, he is reprogrammed as a number, in my case, JC4997, and his previous self is subjected to harmful acts. As someone with experience of long-term imprisonment, I am familiar with these conditions and in my view it would be wrong to ignore their substantial and cumulative impact.

At this stage of my life, I held no educational ambitions and was indifferent to the learning process. Significantly, prisons are not designed to educate but rather to punish. Of all the things offered in prisons, I did not think education would be one of them. Yet, according to Prison Service Instruction (PSI) 06/2012,[1] which relates to prisoner employment, training and skills, prisons have a responsibility to ensure that prisoners are able to access employment, training and skills dependent on their identified needs, the needs of the establishment and commercial commitments. In addition, PSI 06/2012 states that 'all prisoners must on entry to custody be given assessments to determine their functional skills needs which should be recorded on an Individual Learning Plan'. In these circumstances, the needs of the establishment and its commercial commitments always take priority and I was allocated a job within the prison's industrial complex, assembling paper hats for the catering industry.

Initially, I welcomed the opportunity and benefits of the immediate income; however, it was monotonous, mind-numbing and unskilled work. As time progressed and in line with the above PSI, I was assessed to determine my functional skills level and needs. The process involves completing an initial assessment designed to establish each prisoner's skills level and identify those who need support to address any gaps. Education providers who operate in prisons are tasked with ensuring that every prisoner is given the opportunity to address this important skills gap if they have one, and success is demonstrated by the achievement of level 1 and 2 certificates in literacy and numeracy. Prison education providers are private entities contracted by the government to provide specific services in prisons and payment is often by results. Therefore, there is a financial incentive for prisons to focus on these qualifications.

My assessment indicated ability well beyond level 2, however, the lack of these qualifications meant that I was instructed to work towards gaining them. At the time, it was a bit irritating having to start from scratch, but it provided a solid basis for my future learning. Starting with entry level 3 literacy and numeracy, I was able to work my way up to the required standard of level 2 in just over nine months. During this period, my involvement with prison education resulted in a reduction in the time I spent making paper hats and consequently, a reduction in my pay from approximately £10 to £4 per week. Despite the loss of the immediate benefits of having a larger wage, I was rewarded with the achievement of my level 2 certificates. This had an unbelievable effect on me and boosted my confidence a great deal simply because, they were my first formal qualifications. House of Commons (2018) data suggests approximately 47 per cent of prisoners do not have any formal qualifications and I could relate to that. The positive experience left me thirsting for more learning. But the prison curriculum was extremely limited with nothing above level 2. Various level 1 and 2 vocational courses were proposed, but none captured my interest.

A chance encounter with the prison's education manager, who knew the results of my assessments, proved to be a turning point. I was offered the opportunity to study with The Open University (OU), which at the time seemed a bit surreal. Never in my wildest dreams had I ever expected to go to university. It went against everything I had been told and came to believe. The idea of a university adopting an open access policy is one that I think goes to the heart of what education should be about, an individual's ability above anything else. Thanks to a programme of government funding for prisoners studying higher education courses, I secured the funding to pay for my studies. Access to this government funding was a crucial factor in my decision to study with the OU. It meant that as long as I successfully completed my last module, funding would be available for the entire degree. In turn, this allowed me to focus on my studies and not worry about how to fund them. Unlike today, where prisoners have to be within six years of their earliest release date in order to access a student loan, there were no such restrictions to eligibility for this government funding and I was able to secure what I needed to pay for my first OU module. With funding secured, and after a brief exploration of available subjects, I decided to study towards a social sciences qualification. I had an interest in both psychology and sociology, a need to better understand people, issues around social justice, order and the law. On reflection, it seemed I was trying to understand myself.

For many people, going to university is one of life's major decisions and a lot of thought is put into it. Prospective students are expected to access information, advice and guidance from a variety of sources before making their decision. However, in prison, things were totally different. Access to up-to-date information and advice is problematic on many levels so that, in effect, prisoners often make important decisions about their studies in the 'dark'. This can create problems further down the line for students who find that they have got on to the wrong course or are registered for the wrong qualification. In my case, I received minimal information or advice about my university studies before registering for my first course at HMP Lowdham Grange in 2003; I was determined to give it my best shot, however.

I embarked on my first 60 credits module: DD102, An Introduction to the Social Sciences, in 2003 at the age of 38. For the first time in many years, I felt intuitively that there was nothing more to lose. It was like I had tried everything else and failed. I remember receiving my first course materials and being completely overwhelmed by them. The books, assignments and study calendar which set out my programme of study all contributed to a scholarly, learning feeling. Reading about issues that were of interest to me as well as having responsibility for my studies proved to be a perfect combination. It completely suited the restricted environment in which I was forced to study. The OU's flexible approach and its structure of support available to students in secure environments like prisons and secure hospital units enabled someone with little experience of higher education to successfully come to grips with learning at university level in less than ideal circumstances. In 2016, the Coates Review (Ministry of Justice, 2016) into education in prisons in England and Wales comprehensively set out many of the barriers to learning in these establishments.

All of this study enabled me to rise above the daily routine of prison life while focusing on doing something positive with my life. This level of learning was totally new terrain for me: reading, taking notes, analysing, constructing arguments and developing points of view. Working on course assignments and preparing for exams required a great degree of commitment and determination, and I had never worked this hard to complete a course before. My first OU tutor had extensive knowledge of his subject area, but, more importantly, was able to guide and inspire me throughout the course, which I passed with an overall score of 77 per cent.

At this stage in my sentence, I had settled into a routine at HMP Lowdham Grange, a medium-security prison holding long-term prisoners in the Midlands and described as a training prison on the Ministry of Justice website. Working on the wing servery at mealtimes meant that I was allowed to remain on the wing throughout the working day and this gave me more access to my course materials. Due to the deafening noise levels on the wing, I would usually study in my cell at night. Simultaneously, I was aware that returning to a life of drug dealing after my release would be predictable, but not wise. Equally, I was increasingly conscious of the fact that my lack of any formal qualifications would be a major obstacle to employment in the future. This issue occupied my mind endlessly and I was keen to find a way out of what seemed an impossible set of circumstances.

Successful completion of my first module seemed to increase my confidence and I registered for the next module, ED209, Child Development, almost immediately. During the course of this module, I was transferred from one medium-security prison, HMP Lowdham Grange to another, HMP Lewes on the south coast. Unfortunately,

HMP Lewes was extremely overcrowded and was experiencing severe issues with low staffing levels. This resulted in regular 23 hours bang-ups, restricted regimes – including limited access to the prison's Education Department or library – as well as the doubling up of single cellular accommodation designed to house one prisoner to hold two. Social visiting was restricted to 45 minutes if you were lucky, which is no time at all especially when it involves long-distance travel, as it did for my family. It was a prison seemingly unable to provide a learning environment that was conducive for studying at any level. However, I was able to successfully complete my course and, in the process, accumulated 120 credit points towards my degree. This was a particularly pleasing achievement because the main reason for studying this module was my baby daughter, who was now just over a year old. Although I receive regular social visits from my wife and daughter, there was a real nightmarish fear that she may not have fully bonded with me as her dad. Studying this specialist module was a way of demonstrating my commitment to be a good parent in the future as this had not been the case in the past.

According to recent research conducted by the third sector organisation the Prisoner Learning Academic Network (PLAN), there are specific benefits that prisoners can gain through engagement with education in prison. These benefits include health and wellbeing, increased human capital, social capital, knowledge, skills and employability (PLAN, 2016). Through my OU studies, I have experienced many of these benefits while incarcerated and I would be right in saying that some of these benefits acted like a coping mechanism in prison, giving me the opportunity to look forward rather than backwards as is necessarily the case in prison; the need to be hopeful in an environment devoid of it. Indeed, some of these benefits extended to my wife who was encouraged and optimistic about the possibility of a future that is free from crime with me and our daughter.

In 2006, the success of completing my last two stage one modules propelled me towards my third module, DSE212, Exploring Psychology. Understanding issues around individual characteristics, traits and personalities was an eye opener. Slowly and a full two years after commencing my OU studies, the potential benefits of getting an education began to dawn on me. I consciously started taking my studies very seriously and any time a problem relating to my OU studies arose, I would use the prison's complaint system to try to resolve it. I was using the writing and communications skills that I had learnt through my OU studies to good effect. After completing the psychology module, I was transferred from one medium-security prison, HMP Lewes, to another, HMP Erlestoke. HMP Erlestoke prioritised prison education within their daily routine, which provided good access to educational and learning resources such as PCs to word process your essays. Prior to going there, I had become accustomed to hand-writing my assignments, which was extremely time-consuming and impractical. At Erlestoke, I was able to take advantage of their education-friendly regime to study towards my next two modules, DD307 – Social Psychology: Critical Perspectives on Self and Others, and D315, Crime, Order and Social Control. The first was completed in 2007 and the second, 2008.

By early 2008, I had served more than five years in custody and a prison review panel tasked with assessing the level of risk posed by each prisoner concluded that the risk I posed to staff and members of the public was low. This was a significant development in my sentence because being a low-risk prisoner made me suitable and eligible to be transferred to an 'open' prison. Unlike the 'closed' prisons I had resided in up to this point, open prisons are designed to hold those coming to the end of a long sentence. They offer the opportunity for prisoners to be released on temporary licence (ROTL) into the community at specific times and for specific purposes to aid their eventual resettlement post-release. It is also a good barometer of the progress being made by a prisoner and is generally recognised as such.

The arrival of the results of my last module, D315, Crime Order and Social Control, coincided with my transfer to an open prison, HMP Springhill in Aylesbury, Buckinghamshire. My successful completion of this module meant that I had achieved a Bachelor of Arts Open degree with the OU. It was an amazing feeling, knowing that gaining a degree would only enhance my future prospects. This is in line with research from the US, which suggests that prisoners who gain college qualifications while incarcerated are more likely to secure employment after release (Fabelo, 2002). The study evaluated the ability of the prison educational system to improve the educational level of inmates in a Texas prison, enhance their employment prospects and lower their recidivism rates. Findings from this research demonstrated that inmates with the highest levels of education were most likely upon release to obtain employment, have higher wages, and lower recidivism rates. The study concluded that higher level learning in prison can lower some 'natural' barriers to positive community reintegration by strengthening the intellectual, cognitive and life skills possessed by prison leavers. I had high hopes for the future.

As per the now familiar PSI, I was reassessed for my basic and functional skills level and needs again upon arrival at HMP Springhill.

It was during this assessment with a member of the prison Education Department that we discussed what my educational goals were, and my reply was none. I was aware of the restrictions prisons place on educational activities and as I had accepted and received my degree from the OU, I simply did not think there was anywhere else to go for me. But to my surprise, I was informed of a scholarship opportunity at Oxford Brookes University for prisoners from Springhill to study a Master's degree. It would be the first time a prisoner from Springhill would be granted ROTL to attend a 'brick' university and, depending on the success of the trial, it would be rolled out more widely. No pressure then. The only problem, or so I thought, was that it was in International Relations, as area that I had not studied previously. I decided this was not a barrier in itself and applied anyway. I had nothing to lose and was delighted to be accepted to start in the autumn of 2008.

The prison provided daily transport to and from Oxford, and a packed sandwich for lunch. Over the next nine months, other prisoners and prison officers would regularly ask me what exactly I hoped to achieve by studying so much. After all, I had a long criminal record which would never be 'spent' under current legislation because, under the provisions of the Rehabilitation of Offenders Act, 1974, sentences over four years cannot be 'spent' and must be declared when making applications for employment. I always gave the same reply; I do not know! I had learnt the lesson of not planning too far ahead because there are many things that could go wrong. However, I had an innate feeling that my efforts would be rewarded in one way or another. This proved to be the case as I successfully completed my MA in International Relations, achieving a lower Merit. My elation at this achievement was further enhanced by the offer of another scholarship, this time to pursue a research degree, a PhD. I could hardly believe my luck, all that hard work seemed to be paying off! This was in the summer of 2009 and less than a year to my release in June 2010. With this in mind, I explained to Oxford Brookes University that the unforeseen impact of my eminent release could have an adverse effect on my ability to commit to a four-year programme of study and I was concerned about dropping out and wasting these funds in the process. My honesty was rewarded with the offer of yet another scholarship to study a Master of Laws programme. Again, this could be achieved in nine months and, while the final three months of study would take place in the community, this was something that was achievable, and I accepted the offer.

Following my release in June 2010, I was able to complete the Master of Laws degree. The significance of these high-level qualifications soon became apparent. After my release, I volunteered for a national charity that worked with former prisoners to support their reintegration back into the community. This involved working with local probation service providers to support their service users using our experience of the criminal justice system. This was a great way of giving something back to society and led to my first offer of employment as a programme manager for the charity. The demands of family life and working full time left little time to consider what my next educational goals should be. However, this changed when I applied for and successfully secured my current position with the OU as a regional manager for the Students in Secure Environments team. The team is tasked with supporting OU students in secure environments, namely prisons and secure hospital units. My experience of being a student in some of these environments made it an ideal role for me and provided the opportunity to support some of the most committed students in the university.

Working in my position brought back a lot of memories about studying in prison including the barriers faced by students in secure environments: a lack of access to IT and other basic educational resources, including access to a library, computers, other university students and a lack of understanding by many prison officers of what studying at higher education level involves. I also missed studying regularly and the structure that it brought to my life. After joining the OU as part of their Academic Services department, I registered for a part-time PhD programme in criminology. My decision to return to the OU to pursue a research degree owes much to my previous experience of studying with them. The flexibility, high quality of teaching and incredible support offered to students won me over. In addition, being part of the OU's Academic Services department has given unique insights into the workings of the university and just how much effort is made to support students. Going forward, my intention is to investigate, for the first time in the UK, the conditions which best support or hinder prisoners seeking higher education qualifications. The hope is that this ground-breaking study will help to improve our understanding of the needs of this particular cohort of prison learners, as well as provide the basis for future research in this important area.

One of my childhood heroes, Nelson Mandela famously declared that 'education has the power to change the world', it has certainly changed my world and that of my family. I strongly believe that my learning journey has been nothing short of amazing and my gratitude to the OU is eternal, mainly for giving me the opportunity to realise my potential academically. The university has provided the perfect platform for me to go on and make the most of a pretty bad situation. As a school dropout, who perhaps predictably ended up in prison without any future prospects, it is remarkable that I have managed to turn my life around through education and with the help of a forward-looking and socially progressive institution. It is a privilege to have the opportunity to see things from the perspective of both student and employee. This knowledge has allowed me to inform the work done by the university to improve the study experiences of many students in secure environments while enabling my professional and career development as an academic and manager.

In many ways, gaining my undergraduate degree in prison was a seminal moment in my life and, consequently, I have no regrets about going to prison. Despite the prison environment being unconducive to study, I welcomed the opportunity for personal development and growth while gaining high-level transferable skills and knowledge. They have helped immensely to improve my future life chances and prospects. The university's delivery of tuition via distance learning worked well for me. Unlike the traditional top-down method of teaching in traditional 'brick' universities, studying by distance learning worked perfectly for me. I loved the idea of taking responsibility for my learning and, as a result, have become an independent learner. The modular approach to gaining a higher education qualification provided the flexibility needed to navigate the prison environment in order to complete my degree. Coupled with the tutorial support offered, studying in prison proved to be extremely rewarding and life changing. With a BA and two MAs under my belt, as well as a soon to be completed doctorate degree, my learning journey is far from complete. It is a journey that is likely to be lifelong.

Note
[1] Prison Service Instructions are guidelines issued by the government to prison governors.

References

Christie, N. (2013 [1977]) 'Conflicts as property', in E. McLaughin and J. Muncie (eds) *Criminological perspectives: Essential readings*, London: Sage.

Cohen, S. and Taylor, L. (1972) *Psychological survival: The experiences of long-term imprisonment*, Harmondsworth: Penguin Books.

Fabelo, T. (2002) 'The impact of prison education on community reintegration of inmates', *Journal of Correctional Education*, 53(3): 106–10.

Goffman, E. (1968) *Asylums: Essays on the social situation of mental patients and other inmates*, Harmondsworth: Penguin Books.

House of Commons (2018) *Support for ex-offenders*, House of Commons Work and Pensions Committee, Fifth Report of Session 2016–17.

Mathiesen, T. (2000) *Prison on trial*, 2nd edn, Winchester: Waterside Press.

Ministry of Justice (2016) *Unlocking potential: A review of education in prison by Dame Sally Coates*, London: Ministry of Justice.

Ministry of Justice (2018) *Safety in custody quarterly: Update to December 2018*. www.gov.uk/government/statistics/safety-in-custody-quarterly-update-to-december-2018.

PLAN (Prisoner Learning Academic Network (2016) *What is prison education for? A theory of change for prison education*, London. Prison Education Trust.

Sykes, G. (1958) *Society of Captives*, Princeton, NJ: Princeton University Press.

9

From Open University in prison to convict criminology upon release: mind the gap

Michael Irwin

As I sit down to write this chapter that old cliched phrase "What did the Romans ever do for us?" plays softly in the back of mind. My brain doesn't quite function in a normal way so this phrase has been transformed to "What did The Open University ever do for me … ?"

In 2007 I was arrested at Gatwick Airport with 1.1kg of cocaine hidden in the lining of my bag. After a short period on remand I was convicted and received a 12-year sentence for drug trafficking (six in prison, six on licence). I was 40 years old at the time and had never really paid any heed to The Open University (OU). The only thing I ever remembered about the OU would have been those early morning programmes on BBC2, way back in the 1970s – my mother being the enthusiast as I was only eight or nine. I had different priorities; mainly football. However, upon receiving my sentence and being acutely aware that I would have a lot of time on my hands I decided to make a few enquiries about the OU.

After a few false starts in England I arrived back in Northern Ireland in 2009 and received my first parcel K101, An Introduction to Health and Social Care. I distinctly remember thinking to myself "What on earth are you playing at? The last time you ever wrote an essay was in high school for GCSEs. Send it back and forget about it." Fortunately for me, the OU have people in prison who are there to coordinate and guide doubtful Thomases like myself through this daunting process.

After much procrastination (we all have it) I got myself set up at a desk in a prefab unit called the Education Department in HMP Magilligan. I had just under four years left of my prison sentence and by this stage I was well versed in the politics of the institution of prison, its attitudes to 'pond life' like myself. I thought, "Hold on a second here, where better to study crime, criminals, social justice and psychology than in the middle of it all?" Not only that, I realised that in reading and learning more about myself that I could actually leave prison with a degree.

This is where my problems truly began. My first realisation of this lived experience had already happened; but I'd buried it.

> Behind your thoughts and feelings, my brother, there stands a mighty commander, an unknown wise man – he is called Self. He lives in your body, he is your body. There is more reason in your body than in your best wisdom. And who knows to what end your body requires precisely this your best wisdom? (Nietzsche, 2007 [1885], np)

For many prisoners it is this Nietzschean (somewhat deranged) view of 'self' that becomes part and parcel of the mental process involved in becoming a prisoner. It feeds on a sense of personal injustice being generated by the procedures of justice. For many prisoners the only person you don't expect to meet in prison is indeed your 'self'. I distinctly remember looking in the little scuffed, square metal plate above the sink, used as a mirror and thinking "Who are you?" When that door closes and the penny finally drops that it's just you, the bed and the four walls, you start to realise that you are well and truly alone and all you have to keep you company is your thoughts. It might be this awakening of 'self' that allows a certain mindset to question what we do to society in the name of justice. During my introduction to Zimbardo's (1999) work on identity, I was ordered in the most demeaning manner to report to the Senior Officers office as I had allegedly just failed a piss test (mandatory/voluntary drug test). At that precise moment it hit me that I was 'living' what Zimbardo had hypothesised! What was it that allowed that officer to speak to me the way he did? I was still on remand, not yet convicted, entitled to be assumed innocent before being proven guilty, but in prison I was immediately assumed guilty by staff. Naively I had thought they, the staff, were there to help me.

Some of Zimbardo's questions worried me and got me thinking: 'What happens when you put good people in an evil place? Does humanity win over evil or does evil triumph?' (Zimbardo, 1999), and I couldn't help but wonder what if anything had changed between Zimbardo's experiment and the prison I found myself in years later. However, the question that truly got my juices flowing was one to myself: "Would I be like the officer if the roles were reversed?"

The journey into criminology as a convict

As most of us know when embarking on this academic malarkey, we sort of stumble along for a while until something finally clicks and, in a non-academic term, one simply 'gets it'. When I came across the term 'Convict Criminology', it fascinated me, and by the time I was completing level 2 of my OU studies (in and around 2011/12), I realised I could maybe have a future in it, perhaps even helping to shape future prison policies and shaping the cultures therein.

I was fortunate enough to have a visit from Professor Shadd Maruna, a prominent advocate of Convict Criminology, who had recently written an article about Redemption Scripts (see Maruna, 2010). Unbeknown to me, Shadd had been speaking to one of my governors at an academic conference in Cambridge and the governor told him "If you believe in this redemption script, I've got a guy at HMP Magilligan going through the very process your paper describes." This coincided with me reading an article in *Inside Time* (UK prison newspaper) about a guy called Dr Andy Aresti who was a former prisoner and now taught criminology at Westminster University. I was also a Listener[1] at the time and the combination of these events made me realise that my experience of prison did not solely belong to me and that I was in a unique position. I began to realise that by combining my studies, the experiences of other prisoners, and spending prison time in England and Wales and Northern Ireland I could fill in the gaps on much of the academic work I was reading. I then read a book called *The felon* (1970) by John Irwin, a founding member of the Convict Criminology group in the USA (but no relation) and this truly got my juices flowing. Irwin described how I was feeling. He had done five years in prison for robbery and I suppose it was a bit like looking in the mirror and deciding that I not only had an interest in radical and critical criminology but also a personal connection, and that I could actually do something with it.

Traditionally criminology emerged as a sub-discipline within the social sciences which drew from a range of other disciplines, particularly psychology and psychiatry. Loosely described, this early criminology was very much an official criminology of the state. Two of the founders of Convict Criminology, Jeffrey Ian Ross and Stephen C. Richards (2003) suggest that the history of criminology consists of a series of reform movements. As early as the 1920s biologically based arguments of criminal causation were being supplemented by environmental, socioeconomic and behavioural explanations.

Convict Criminology attempts to fill a gap in criminology and focuses on several main areas; developing a critical theory for Convict Criminology, policy analysis and suggestions, developing methods for ethnographies and autoethnography, as well as supporting and mentoring convicts in higher education. Convict Criminology attempts to challenge the status quo on what counts as valid academic knowledge production, whereby it might bring in the voices of the subjects as a correction to the problems in criminology and criminal justice. Much of Convict Criminology was born from the frustration and anger of people with first-hand experience of criminal justice being denied the opportunity to use what they knew about the criminal justice system. Personal knowledge was not acceptable as valid academic work. Convict Criminology tries to combine the use of theory, conventional research data, ethnographies or other methods with the insider voice (see Earle, 2017, 2019 for a full account of the emergence of Convict Criminology).

Convict Criminology tends to exist in tension with administrative criminology, an approach where academics are hired by the state which is likely to control everything the researcher will ultimately write and discover. The theoretical grounding of this is that administrative criminology assumes that the criminal justice system works and that all you need to do is make it run better. A relationship between the state and criminology develops and 'the goal of administrative criminology is to make crime less attractive to offenders' (McLaughlin and Muncie, 2012, p 7).

I had wondered what Convict Criminology was and it is best summed up like this:

> convict criminology is a branch of critical criminology started by convict and ex-convict academics who were dissatisfied with mainstream criminological considerations of crime, crime control and criminal justice. This failure, according to convict criminology, is evidenced in the persistent representation as of convicts as 'inferior' or 'deviant' and the continued tolerance of criminal justice processes that are inhumane and counterproductive. (McLaughlin and Muncie, 2012, p 79)

Education was my weapon of choice against an unfair and unjust system. Prison staff used to sneer and mock me as I walked past them to the study room I'd helped set up on the wing, with armfuls of OU material. At the start there was only me and another guy. By the time

I had departed prison the room had eight computers installed and there was a study room on each wing in the prison. The attitude of prison staff is highly significant as many fear knowledge. After all, what do you not want in a prison? Someone asking 'why?', questioning, debating, discussing harmful and irrational policies? Some staff loved it as I could also challenge the policies they disliked. These staff members wanted an easy working day, without incident and to enjoy many more cups of tea. By my questioning and challenging I was able to do this on their behalf, a somewhat sacrificial lamb, without them losing face with colleagues. It was like walking a tightrope at times, but this is what the OU allowed me to do.

However, where is the voice of the insider in academia? This voice is scattered throughout the academic discourse as hard-hitting quotes and statements from within the research but has little or no validity in the science of criminology as it can be swept away as 'sour grapes' or someone having 'a chip on their shoulder'. Due to the petty punitive regime of the institution it may be worth considering that after all irrational forms of protest have been exhausted there is very little left to bargain with and it is then the case that 'education' is the last bastion of rebellion within the psyche of a disenfranchised identity.

In 1913 Oscar Wilde was imprisoned in the UK as a result of his homosexuality, then illegal. He writes:

> When first I was put into prison some people advised me to try and forget who I was. It was ruinous advice. It is only by realising what I am that I have found comfort of any kind. Now I am advised by others to try on my release to forget that I have ever been in a prison at all. (Wilde, 2007 [1913])

What Wilde alludes to here is the deconstruction and reconstruction of self. It is this quashing and reconstruction of 'self' that enables those who have been to prison to argue that you simply cannot walk away or forget the destruction of 'self' for whatever period of incarceration.

Having spent my first 48 hours being interrogated by Her Majesty's Customs and Excise at Gatwick and a night in the cells at Brighton police station I was transferred to HMP Lewes. In the fog of withdrawal from alcohol and cocaine it was with much trepidation that I was led from the meat wagon to the induction wing, still in handcuffs. I distinctly remember asking the officer escorting me "What's this place like then?". His reply will never leave me "Don't trust no fucker, they're all a bunch of manipulative bastards. Especially the ones wearing white shirts. You're a big tough lookin' fella with a Belfast accent. Keep your head down and you'll be fine." This took me back a bit as I'd always imagined some sort of camaraderie between prisoners, "thick as thieves" for want of a better phrase. I realised very quickly that I'd have to walk-my-own-walk but would I have the strength or courage to do it? Upon reading *Society of captives* by Gresham Sykes (during my OU studies in Northern Ireland several years later), I was intrigued by the so-called 'code of honour'. Sykes (1958) attempts to describe this code via the barter system in prison whereby there is a hidden set of rules that all prisoners share, and the prison society is founded upon this. It always reminds me of the image on the cover of Thomas Hobbes' *Leviathan*, where the King is made up of hundreds of individuals. Hobbes (1996 [1651], pp 9–10) states:

> And though by men's actions we do discover their design
> sometimes; yet to do it without comparing them with our
> own, and distinguishing all circumstances, by which the
> case may come to be altered, is to decipher without a key,
> and be for the most part deceived, by too much trust, or
> by too much diffidence; as he that reads, is himself a good
> or evil man.

There is no 'King' in prison. There may well be a 'number one' or 'top dog' but at the end of the day the system, the state, is King, and prisons are a society within a society; those within form a secret bond that will be carried with the person for the rest of their life. In contradiction to the previous characterisation of king and society within a society, for me that is what prison is, a complete and utter paradox, it is not a collective experience. Despite what many may think, the 'inmate code' referred to by Sykes (1958) in *Society of captives* is more akin to the fictional adaptation of 'The Code' in *Pirates of the Caribbean*, where everyone adheres to the code only providing it suits their own purpose (Sykes, 1958; Bruckheimer, 2003).

Prison is personal, it is lonely and it is 'self'-contained in that, for many, it is effectively a form of solitary confinement, namely single cell occupation. Even the bunk in a shared room becomes the only place claimed and defined by albeit temporary ownership. John Irwin defined his life by overcoming the degradation of imprisonment, became a widely respected professor and dedicated the rest of his life to helping others recognise what many now call the reintegration process and 'desistance' (see McNeill, 2006).

Interestingly and importantly, although twenty years apart, when one compares the phenomenological rationale behind Andy Aresti's and John Irwin's decision to become 'educated', they are not that different. Aresti suggests his research particularly focused on what it is like to live with the stigmatised 'ex-offender' status and explored how this identity is negotiated in everyday life. Andy has lived experience of imprisonment, having served a three-year prison sentence, and having lived a 'colourful life' prior to his academic career (Aresti et al, 2010).

Similarly, Irwin states:

> ... prisons in some ways are like exotic, isolated island societies with their own language, worldview and cultural patterns. Skilled anthropologists have come close to these primitive societies and produced good ethnographies. But it takes time and special effort. To do it with indigenous people or convicts one has to go native. (cited in Ross and Richards, 2003, p xix)

I suggest that lived experience is crucial to the advance of criminology as academia can 'science' the hell out of prison life but most academics have never been on the receiving end of criminal justice processes and as a result they will always be on the outside looking in. When it comes to the raw experience of imprisonment there is no doubt that this is something which most academics miss out on. Irwin elaborates on this: 'they [ethnographers] come close don't they? And close is good enough. The trouble with this is that they often misunderstand crucial meanings and motivations of convicts' (cited in Ross and Richards, 2003, p xix). This is indeed a crucial point. Erwin James, a former prisoner who has become a respected journalist (see Chapter 14), suggests that no person will ever fully understand the sheer energy it takes to get through a day in prison. Unless you've been there. To the uninformed or the inexperienced this might suggest men and women in prison are fighting toe to toe, day by day and for the length of a sentence, but it is more subtle than that. It is more to do with the deconstruction of your being, the petty punitivity of life on a prison wing and the mountainous levels of bureaucratic malfeasance administered to anyone who dares reason with or question authority; this on top of the daily drudgery and monotony of the prison regimen. As Irwin clearly states, there are consequences to this misrecognition of prisoner experience:

> this leads to the most important reason for a Convict Criminology. The general public, most functionaries in the criminal justice system and many criminologists fail to

fully understand and appreciate the viewpoint of the convict and because of this see them as less than human, as inferior or evil deviants. Consequently, they participate in the inhumane and counterproductive treatment of them that is occurring today. (Cited in Ross and Richards, 2003, p xix)

The discovery of one's sense of self in prison is a unique and personal experience, exposing how it is an evolving and continually changing entity. Self-discovery via education in prison can be a self-rewarding and self-fulfilling endeavour which not only serves a personal self-satisfaction but can create the will to impart this experience, this self to others. Convict Criminology recognises how this phenomenological approach to self via education is relevant to lived experience and how we recognise our self within the world. Habits and routines inside prison make the world feel secure to the individual who unavoidably maintains a blind obedience to established routines, initiating a loss of autonomy that ultimately has a negative impact on one's ontological security (Jewkes, 2013). As the sociologist Anthony Giddens argues: 'Where individuals cannot live creatively, either because of the compulsive enactment of routines, or because they have been unable to attribute full "solidity" to persons and objects around them, melancholic or schizophrenic tendencies are likely to result' (Giddens, 1991, p 41). Therefore, it might be worth considering how the modern prison's aim, which Foucault (1977) suggests is to punish and create docile bodies, may also work to produce insecure prisoners who manifest an unhealthy mental attachment to prison routine; indicative of what it means to be institutionalised.

How then, did I end up sitting in an Education Department in a prison with Oscar Wilde discussing how I should forget who I was, keep my head down and get on with it? Only through trial (no pun intended) and error and much reading did I realise that the actual problem with prison is the institution itself. How has it survived for all these years while society itself has changed? I could see that the system was weak; it could be challenged. One of my personal challenges was the checks on prisoners during the night. After many years of sleep deprivation (we were checked every hour on the hour), I initiated a Judicial Review against the Northern Ireland Prison Service in 2011. I lost in court but in many ways, succeeded as I got the issue out there, beyond the prison wall and into the public domain see (Irwin, 2011). The authorities reduced the number of checks and promised a review of their suicide and self-harm policies. My question has always been "How can you expect a person to function as a human being if they can't get any proper sleep?" My challenge was that the very same rules that were there to protect and safeguard prisoners and fulfil the state's duty of care were in fact doing the complete opposite.

Goffman (2017 [1961]) examines the total institution from the point of view of the prisoner, observing the disciplinary programming procedures that work to institutionalise a new prisoner. He or she enters an all-male or -female prison, and carries a certain conception of their 'self' formed by arrangements in the outside world, which is immediately stripped away by a series of mortifying procedures and processes (Goffman, 2017 [1961]). He or she must submit to the indignity of strip-searching and, where personal belongings are confiscated, a symbolic de-personalisation of the self occurs. He or she is given a prison number instead of a name. Through these many and various processes and procedures, a prisoner is presented with a new set of beliefs about the world and is encouraged to build a representation of the self constituted by the institution. Goffman (2017 [1961]) refers to this process in terms of primary adjustments of selfhood, through which the inmate's self-identity is first mortified and gradually broken down, only to be reassembled in an attempt to fit the requirements of the institution. This is where the concept of fear takes a dramatic turn as the student convict criminologists, such as myself, can testify as they start to do well in their studies. Attaining critical knowledge of institutional practice, a student may find themselves in a position to question or resist the practice, only to find that they are suddenly not permitted to progress through the system until they learn to conform to the institution's expectations. Goffman's (2017 [1961]) assertion is that the 'fraternalisation process' marks one of many routes by which the individual's process of institutionalisation is accomplished: 'More important as a reorganization influence is the fraternalization process, through which socially distant persons find themselves developing mutual support and common counter-mores in opposition to a system that has forced them into intimacy and a single egalitarian community of shared fate' (Goffman, 2017 [1961], p 56). Moreover, a constant state of conflict between various inmate factions may be desirable for the smooth running of the institution, considering a divided prison population better lends itself to authoritarian control. Liebling argues that 'the observational nature of research on total institutions has largely failed to convince scholars that incarceration causes psychological harm. This failure, such as it is, stems in no small part from the many complications involved' (cited in Schnittker et al, 2012, p 450).

What most prisoners and researchers do not realise is that every interaction between a prisoner and another person, be it staff from psychology, probation, education, the Samaritans, or offender programmes are all recorded and reported on. One might think that good behaviour as well the risky is taken into consideration also but it is not, in my experience. The reality is that the institution tries to satisfy both public opinion and the human rights of the UK population, embedded in law, and that all prisoners must feel the full weight of the punishment of prison until the day they leave. What Convict Criminology can bear witness to is that if there are 19 entries in a prisoner's file about achievement and one about a minor indiscretion you can guarantee the only questions asked will be about the single negative entry on the file. In June 2013 I sat my final OU exam 12 days before my release. At the time I was allowed weekend- and day-release (semi-open conditions) so you can imagine where my head was at. There was one room set aside for education on the unit. The Education Department made sure that the room had been set aside for me to do my final exam. When the day arrived, the governor in charge of the unit had deliberately double-booked the room and the teacher who had to administer and observe me spent 20 minutes trying to find another room. The governor was off that day, so we used his office. My point being that this governor, in charge of rehabilitation, appeared to do everything in his power to disrupt my final exam. Instead of calmly walking into the exam prepped and relaxed I was completely stressed and unsure whether I was going to be able to do it at all. I managed to pass the exam but in hindsight have to wonder would I have done better without the disruption. The Prison Service and this governor, in particular, did not seem to me to believe that education was part of the rehabilitation process and refused me home leaves to attend seminars and lectures at Queen's University Belfast and other places. Thankfully, the ethos has changed now and people like that governor are no longer in charge, but it does demonstrate what I and others were up against at the time.

In recent years, there have been leaps and bounds in the relationship between academia and prisons. The one I am most impressed with is between Westminster University and HMP Pentonville, whereby students studying criminology at the university go into the prison and study alongside prisoners doing exactly the same. And right there in the middle of it all is Dr Andy Aresti. Despite years of being denied access he was finally able to work inside a prison. I too have visited a few prisons in England to share my experiences and eventually made it back into HMP Maghaberry in Northern Ireland to introduce *Prison Smart*, a breathing and meditation course. Some of the staff who knew me from HMP Magilligan, now working in Maghaberry, came to the

Education Department to meet me. One member of staff in particular said: "I heard Elvis was in the building and I had to come and say hello." He didn't ask for my autograph but the laughter and stories we shared is testament to the understanding and warmth that can develop between staff and prisoners. The OU allowed me to survive prison, it enabled me and gave me confidence. Eleven days after my release I attended a British Society of Criminology conference at Wolverhampton and met some of the academics mentioned in this article, who I now call friends. I now help and teach others (albeit privately) adhering to the ethos of Convict Criminology of which I'm proud to be a part. It was a bumpy ride but by continually chipping away, myself and others have made it easier for those who come behind us to follow this kind of education in prison. Without the OU in prison I wouldn't even be writing this.

Note

[1]   Listeners are prisoners who volunteer to operate a service similar to the Samaritans in free society, listening confidentially and without judgement to someone's troubles. Listeners are trained and supervised by the Samaritans.

References

Aresti, A., Eatough, V. and Brooks-Gordon, B. (2010) 'Doing time after time: an Interpretative Phenomenological Analysis of reformed ex-prisoners' experiences of self-change, identity and career opportunities', *Psychology, Crime & Law*, 16(3): 169–90.

Bruckheimer, J. (2003) *The Pirates Of The Caribbean*, Walt Disney Studios Motion Pictures, United States.

Earle, R. (2017) *Convict criminology: Inside and out*, Bristol: Policy Press.

Earle, R. (2019) 'Narrative convictions, conviction narratives: the prospects of convict criminology', in L. Presser and J. Fleetwood (eds) *Handbook of narrative criminology*, Basingstoke: Palgrave.

Foucault, M. (1977) *Discipline and punish: The birth of the prison*, New York: Random House.

Giddens, A. (1991) *Modernity and self-identity*, Cambridge: Polity.

Goffman, E. (2017 [1961]) *Asylums: Essays on the social situation of mental patients and other inmates*, New York: Routledge.

Hobbes, T. (1996 [1651]) *Leviathan*, edited by R. Tuck. Cambridge: Cambridge University Press.

Irwin, J. (1970) *The felon*, Berkeley: University of California Press.

Irwin, M. (2011) Judicial Review. www.casemine.com/judgement/uk/5a8ff87360d03e7f57ec0b44.

Jewkes, Y. (2013) *Captive audience*, London: Routledge.

Maruna, S. (2010) 'Redemption scripts and desistance', in F.T. Cullen and P. Wilcox (eds) *Encyclopaedia of criminological theory*, New York: Sage.

McLaughlin, E. and Muncie, J. (2012) *The Sage dictionary of criminology*, 3rd edn. London: Sage.

McNeill, F. (2006) 'A desistance paradigm for offender management', *Criminology and Criminal Justice*, 6(1): 39–62.

Nietzsche, F. (2007 [1885]) *This spoke Zarathustra*. Lexido. com. www.lexido.com/EBOOK_TEXTS/THUS_SPOKE_ ZARATHUSTRA_.aspx?S=5.

Ross, J.I. and Richards, S.C. (2003) *Convict criminology*, Belmont, CA: Wadsworth.

Schnittker, J., Massoglia, M. and Uggen, C. (2012) 'Out and down: incarceration and psychiatric disorders', *Journal of Health and Social Behaviour*, 53(4): 448–64.

Sykes, G.M. (1958) *The society of captives: A study of a maximum security prison*, Princeton, NJ: Princeton University Press.

Wilde, O. (2007 [1913]) *De profundis*. Gutenberg ebook. www. gutenberg.org/files/921/921-h/921-h.htm.

Zimbardo, P. (1999) The Stanford prison experiment, homepage of Philip G. Zimbardo. http://www.prisonexp.org/.

VIGNETTE 6

Message to a prisoner

Gordon McDonald

Oh, there you are.

I was wondering when you would turn to this page. The fact that you have read this far would suggest that you are, at the very least, interested in doing something constructive with your time while in prison. To be honest, and how many of us have been in the past, this is the sole reason that I looked at the possibilities of studying with The Open University (OU) back in 2014. I left school with a few qualifications, worked in various jobs, then everything went wrong and I found myself looking at a lengthy prison sentence. But enough of that!

The OU opened up new horizons. I had always liked reading and when I first looked through the OU prospectus for study in secure environments, I was taken by the Humanities courses (that's the academic name for the study of literature, philosophy and the arts). The modules looked varied, interesting and something that I believed I would enjoy. The key word here is 'enjoy'. It's no use starting on a course that you think might be OK only to find that by your second TMA (tutor-marked assignment) – it's not only the Prison Service that exists in acronyms! – you are not enjoying the challenge. You already know about challenges after all. Prison is a challenge, and if you want to make constructive use of your time, read on.

I chose a module which I thought would give me a good introduction into the academic world, hoping that if everything went well, I could maybe move forward to further modules. There was no thought at that point that I would try to achieve a degree but as the modules came and went, I realised that I could really do this, and the added bonus was that the days and weeks seemed to be passing with alarming frequency.

I remember opening my first module material with a sense of apprehension, thinking that maybe I had been a bit too ambitious. There seemed, at first glance, to be an overwhelming amount of detail to take in, but on looking through the material, it became clear that this was part of the challenge of studying – organising TMA dates, making sure that I had an achievable study plan and that I had confidence in the support of the prison Education Department and the OU. In other words, getting into a routine that I was happy with – we all know about routines!

As time went on and I received feedback from module tutors, I started to feel a sense of worth, something that I had personally struggled with. There were, of course, comments from other prisoners who thought it was all just too much hard work. In reality, they were not wrong but in a strange way that just made me want to achieve even more and I felt that it also helped my family to understand that I was changing, that my horizons were changing and I was using this opportunity to move forward with a life that had all but fallen apart.

With hindsight, was my decision to complete the OU module application form back in 2014 a good one? Resoundingly yes! Was it hard work? Undoubtedly! Did I feel a sense of achievement? The process was and still is, life affirming, so I guess that's a 'yes' as well.

I hope to graduate with a BA (Honours) Arts and Humanities degree in English Literature and Creative Writing in the autumn of 2020. Six years hard work but worth every second.

Your journey within a journey – OU study within your prison sentence – can start right here. Grasp the opportunity. As Katherine Mansfield once wrote 'Would you not like to try all sorts of lives? One is so very small.'*

---

* Mansfield, K. (1906) Letter from Katherine Mansfield to Sylvia Payne, April 1906.

10

From the school of hard knocks to the university of hard locks

Abdulhaq Al-Wazeer

Criminal, trouble-maker, thug, failure, drop out … what do all of these descriptions have in common? They all comprise some of the only descriptions I used to think could, or would ever apply to me.

Academic, public speaker, community leader, scholar, university graduate … what do all of these descriptions have in common? They all represent descriptions which I never thought could, or would, ever apply to me.

What follows is an intimate account of how I went from the only thing(s) I thought I would ever be to something I thought I would never be, and the pivotal role which my engagement with The Open University (OU) played to that end.

Early days

Growing up for me wasn't all rainbows and unicorns. I was born and raised in the London borough of Hackney, where I lived for pretty much all of my pre-adult life. I had one (older) sibling and I used to see my father occasionally up until I was around six years of age, after which he disappeared; my mother was thus forced to play the role of two parents – which she wasn't the best at managing. I was very bright, even in primary school. I used to receive a lot of praise about this, however, perhaps unbeknownst to many around me, I used to suffer from an acute feeling of loneliness and perhaps what I may in refer to in hindsight as mild depression. I was always a very popular figure, yet I had very few friends and my extra-curricular activities were greatly restricted by my mother. In addition, I found her very difficult, if not impossible, to communicate with for constant fear of getting in trouble, or not being heard out. This meant that expressing my feelings to her were out of the question. Even if I had been able to do so, it would perhaps have been futile as it was clear that we were living in two different realities – she was a first-generation African woman who didn't understand the reality of the world of a young black boy born in the 1990s and growing up in Hackney, facing the various multifaceted challenges associated with doing so. All of this, over time, caused me to develop a very raw concentration of anger, an anger which I allowed to continue to grow in increments, and which I harboured in silence for years before any manifestation thereof.

Moving forward a number of years, my school days started to become hectic from around Year 8 onwards; I was constantly implicated in violent incidents which led to me being excluded for pretty much the bulk of years 10 and 11. The anger and frustration which had been building up over the years had remained unchecked and began to manifest in increments over the years, having a major effect on the personality I was developing and the type of person I was becoming. I started sneaking out of the house to meet friends when my mum went to work as well developing numerous other bad behaviours. I became embroiled in different types of criminal activity and also various conflicts as a result of my own personality, as well as my affiliations with various individuals and groups. To indicate just how serious the situation was, suffice it to say that I was first arrested and charged when I was only 12 years of age, and during the GCSE exams period I was stabbed in the head outside of my school by some individuals who had come looking for me. By the time I reached the age of 18, my relationship with my family members (especially my mum) had become rotten, I had respect for hardly anyone, and I had developed something of a vendetta against the world, coupled with an acute sense of paranoia. By this time, I had gained no qualifications besides a few GCSEs which I barely scraped; my first attempt at college had resulted in an indefinite ban from the premises, my second in my being implicated in a violent incident and thus unable to return, and my third interrupted by my being sent to prison, wherein I subsequently remained for the next nine years of my life.

Graduation from the school of hard knocks ... enrolment into the university of hard locks

After being sentenced, I remember thinking to myself that there was no way I could leave prison knowing no more than I did coming in. That being the case, it was only words at the time. I had been handed an 18-year sentence, but at that time it didn't affect me more than perhaps scratching my nose would; the reality of my situation hadn't really hit home. At the time I had already completed a year behind bars – hardly enough for me to develop any drastic change in mentality or behaviour. In the same manner in which I started my period of incarceration, I continued to be involved in – and sometimes at the forefront – of incidents and activities that were far from indicative of any intention of self-development or progression.

In 2010, however, things began to change. The growing strain of a repetitive lifestyle began to wear me down. I had been through various phases of repetitive activity and exhausted each; of these perhaps the most frustrating was the educational routine. At this point I had experienced life in three different establishments and a trend with respect to the nature of education on offer had begun to manifest; there was very little on offer in terms of both subject and level, and very little promotional encouragement for people to pursue learning. Additionally, just as the average prisoner would approach attending education sessions as something of a 'tick box' exercise, it was even more surprising to notice that the same seemed to be the case on the part of the prison establishment. I hardly felt challenged or stimulated by any class I walked into; this really began to wear me down. I used to express this frustration to various people – both fellow prisoners as well as officers. Then one day a person whom I had met once at Friday prayers, and would speak with around the prison estate from time to time, made a recommendation to me. That recommendation was to give the OU a shot. This was the first time I had ever heard of any such organisation. I followed his advice and submitted an application and was subsequently invited to an OU workshop. When I attended, the first thing I noticed was how informal the setting was; it was led by two members of staff whom I had never seen around the prison before in a very small classroom situated on one of the residential units; it had connection neither to the Education Department nor to the library, and there were only around five other prisoners there. I felt like I had walked into the initial stage of some sort of cult initiation. I was subsequently given an initial brief about the idea of distance learning at the prison. Hitherto, the OU was a foreign institution to me and I had no idea about the implication(s) of studying with them; actually, despite the name, I didn't even recognise it as a university in the conventional sense of the word. It didn't occur to me that, by going down this path, I would be pursuing university-level study. I just knew that it offered a higher level of education than that offered by the prison service and that was good enough for me. I was instructed with respect to the process of enrolling on an OU module and I did just that. I applied for, and subsequently received funding from the Prisoners' Education Trust (PET) to study with the OU. Little did I know that this would be the first milestone on a long road to change.

I enrolled onto an Openings module which was, quite auspiciously, entitled Learning to Change. It was really hard at first; all the years I had spent out of formal education had made me rusty. In actuality, I don't think I had ever completed a book in my life before entering the prison system, despite having been capable of reading novels since year three. My vocabulary was very limited; I spent more time reading the dictionary than the actual book(s) which caused me to consult it in the first place. The same was the case when I would try to watch the news and other current affairs programmes. In addition to this, distance learning wasn't recognised as a form of 'purposeful activity' at that particular establishment. This meant that I had to figure out for myself complex ways of getting out of work to access the library for books, or to arrange sessions where I could use some of the facilities which were available for the purpose of accessing my audio-visual course materials – effectively trying to find a way out of 'purposeful activity' for the sake of 'non-purposeful activity'. It was very clear that the concept of distance learning was not highly regarded within the prison establishment. Far from the cult-like image that came to mind when I was first introduced to it, I now begun to understand that the reason for the way distance learning had been facilitated at that prison was due to the lack of support it had on the part of the establishment. Nevertheless, I slowly began to find my rhythm. Although it was only an Openings module, I actually felt that I was achieving something for the first time since entering prison; I was reading, writing essays, reflecting, working to deadlines and more. During this period, I was in regular contact with my closest childhood friend on the outside, who had extricated himself from going down the path of life which I had. I told him about my studies and he was very pleased and supportive. I don't think he had ever imagined I'd one day be phoning him from prison talking about degree-level study. He recommended some books, which I subsequently read. It was actually an amazing feeling. Quite literally for the first time in my life, I was beginning to develop something of a feeling of purpose. I was exposing myself to new things and was gradually beginning to develop new interests.

Out of all the interests I was slowly developing, there was one which stood out in particular; I began to develop an acute, yet quite accidental interest in politics. Accidental in the sense that my first engagement with political viewing wasn't actually intended to be just that. After having come across it while flicking through the television channels one day, I became an avid viewer of Prime Minister's Questions on Wednesdays, but perhaps for the wrong reason(s). You see, I previously had no active engagement with anything to do with politics or current affairs – I had been living in a kind of bubble, trapped in my own surroundings, surrounded by like-minded individuals for the most part. Thus, when I first started watching Prime Minister's Questions, I did so purely for entertainment purposes. That is to say, I didn't initially realise – quite embarrassingly – that PMQs was a real thing; I thought it was a type of satirical comedy, along the lines of programmes such as *Yes, Prime Minister*, or (the more exaggerated comparison of) *Spitting Image*. One can imagine my surprise when I found out how far from the truth I was; I never guessed that the elite (as I saw them to be) – the political class within whose hands my affairs had been placed, as well as those of my family and the rest of society at large – would be a collection of individuals who shout each other down in the manner in which they do, and are capable of conducting themselves in a way more suited to a hip hop battle rap scene than an institution home to the main legislature of a leading country of the Global North. This was a real eye-opener, especially when I began to pay more attention to debates and discussion of legislation which was closer to home (such as talks of a harsher stance on prisoners).

As time progressed, the more I followed current affairs, the more I realised how much of an interdependent world I had been living in, all the while plodding on oblivious with my head in the clouds. I began to understand how an event taking place in a completely different part of the world could have ramifications for me living here in the UK, even as a prisoner. I realised at this point that there was much more to life and the world than I previously perceived, and along with this realisation came also the realisation that if I wanted to be able to hold my own in such a vast and complex world, then I would need to know what I was doing, and that that would require education. Thus, I began to take my reading all the more seriously.

The inception of the personal process of self-development, which I began to undergo as a result of the culmination of all of the aforementioned events of 2010, was exacerbated by a major event which took place in the same year: the 2010 UK general election, which resulted in the first hung parliament since 1974, and subsequent coalition government. I had followed the whole thing – that is, from the time I had started my Openings module in the same year. Following the news reports, debates, analyses, commentary and the rest of the inputs which shaped the socio-political landscape really had an impact on me, an indelible one. I began to remember the promise I made to myself on the day I was sentenced: there was no way I was going to allow myself to leave the prison system knowing no more than I did coming in. Upon completing the Openings module, I made an application to study a level 1 Introduction to Business Studies module, for which I was once again granted funding by the PET. Business courses were a popular choice among students in prison. Probably part of the reasoning behind such a common choice was that by studying business, one would automatically go on to become some sort of millionaire mogul; that was at least part of the thought process which led me to do so, in addition to having been influenced somewhat by some of the strands of the Conservative Party ethos. However, the more I began to read and expose myself to new information and perspectives on the world and current affairs, the more I began to learn about my own self. I realised I had skills and characteristics I had never previously paid attention to, as well as interests I would never have previously attributed to myself. I developed a real interest in politics, both local and international. Likewise, I really enjoyed debates and analysis, as well as trying to make sense of the various phenomena which make up the world as we know it. This led me to move away from studying business, in favour of a shift to the social sciences.

At this point I was in full commitment to study. However, I was still suffering from a major impediment to my progress – my social circle. As my interests began to develop, so did the nature of my conversations, meaning it wasn't the easiest thing to find someone to speak with, as many people in were not into what I was. At times I ended up going to the library just to have a general chat with the librarians about various topics. As a result, I naturally began to drift away from my former group of peers. However, the transition had not set in place 100 per cent, and so I still found myself getting involved in things which I knew were totally not in my favour. One day, one such event caused me to undergo a major setback after all the progress I had been making. The result was that I ended up in the segregation unit for 10 days, before being transferred to another establishment. This had a major impact on my mindset and sent me into a downward spiral. I had now been reminded that I hadn't been spending the last year or so as a student in some university halls of residence – rather I was a prisoner and was still in prison. I was battling with myself. I hadn't figured out how to reconcile between the mindset and personality I was now developing and the one I was trying to abandon. It was as if I was stuck between being two totally different people. That fact alone caused me to become all the more frustrated on a daily basis, as my environment continued to wear me down. I was certain that I no longer wanted to be a particular kind of person, yet I was surrounded by scores of exemplars of the very type of person I was trying to break free of being. Eventually, I snapped and gave into the pressures, and what followed was a series of events which led me to being expelled from two prison establishments in succession. Just as I thought my newly discovered path to progress had taken a turn for the worse, it turned out that having been expelled from the previous two prisons worked in my favour. I ended up in a private establishment, relatively calm, which had set distance learning as form of purposeful activity within its regime. Funnily enough, I had not given up with my studies. I had, somehow in the midst of all the madness, found a way to complete the business module and enrol on an introductory social sciences one.

When I first arrived at the establishment, I almost made the same mistake again – having met up with a number of people I already knew (some of whom I had previously had problems with) – but this time I didn't give in. All of these experiences led me to sit down and have a serious conversation with myself. I had to question my identity – who I was and who I wanted to be. I had begun to realise that a major aspect of my problem of was that I had not yet begun to undergo a redevelopment of character and heart as much as I had begun to reshape my mind; I was thinking differently, but my values and overall character hadn't changed much. I then began to turn my attention to an aspect of my identity that I had allowed to be overshadowed as time went on – my religion. I was born into a family which was originally comprised of Muslims (nominally). However, my mother, as well as all of her siblings, later became Christians – which is what me and my sister grew up on. However, neither of us were ever truly that way inclined. My own investigation had led me to incline towards Islam, but my previous lifestyle and mentality could not be reconciled with the values and prescriptions of the religion, and I was not very interested in amending that reality. However, things were different now. I was ready for change. I had already begun the intellectual pursuit, now my principles and core values were in need of fine tuning. As I was now (somewhat) already into the routine of studying and learning, I thought to myself: "Why not do the same with my religion also?" And that I did, and it was the best choice I ever made. I began teaching myself Arabic, and later memorising the Qur'an and studying the religion in a like manner to the way I was studying for my degree. As a result, I was able to combine between mind and soul (as they say), and what ensued was a long road of intellectual as well as spiritual development. I started looking at everything differently. And it was at this point when I truly started to realise the impact(s) of my past criminal behaviour – the immediate ones as well as the knock-on effects. The deep reality of my past behaviour had set in, and I knew that I could never allow myself to be that person again.

Over time, everything about me began to change – my speech, my demeanour, my daily activities and, of course, my associations. My relationship with my family (especially my mother) began to improve a lot. Perhaps most shocking to me was not this change per se, but the change it elicited in those around me. I started realising that people would no longer approach me to talk about the kinds of thing they previously would have. I used to think to myself that perhaps they believed me to be some kind of prison informer now, but it wasn't that at all. I became the person who people would come to speak to about things they didn't find themselves able to even with their immediate associates – regrets, feelings, dreams, aspirations and so on. Likewise, I would also open their minds to new discussions and lead them to think in ways they had never done and about things they had never done. I had finally struck the balance between who I previously was, and who I was now trying to be.

The establishment I was in at the time allowed us to have access to Free View, which helped me a lot because I could access more news, history, documentary and current affairs channels and programmes, and as distance learning was considered a purposeful activity there, I didn't even have to leave my cell. One channel I became very fond of watching was BBC Parliament. I would watch debates, parliamentary and select committee sessions and more. Every so often there would be short 5-or-so-minute programmes dedicated to taking a brief look at the profile of various Members of Parliament. The more of these I watched, the more I kept hearing the same phrase over and over: that they had studied something called PPE. I became fascinated by this, and almost obsessed with finding out what it was – and one day I finally did. PPE stood for Politics, Philosophy and Economics – one of the most prestigious degrees ever to grace the world of intellectual pursuit and academia, the elite of the elites, the crème de la crème (so to speak). If my brain had a mouth then it would have watered every time I read more about this degree. It was perfect for me. It was interdisciplinary, encouraged utilising the mind to the fullest extent and also incorporated numerous hard skills. Even more, it brought together the three subjects I had hitherto developed the most interest in. I had to have a taste. I had already been registered on an Open degree at the time, so I thought I'd just tailor the modules I chose to study in a way so as to replicate as closely as possible the PPE qualification. Then, one day as I was flicking through the current OU prospectus selecting modules to make up my degree I somehow ended up in the 'named degrees' section and was completely shocked by what I saw next: staring me in the face was the big bold title 'Politics, Philosophy and Economics'. It took me a moment to process what was actually happening, and to make sure that I was seeing what I actually was. The next step was a no-brainer: switch from an Open degree to a PPE one, and that I did. And what followed from there was a whirlwind of a journey of progression, change and self-development – the details of which would require a whole book in itself. What I can say, however, is that six years on from then, I could barely recognise myself as I stood, almost nine years after walking into the prison system, to address a crowd of people – including professionals, academics, prison chaplains and others – who had all come to see me graduate with honours, only two weeks prior to the date I was set to make my return to the outside world. I thought back to what I had told myself the day I was sentenced: there was no way I could leave prison knowing no more than I did coming in. I stayed true to that realisation, but never in a million years did I think that this would be the manifestation of those words to myself.

Graduating from the university of hard locks: hindsight v foresight

It is said that hindsight is a wonderful thing, and indeed it is; without hindsight, one could never develop foresight. In 2009 I was officially made a convicted criminal; at the time of both my crime and conviction I was a young man – I had literally just reached adulthood. I had a very poor mentality, few qualifications, next to no experience and little direction in life. All of these factors led to me becoming involved in an incident that has remained indelibly in my mind due to what it elicits of regret and embarrassment. The image of a 'happy ending' to this story of mine will always be overshadowed by the reality of the fact that it came at a price, and that myself and others were forced to split the cost in order to cover it. That being the case, it so happens that my imprisonment was perhaps the best thing to have happened to me. I vowed to become a better person and used my time to redevelop myself from top to bottom. I addressed my offending behaviour by completing thinking skills as well as victim awareness programmes; I then went on to educate myself and improve my functional skills; I taught myself a foreign language and went on to become a teacher and practitioner of the said language, and, perhaps most notably to many, worked hard for six years to achieve my BA (Hons) degree in an environment wherein literally almost every odd was stacked against me. My imprisonment gave me my life back and made me a person I did not even know I had the potential to be.

I have learned much in prison and, as such, have become very concerned with the issue of education as a means of rehabilitation. One of the most important things I have realised is that education is not just an academic pursuit, rather it is a mentality; rarely will an individual see something through unless they perceive what they personally gain from doing so. The kind of feedback and reaction I have received from those who hear about my journey has made it apparent that my story is not one which is heard every day, and I can't help at questioning why exactly that is. We are not in the context of discussing prescriptions for curbing society's soaring crime rates and increasing prison population; that is speculative. We are talking about the here and now – the fact that there *are* people – men, women and youths who, like myself, have committed crime(s) and are now resident within the prison system. Why, in that case, can't stories like mine be the norm as opposed to the exception? The prison estate is filled with a vast store of untapped talent, individuals with some of the greatest potential I have ever seen. Individuals who gather within themselves all of the requisite ingredients for a recipe of reform of the greatest scale. However, no Michelin star chef ever got to where they are simply by having their cupboards stocked. Whether we like it or not, such a pursuit is not one that can be left to the individuals who undertake it alone. Everyone needs support of some sort, no matter how little. I once said to an audience of people at the OU, that when you look at my degree certificate, all you will see is my name and achievement. You will never be able to see the names of the numerous individuals who supported and assisted me along the way to that end, no matter how little. Those names are numerous indeed, and I know because I have been keeping a list since the day I first embarked on this journey.

It is my view that failing to recognise the power of education in the process of rehabilitation is one of the worst phenomena prevalent within the prison system and in society as a whole. It is my suggestion that education is a mandatory tool to this end. But, as I said earlier, it is more than just an academic pursuit, it is also a mentality; each individual is responsible for his/her own progress and development and there will be no change unless they themselves opt for there to be, irrespective of whatever external assistance they may have access to. Each has to understand the relevance of his/her own learning to his/her own long-term goals and ambitions (which necessitates that they have goals and ambitions in the first place), otherwise their learning will be nought but an aimless endeavour which may or may not bring about benefit; and what use is gambling in this respect? On the other hand, it is also a mentality on the part of the prison system, which needs to engender within its staff and infrastructure an ethos of promoting, supporting and facilitating prisoner learning. Politicians can promise everything under the sun, but policy makers are only effective if they can actually ensure that their policies are actualised through implementation by the institutions and actors on the ground. There is no doubt that this is a collective endeavour, for, as I also said once: if the whole society can be afflicted by just one crime, then likewise the whole society can stand to benefit from the education (and thus rehabilitation) of even just one prisoner. It is a positive sum game, while turning away from this issue and allowing the status quo to remain is it is a zero sum one – everybody loses in the long run.

Criminal, trouble-maker, thug, failure, drop out ... what do all of these descriptions have in common? They all comprise some of the only descriptions I used to think could, or would ever apply to me.

Academic, public speaker, community leader, scholar, university graduate ... what do all of these descriptions have in common? They all represent descriptions which I never thought could, or would, ever apply to me.

Change is a real possibility, and no one should ever give up on it.

11

Becoming me with
The Open University

Edwin Schreeche-Powell

'Mr Schreeche-Powell, you may remain seated for the
sentence that I am about to deliver ...'
    (Chelmsford Crown Court, 15 December 2012)

Guilty! The impending doom struck in abundance and following very
shortly after was the realisation that life as I knew it had ended. I was
guilty of a lot of things looking back; a lack of consequential thinking,
a lack of foresight, a lack of common sense, immense stupidity, wanting
and pursuing something that I didn't need, an inability to accept and
be comfortable in my own skin and self and to be me. Hindsight and
reflection is a wonderful thing and I can know, identify and accept that
the combination of these things contributed to me receiving another
guilty conviction leading to the words "You shall spend not a day more
than 15 years in prison". The judge labelled me a "skilful and clever
manipulator of the criminal ropes" and delivered a narrative effectively
describing me as Beelzebub incarnate.

Do I regret what I got myself involved in, what I did and all those
errors and deficiencies? Yes! Do I wish I could turn back time? Yes!
– and I would in a heartbeat. Dwelling in the past and ruminating
on those things was never going to rewrite them but I do have an
opportunity to write my future and equip myself to learn from those
mistakes, not make them again, and build a new future.

I make it clear from the outset that I don't seek to preach or claim
be an authority on prison, merely that I am a commentator sharing
my experiences of prison and The Open University (henceforth, OU).
From the humble beginnings of my youth, I walked a path that although
long-winded and fraught with adversity brought me into contact with
the OU. It is an institution that I describe as a force of nature in the
best possible way – a force that carried me along with gusto to achieve
goals and develop skills and characteristics I can take pride in.

I had a stark choice to take my opportunity with the OU to better
myself or waste my time in prison, merely existing rather than living.

The OU has underpinned my journey from being what I refer to as the lowest common denominator, to someone on the path to feeling like a fully paid up and contributing member of society, with options for a crime-free and pro-social lifestyle.

My aim is to chart the development of my identity through three different stages; as a person, a prisoner and an academic, especially in the context of my journey through the prison system from the high-security estate to the low-security estate.

Identity is a deeply personal part of our everyday being yet so vulnerable and malleable to context. It is influenced by and accessible to so many people. The OU was one context which had a profound impact on my identity and sense of self. I call the first contextual stage of my development the 'anti/ante OU stage'. It includes my stance of negativity toward education and the OU as an institution. It was a stage when ignorance, a lack of knowledge and confidence in my own beliefs and values dominated my identity and my life choices, which resulted in me going to prison.

The next stage is what I call the courtship stage. This explores how I came into contact with the OU and my reasons and motivations for doing so. It involves how my study with the OU and interaction with this institution shaped and developed my identity as a man, an academic and a prisoner. The OU gave me an opportunity and support when I was at my lowest and weakest, helping me to summon the strength and fortitude to keep challenging, bettering and educating myself to achieve a better future. As the poet Edward Hirsch (2014) says 'Look closely, and you will see almost everyone carrying bags of cement on their shoulders, that's why it takes courage to get out of bed in the morning and climb into the day.'

I'm not ashamed or too proud or too 'hard' to admit there were days and times where I wondered just what my limit was and just how many more blows I could absorb before I finally succumbed and just couldn't take any more – but somehow I always, always managed to hang in there and fight and suck it up no matter what the system threw at me. I refused to yield or to break no matter how much I was beaten down by the system and made to bend and fracture. Each step drove me on to learn and achieve more and, in that sense, the OU is an institution like no other, an ever-evolving supportive mechanism. It does not stop and has exposed a thirst for knowledge that I never knew I had. It has developed a range of valuable aspects of my identity that had remained hidden or unknown for many years. The sense of achievement I now feel is immeasurable and what I learned invaluable.

The journey was not easy but support was never not to hand. With the commitment of a range of OU staff who knocked down barriers alongside me and looked past the man I was, I was able to become the man I now am.

The final stage, the one I currently occupy, is what I term the post-OU stage. Now, as I venture into the postgraduate world of study away from the OU, I want to express how the OU still shapes my identity as a researcher and academic, providing the foundations of my knowledge as part of a new community as I attempt to establish myself in the field of criminology and back in society.

The anti and ante OU stage

I don't think I was a bad guy personally. In fact, I think that I was a good guy who made very bad choices. If I ever expressed that personal evaluation of myself to a probation officer or a prison officer I would be slapped down straight away for 'minimising' my offences and not accepting my offending behaviour. I understand their professional perspective, yet it doesn't make it right. For years I have accepted that perception of myself at various parts of my sentence, but I have never been able to shake the internal belief that I am a good guy who lost his way a bit. However, that being said, I am all too aware of the wholly inappropriate errors and mistakes that I made.

I was always told that I had the skills and abilities to achieve anything that I wanted and rather than accept that and embrace it, this knowledge served as a catalyst for me not applying myself. In fact, the more I knew I could do something, the less I would do it. I had a blasé attitude reliant on the fact that I could 'turn it on' whenever I felt the need to do so; call it arrogance, call it ego, either way, I had it in abundance. I thought I knew best and I knew that I could just amble through life being a 'Jack the Lad'.

I remember my Dad on countless occasions sitting me down and saying to me in his sternest yet most fatherly voice: 'Edwin, you're in danger of throwing your life away and you'll regret it forever when you look back.' His voice and the words would drone on, again and again, time after time, yet my dear old Dad has proved to be prophetic!

At this point, in my life in my teens, I was anti-education but more anti-people-telling-me-what-to-do. Both in the community before, and in prison, I remember adopting other people's negative perceptions and viewpoints of The Open University. People said things about it not being a 'proper university' or a 'university for those not good enough to get into a proper university'. At a time when I lacked confidence I found myself agreeing and actively projecting these positions, in part due to my own anti-education perspectives at this point. My earliest memories of the OU stem from a television advert I regularly saw as a child, that I would stare at waiting for the cartoons to start. I remember how growing up I heard many people stating these negative opinions about the OU. I must admit that very naively I fell in line with these poorly informed perspectives through my own ignorance. However, what I came to discover through personal experience is that the OU is an institution that provides the knowledge and opportunity to overcome ignorance.

Sociological research has consistently identified penal establishments and the mechanisms of imprisonment as an application of power that is 'brutal, mortifying and damaging' (Sykes, 1958; Goffman, 1961; Cohen and Taylor, 1972). Sykes advanced the idea that the subsequent 'pains of imprisonment' emanating from these mechanisms challenge and attack an individual's personality and self-esteem: 'In the custodial institution of today ... the deprivations and frustrations pose profound threats to the inmates personality or sense of personal worth' (Sykes, 1958, p 64). Cohen and Taylor (1972, cited in Liebling, 1999, p 323) describe prisoners as living in a 'constant state of anxiety'. I can certainly vouch for all of the above to varying degrees from my own experience of imprisonment! According to Matthews (2014, p 43), 'every facet of law and order is infused with power ... from the interpersonal to the structural, power operates at every level'.

Prison is an institution which typifies and illustrates the complex entanglement of power relations embedded within its walls. 'Weight' is the metaphor that people who are imprisoned tend to use to describe the psychological effect of imprisonment – the degree to which it weighed down on them (Crewe et al, 2014). The concept of weight is associated with its suppressive nature rather than considerations of how differing power formations may bring about a range of positive outcomes such as support and 'buy-in' to the regime. Foucault (2002) argued that the exercise of power has to become more refined, distinguishing between the custodial apparatus's effects on individuals in a more continuous connection.

Custodial regimes with the appropriate 'weight' and high levels of legitimacy can promote personal wellbeing, cooperation and long-term compliance. Legitimacy 'is the perception that one "ought to obey" another' (Hurd, 1999, cited in Tyler, 2006, p 337). The most concrete influence of legitimacy occurs when 'people make decisions or create rules designed to shape the behaviour of others. The question of whether others will accept those decisions and rules is always a key one in social settings, particularly when decision-makers are not backed up with either credible coercive potential or the promise of rewards' (Tyler, 2006, p 379).

A core finding of research literature is that authorities and institutions are viewed as more legitimate and, therefore, their decisions and rules are more willingly accepted, when they exercise their authority through procedures that people experience as being fair (Tyler 2001, 2006). When people who are imprisoned are of the belief that their treatment in prison was reasonable and fair, then they will respond more favourably to those in authority applying power over them, and will also produce more favourable offender-based outcomes (Crewe et al, 2014). Prison research in England and Wales has provided evidence that the most stable forms of prison order in custodial settings are derived from applications of power that produce conditions deemed as legitimate. This is based in the degree to which power is exercised in a manner promoting the respect, dignity and rights of people who are imprisoned.

Although power is often associated with coercion and other negative applications and manifestations in the context of prisons, Foucault argues that power is not simply 'repressive but productive and positive' (Matthews, 2014, p 44). This view is supported by Lukes (2005, cited in Matthews, 2014), who is critical of commentary and rhetoric equating power only with connotations of domination, repression and constraint, and actively seeks to reject these notions. Good power, such as power used with care (legitimate) as opposed to power used with indifference (illegitimate), can achieve such positive outcomes. This builds upon Foucault's argument that power can be productive and positive as well as repressive. He is critical of theories that fail to recognise this variable dynamic of power (Foucault, 1977, 2002). Power, in one form or another, is an underlying theme and everyday current which penetrates the day-to-day lives of both prisoner and prison. Foucauldian theory is interested in the different ways that power manifests itself and its impact upon attitudes and actions, the consciousness and the body of the prisoner. It conceptualises power as embodied within the creation and operation of the modern prison and those within it (Matthews, 2014).

Positive outcomes of power can manifest in many ways. The evolution of contemporary penal practices is symbolic of a reconfiguration of penal power steeped in the assumption that 'power in prison is inherently bad' (Crewe et al, 2014, p 392). These practices have often been viewed from a perspective riddled with scepticism and the perception that they are sinister in nature and 'involving ... repression, domination and subjection' (McMahon, 1992, p 218). This outlook has often served to preclude the fact that coercion is merely one aspect of power relations in prison and is not 'the essence of the phenomenon itself' (Wrong, 1996, p 261). Good power, utilised with the intent to produce positive quality of life through initiatives such as distance learning in custodial settings, and staff using their power productively to promote and encourage it can achieve positive outcomes both supporting resettlement and daily psychological functionality. I found this aspect of power resonates with my development.

Hughes (2016), however, recognises applications of bad power emanating from prison – 'Negative attitudes expressed by those in authority within the prison can be particularly damaging, and may have significant consequences for the prisoner-students' – and I have myself also witnessed this. Hughes (2016) builds upon the potential of positive power applications in relation to education provision in prisons suggesting that, for a purposeful culture to take hold, there needs to be commitment that goes beyond prisoners making decisions about whether or not to engage in education and other related endeavours. Hughes (2016) argues that the extent to which managers of prison establishments, both at local and national level, can officially encourage and recognise prisoners' efforts to make valuable use of their time is crucial. This is usually dependent, she says, on the extent to which prison officers and other prison staff are seen to have a stake in the prisoners' activities in the prison itself. If prisoners' constructive activities are encouraged and seen to contribute to the prison environment in meaningful and helpful ways, they will significantly shape individuals' decisions about engaging and maintaining involvement in such activities.

An absence of opportunities precludes the implementation and development of purposeful activity. It is imperative that prisons have 'permeable cultures', that are receptive to opportunities beyond the prison walls. These must be responsive to the needs of prisoners, and this is especially important with distance learning. This is a vital provision to engage with prisoners. It can equip prisoners with an offering and subsequent skill and knowledge base to engage and build bridges with the outside world, both while they are in prison and later, on release (see Hughes, 2016).

It was an officer in the early days of my imprisonment who took the time both to recognise my talent and potential and then give his time above and beyond his job remit to continue to encourage me to push myself and acquire new skills, and not to waste my talent and intelligence by adopting an offender identity that accepts what the system gives him. He urged me to rise above that mentality and beat it by coming out of prison better than when I entered it. I think every prisoner harbours hopes of 'beating the system' and by gaining an education, I would not let the weight, depth, tightness of imprisonment, and how power was applied to me, to bring me down. 'Each man brings to the custodial institution his own needs and his own background and each man takes away from the prison his own interpretation of life within the walls' (Sykes, 1958, p 63). I believe that the development of my 'self' and identity has ensured that I take away from prison an identity that I am proud to have crafted through engagement with higher education.

Some people at their lowest ebb in prison find religion to help set them back on the right path and guide them. For me, it was the OU that became my light and my guide, having a crucial impact on shaping and developing my identity as a man, an academic and a prisoner. It gave me opportunities and support when I was at my lowest and weakest, helping me to summon the strength and fortitude to keep challenging, bettering myself and educating myself so that I might achieve a better future.

The evolution of (this) man

I feel my experience demonstrates that the self is not a passive, rigid concept and is in a constant flux of shaping through interaction and interpretations of our social environment. This includes the influence of other people and institutions, with the OU representing one such institutional example. It is said that, as individuals, we 'act to promote the self, developing a narrative of who we are, who we have been and who we plan to become' (Nicolson, 2018, p 31). The mechanism of reflexivity helps us to work out our position in a range of wider and both short- and long-term contexts. As an active and responsive social agent, I am continuing to make sense of my social world and myself, longitudinally, throughout my life course. This involves processing and reflecting upon information about my life and its contexts so that I 'manage the story that I tell myself of who I am and project it to those around me' (Nicolson, 2018, p 31). As such, the more knowledge and understanding I have gained from my experiences and interactions over my lifespan, the more they have contributed, and continue to contribute, to my sense of self-identity.

I came to prison having largely held what I would describe as a positive, socially oriented identities. I had both successful employment and educational records before entering custody, although I had diminished both by living on cruise-control and making poor decisions and life choices. There is a school of thought (Crawley and Sparks, 2005; Jewkes 2005) that argues there is a systematic spoiling of the positive former identities of people sent to prison, including their work identities. It is a consequence of long-sentenced prisoners' sustained exposure to the mechanisms of the penal establishment. As such, prisoners face the prospect of losing the very of identities and roles that 'locate them[...] within the social world' (Jewkes, 2005, p 369) and they can be left with simply the identity of prisoner (Hughes, 2009). Education in prison can serve, however, to reclaim the positive identities that were held before prison, or even develop new ones. My education experience with the OU has led to me acquiring a whole new skill set and knowledge base. These acquired resources may help me to reduce the tarnish of a blemished and 'spoiled' identity conferred by my criminal conviction (Hughes, 2009).

In my personal experience, and from observations of other OU students, involvement in education and related activities both improves and consolidates prisoners' self-confidence. This is particularly the case in relation to mental abilities that inevitably and closely form their sense of place and role within the prison, or the society beyond its walls. However, the impact upon the general sense of self goes beyond the confines of educational parameters – they spread out and impact positively with the wider social world.

I'm not the person that I used to be, in the sense that I have developed areas of my identity and crafted this new 'scholar' identity while developing other areas of my life that also needed to be nurtured and grown. I am comfortable and happy with the person that I am now – the direction that my life has taken and the path that I am now following. It is path discovered and underpinned through my interaction with the OU. I have undergone and feel a huge sense of personal change arising from my educational engagement and attainment.

A community of isolation

I was fortunate to feel part of a community. I had a range of supportive lecturers and operational support staff from the OU who were on hand to make the learning experience as smooth and beneficial to me as possible. The associate lecturers were always available and never tired of fielding the various emails from the prison on my behalf, sometimes questioning work, asking for more material, requesting support and guidance, or just ranting in frustration when I was struggling to grasp things. They did so with tremendous enthusiasm and understanding. There were more than a few times when I despaired and felt that I 'couldn't do it' and each time I was met with patience, support and guidance – invaluable!

However, although I was part of a community, I also feel that there is a certain degree of isolation when you learn with the OU. Yes, the staff and support structures are on hand, but when you get your pack of resources at the start of the module, you realise that in some respects you are very much on your own. There are no lectures. There are no other students you can contact and no internet in prison to look things up if you are unsure of something. However, for me this isolation was hugely beneficial, especially in relation to my clarity of thought and decisiveness in my academic work. This isolation and the support structure of the OU also had a range of other tangible benefits for me.

It is argued that when we study on our own, we can focus on our own weaknesses and hone only the skills that are lacking. Ericsson (cited in Goodrich, 2017) who did extensive research on expert performance, suggested that 'the best way to master any subject is to work on the task that's most demanding for you personally and that this is best done alone'. I found studying in private away from a group maximised my focus. In fact, two separate studies offer evidence that studying on your own is better as it improves your ability to retain information and reproduce it. As someone who likes his own company and space, and who can become distracted more easily in a group, the isolating aspect was a godsend as it increased my potential focus, while others may feel like they get more done in a group. Working solo allowed me to maintain awareness of when I was getting off topic or when my mind drifted. Furnham et al (2013) found that, despite the benefits of group study, it hampers creativity and efficiency. The aspect of isolation also allowed me to pace myself and manage my time, ensuring that I was fully engaged, and this also positively impacted my clarity of thought. Group work promotes laziness in my experience, and people in groups tend to sit back and let others do the work – and as someone who used to operate in my youth on cruise-control this is not productive or conducive with maximising my potential.

Postgraduate – post-OU

Since graduating from the OU with a first class Honours degree in Criminology and Psychology, I have studied for an MA in Criminology at the University of Kent and will be commencing my PhD and teaching there. What I learned through the OU has underpinned the postgraduate experience that I currently engage with on a day-to-day basis. It's not just the theoretical subject knowledge but the skills and qualities that I gained and developed which are directly transferable and beneficial. The ability to manage my time effectively, to work independently and to think clearly have held me in good stead to maximise my potential at postgraduate level. I may no longer be actively studying with the OU but it influences my progress and functionality in both my current institution and beyond into my life. The OU gave me an education, a career and a new life and for that I will be eternally grateful. I have spoken about power at length in this chapter and the power of the OU is immense and can underpin and facilitate the positive outcomes discussed – I am living proof of this.

> The depth of darkness to which you can descend and still
> live is an exact measure of the height to which you can
> aspire to reach. (Pliny the Elder, 77 CE)

No matter how much I have worked to change my life and turn it around, and despite all my academic achievements and the positive things that I have to look forward to, my life is always tinged by a sense of regret. It is almost a mourning for the years that I threw away and lost, not just to prison but in my youth more generally. I still feel like the same 18-year-old Jack the Lad I was, and some days I wish I could get that time back, and some days I wonder just how irreparable the damage of imprisonment has been for me. I wonder if I am always going to be stained and tarnished by it and if my prison past will always define my future.

Certain aspects of my identity have now become more relevant and continue to develop. Although more confident in some areas, I am also more aware of the fragilities and weaknesses in my identity these days, and more acutely aware of their impact upon me. For example, I'm still the same painfully shy guy who struggles to tell a girl that he is attracted to her because the fear of rejection is a worse proposition than the stress and anxiety of keeping my feelings bottled up. I guess that some things will just never change, no matter how educated university has got me, although I have made some progress in this area!

My biggest regret is that my Dad is no longer here to see the man that I have become because no matter how many people tell me that he would have been 'so proud', it will never substitute for hearing those words spoken by him. That's something I will never hear, just like my life is something I will never be able to live again. But one thing is for sure, life is too short and precious to waste, and I have already wasted and thrown away too many years. I just want to feel alive again and be the person that I have become – it's time to live the identity and future that I have crafted – an identity and future that The Open University has contributed to immensely. Imprisonment is often described as being experienced as 'an ordeal, an assault on the self to be survived' (Downes, 1988, p 179) but not only have I survived it, I have become a better person for the experience of it.

References

Cohen, S. and Taylor, L. (1972) *Psychological survival: The experience of long-term imprisonment*, Harmondsworth: Penguin.

Crawley, E. and Sparks, R. (2005) 'Older men in prison: survival, coping and identity', in A. Liebling and S. Maruna (eds) *The effects of imprisonment*, Cullompton: Willan Publishing, pp 343–65.

Crewe, B., Liebling, A. and Hulley, S. (2014) 'Heavy–light, absent–present: re-thinking the weight of imprisonment', *British Journal of Sociology*, 65(3): 387–410.

Downes, D. (1988) *Contrasts in tolerance: Post-war penal policy in the Netherlands and England and Wales*, Oxford: Oxford University Press.

Foucault, M. (1977) *Discipline and punish: The birth of the prison*, London: Allen Lane.

Foucault, M. (2002) 'The subject of power', in J. Faubion (ed.) *Power: Essential works of Foucault 1954–1984*, Harmondsworth: Penguin.

Furnham, A., Hughes, D. and Marshall, E. (2013) 'Creativity, OCD, narcissism and the big five', *Thinking Skills and Creativity*, 10: 91–8.

Goffman, E. (1961) *Asylums: Essays on the social situation of mental patients and other inmates*, New York: Doubleday Anchor.

Goodrich, K. (2017) 'Social learning: studying alone vs study groups', Brainscape. www.brainscape.com/blog/2016/04/social-learning-studying-alone-vs-in-a-group/.

Hirsch, E. (2014) *Gabriel: A poem*, New York: Alfred A. Knopf.

Hughes, E. (2009) 'Thinking inside the box: prisoner education, learning identities, and the possibilities for change', in B. Veysey, J. Christian and D. Martinez (eds) *How offenders transform their lives*, Cullompton: Willan Publishing.

Hughes, E. (2016) *Education in prison: Studying through distance learning*, London: Routledge.

Jewkes, Y. (2005) 'Loss, liminality and the life sentence: managing identity through a disrupted lifecourse', in A. Liebling and S. Maruna (eds) *The effects of imprisonment*, Cullompton: Willan Publishing, pp 366–88.

Liebling, A. (1999) 'Prisoner suicide and prisoner coping', *Crime and Justice*, 26: 283–359.

Matthews, R. (2014) *Realist criminology*, Basingstoke: Palgrave Macmillan.

McMahon, M. (1992) *The persistent prison? Rethinking decarceration and penal reform*, Toronto: University of Toronto Press.

Nicolson, P. (2018) 'Family trees, selfies and our search for identity', *The Psychologist*, 31: 28–32.

Sykes, G. (1958) *The society of captives: A study of a maximum-security prison*, Princeton, NJ: Princeton University Press.

Tyler, T. (2001) 'A psychological perspective on the legitimacy of authorities and institutions', in J.T. Jost and B. Major (eds) *The psychology of legitimacy: Emerging perspectives on ideology, justice and intergroup relations*, New York: Cambridge University Press, pp 416–36.

Tyler, T. (2006) 'Psychological perspectives on legitimacy and legitimation', *Annual Review of Psychology*, 57: 375–400.

Wrong, D. (1996) *Power: Its forms, bases and uses*, Oxford: Routledge.

VIGNETTE 7

Catching up with Kafka

Steven Taylor

Prison is like a microcosm of technocratic totalitarianism where every action collapses under the weight of its own bureaucracy. This often requires a member of senior management to override the rules in order to get things done! If you don't have a powerful backer, it's not happening. Most actions, from asking for toilet paper to doing a prison magazine, become a Kafkaesque nightmare rivalling Franz Kafka's novels such as *The trial*, *The castle* and *Metamorphosis*. Things can become incredibly distorted, out of all proportion and it seems like you've just fought the Cold War until you give yourself a reality check and realise that all you've achieved is the ability to wipe your behind. As for doing a degree in prison, if what would be considered a simple task in mainstream society, I'm sure readers can appreciate the sense of achievement every Open University (OU) module provides prisoners with.

I really can't emphasise enough how little things in prison become magnified tenfold. Prisoners and staff alike dig their heels in and become entrenched. Simple things become more difficult in prison, such as computers. In some prisons I've been in, I have only been able to access a computer once a week. I study in my cell because it's one of the only places where I have a degree of control over my study space, although at times it can be like a night club just a matter of feet away from where I'm studying. There are four pool tables, a table tennis table and two public telephones right outside my cell door. Between the hours of 5 pm and 8.30 pm the night club is in full swing.

During the day is the best time to study, but the prison usually requires you to go through what has been deemed rehabilitation. It becomes like a surreal script for a badly written B movie, with everyone going through it in order to get out of their own personal nightmare. Even the worst actors in the world are able to pull the wool over the eyes of the forensic psychologists. It can be surreal, as an observer, to witness this, but then you realise they have built their careers on this and have so much invested in it that they don't want to face the reality that what they're doing is a waste of time. If you've ever seen the cognitive dissonance experiments of the social psychologist Leon Festinger, then you'll understand what I'm talking about. But in order to get out of prison you need to go through the script, submit to the prison psychologists' authority and hey presto! – you're a born-again citizen.

Anyway, not to get too side-tracked, I handwrite all my assignments, then given the limited time I sometimes have on computers, I use them as a typewriter, so I have to do everything twice, once handwritten, then when I access a computer, type it out, read over it, then make any changes that need to be made. Like I've said about bureaucracy in prison, you can have access to a computer five days a week, Monday to Friday, then a couple of days before my deadline for my assignments my name is not on the list at the door. Getting to education can be like going through an airport and finding that just as you are about to board your flight, it's cancelled and you have to go back to your cell which can waste half a morning's study time. You just have to hope that your flight is not cancelled the following day. You may not even get to speak to anyone in education until past your deadline. You sometimes need to be a political ninja to get things done in prison, which can give you a big boost in confidence when you achieve things.

I always wanted to do a degree but never had the time and when I saw others doing a degree in prison, I felt it would help turn my life around. Most things in prison are a failure. Some theorists draw the conclusion from prison that nothing works, but I would argue that nothing has been tried. Most people who come to work in a prison mistake authoritarianism for rehabilitation, which is why nothing works. Authoritarianism is abuse and makes people worse, and rehabilitation is a therapy that makes people better. These two ideas are incompatible and if used in conjunction with each other, only create conflict. Doing a degree, or any education for that matter, seemed to me to be one of the few therapies in prison that make a difference.

I had a strong interest in social sciences before and with my upbringing and life in prison, I felt I had a lot to offer in the field of criminology. I never trusted anyone growing up, including teachers, and have always taught myself whatever I felt I needed to help me out in life. As I've always taught myself, I felt an OU degree would be perfect for me. Many prisoners look up to you and seek help and guidance, as a large proportion have had a poor education, have learning difficulties or mental health problems. But it's hugely rewarding to be able to help others.

There are many other challenges with studying with the OU in prison, such as accessing course materials, accessing research materials and having contact with the OU themselves, as well as other academics. All these things can be challenging in prison but the rewards for me outweigh the added stress in an already stressful environment.

12

From D102 to Paulo Freire: an Irish journey

Laurence McKeown

Prologue

I've often wondered if many who studied with The Open University (OU) found it a lonely experience – in comparison to those who attended a 'conventional' university – working alone at home with only a limited number of engagements with their tutor and/or tutor-counsellor, combined with short group meetings where they had an opportunity to exchange thoughts and opinions on their studies. My experience of studying with the OU was not a lonely one at all; for reasons mostly not associated with the OU but due to my personal circumstances and conditions at the time. I was a political prisoner (Irish Republican Army) in the H-Blocks of the Maze/Long Kesh prison in the North of Ireland. It was because I *was* a prisoner that I had the opportunity to study with the OU but the motivation to engage in the studies, and the choice of courses I took, must be seen in the broader context of what had gone on in the prison in the previous years, and what happened there subsequently. My academic study with the OU (an experience which was shared with other comrades) was closely integrated with my developing political consciousness and activism, just as the materials from a range of OU courses became part of a wider programme of political education of Irish republican prisoners. The two processes were intimately combined.

Introduction

I began my studies with the OU in 1984. The previous year had been an eventful one in the prison as a mass escape of 38 IRA prisoners[1] had taken place on 25 September and we were still dealing with the fallout from that in terms of the prison authorities introducing tightened security and restricted movement, which had implications for education provision.

But then again, the prison had witnessed many eventful years from when the H-Blocks first opened in September 1976. The 'Blocks' as they became commonly known, were built to facilitate a new British government policy of 'criminalisation'. From 1 March 1976, anyone sentenced for IRA (or loyalist) activities would no longer be regarded as a political prisoner (as had been the case up until then)[2] and would instead be treated as an ordinary criminal prisoner. In essence, this meant that they would be forced to wear prison uniform and do prison work.

Republican prisoners refused to go along with the new policy, rejecting the label of 'criminals', and when the first one sentenced under the new regime, Kieran Nugent, was taken to the H-Blocks he refused to wear the prison uniform. He was stripped of his own clothes, assaulted, then put into a prison cell naked. With no clothes, he wrapped himself in a blanket and thus began what became known as the 'blanket protest'. It lasted for the next five years and ended with the death of ten prisoners on hunger strike in 1981 (Campbell et al, 1994).

I was arrested in August 1976 and sentenced to life imprisonment in April 1977 for being a member of the IRA, for carrying out a gun attack on an RUC[3] patrol, and for causing explosions. I immediately joined the blanket protest.

Conditions on the protest were harsh. We were confined to our cells 24/7 with the exception of attending mass on a Sunday for an hour, or for a monthly half-hour visit. We had no access to exercise, no TV, no radio, and no books or reading material other than the prison-compulsory Bible. It is easier to state what we did have; three blankets, a piece of sponge for a mattress, a piss-pot, and a water container. In March 1978 the protest intensified into a 'no-wash' protest. Denied access to proper toilet and washing facilities we smeared excrement on the cell walls. I didn't wash again until 2 March 1981, the day after Bobby Sands began his hunger strike (see Campbell et al, 1994; Bobby Sands Trust, nd). Conditions were indeed harsh.

However, I regard those five years of protest on the blanket as the most educational in my life. In later years I went on to complete a degree with the OU while still in prison, and upon release completed a doctorate at Queen's University, Belfast, but that period 1976 to 1981 was a time when I began to 'unlearn' a lot of opinions, thoughts and views which I had unconsciously, or sub-consciously, held up until then. Opinions and viewpoints which were often contradictory, racist, sexist, or just ignorant or lacking in coherence or substance. Opinions which I had 'soaked up' like a sponge from the state church, or others I had come into contact with in my life up until then. That 'unlearning' process arose through discussion, debate and the personal self-reflection which followed. With no other form of intellectual stimulation available (from TV, radio, or reading material) we had only one another to engage with and discussion and debate thrived. It was through that process that I began to question the 'knowledge' I had in my head and the opinions that seemed so certain, and so 'natural' to hold up until then. I began to question everything. The 'unlearning' had begun.

Post-1981

The blanket protest finally ended on 3 October 1981 following the death of ten prisoners on hunger strike. I had participated in the strike (for 70 days) but survived. It ended with us achieving just one of our demands, the right to wear our own clothes, but achieving that one demand was critical to later developments as it allowed us, for the first time in five years, to get out of our prison cells, to meet together and to strategise about how we would move forward to achieve our outstanding demands. We still refused to do prison work for a period of time, and therefore were denied access to prison educational facilities, including enrolment with the OU. However, we had a thirst for knowledge. Having been denied written material for so many years, and having developed a 'questioning' approach to knowledge and to the world, we were eager to now obtain the widest possible range of reading material. Prison rules, at the time, stated that we could only obtain books of fiction (from our families in the monthly parcel; two books per month) and that non-fiction materials (which we really wanted) could only be accessed as part of a prison-provided educational course – thus a catch 22 situation for us as we were 'on protest' and thus denied access to education courses.

Given the ingenuity that had been displayed during the years of protest this ruling was, however, fairly easily circumvented; our families got the books we really wanted, took the covers off them, substituted them with the covers from trashy novels, and sent them in to us, past the unsuspecting eyes of the prison censor. One of the books we received in such a manner was *Pedagogy of the oppressed* by Paulo Freire and it was to have a major influence on us, not only in terms of how we viewed education and subsequently structured our own political education programme, but on how we developed our structures of command to become less hierarchical and more inclusive and collective.

In October 1982, one year after the ending of the hunger strike, we ended our protest regarding prison work and thus became, in the eyes of the prison administration, 'fully conforming prisoners' and therefore eligible to access all prison education provision, including the OU. However, only a limited number of prisoners were granted permission (by the prison authorities) to study with the OU in any one year so there was always a competition for spaces. I was fortunate enough to be awarded a place in 1984.

First year of study with the OU – D102

I took to my studies with eagerness and the course, D102, Foundation Course in the Social Sciences, could not have come at a better time for me, nor been more appropriate. It offered different perspectives – Marxist, social democratic and liberal – on such topics as the state, gender, class and race. It was like all I had ever wished for. It gave a structure and coherence to my scattered political thoughts and understanding of the world at that time. More inclined to a broadly (if not refined or developed) left-wing politics, I revelled in the Marxist analysis of society that was offered but then would read an alternative viewpoint and see how it also had consistency and a strong argument. My head was buzzing. And the questioning approach to things, the 'Why is it?', gained during the blanket protest was very much to the fore. Looking back on it, there was probably an arrogance too. Coming across a reference in the course text to 'the famine in Ireland' I wrote a letter to the OU news-sheet complaining about their use of the word 'famine'. I argued that there was no famine at the time as food in the form of cereals and livestock was being daily shipped out of Ireland to England, and that the death of millions from starvation was due to colonialism. Laurence Harris, author of the text that I challenged, very graciously wrote me a personal reply and my letter was printed in the OU news-sheet.

My tutor for D102 was Jenny Meegan, who also became my tutor-counsellor throughout my years of study with the OU, and I was very blessed to have her. Jenny not only had a detailed knowledge of the subject matter but was the best – and remains to this day – the best educationalist I have ever met. She 'encouraged' rather than lectured. I still recall, with some embarrassment, when she was reviewing one of my essays (or TMAs – tutor-marked assignments), how she gently pointed out that I should look again at my use of the terms, 'it's natural', or 'it's common sense', to support my arguments as they may not seem common-sensical or natural to others!

The fact that Jenny was aware of the writings of Paulo Freire, and how we were adapting his principles of pedagogy to our own political education programme, created a symmetry between what we were doing in the prison wings and what we were studying with the OU. However, it also led to some challenges. Adhering to Freire's critique of the 'banking approach' to education where the student learns (banks) the knowledge to then regurgitate it come exam time, meant that we had an instinctive opposition to sitting exams and adopted the very political/ high moral position of opposition to engaging in them. Our view was that as republicans we were all equal and were not going to become academically competitive. When Jenny pointed out that completing the end-of-year examinations was compulsory – from the prison authorities point of view, if not from the OU's – to getting access to the next year's course we had to swallow our pride and accept the status quo.

Studying with the OU in prison

In general, republican prisoners studied social sciences, politics or economics. These subjects offered the type of knowledge we sought and fitted neatly with the political education programme we were developing down the prison wings. However, some also studied arts, mathematics and technology. There was also the obligation, according to the OU's own guidelines, to study a subject other than your first preference and while initially I regarded this as an impingement upon my freedom to decide what I wanted to study, I later came to enjoy the diversity.

It was always exciting to get the first batch of course materials and look through the various booklets; always very well presented, both in terms of how they read and how they looked visually. Although I subsequently went on to study for a PhD at Queen's University, Belfast – for which I had to conduct a lot of research and read many books – I have never come across academic texts so well-prepared as those of the OU. Not only was the content very clear and concise but it was easy to follow. It was obvious that the editors of the course materials went to a lot of effort to put themselves 'in the shoes of the student' and how they would engage with the materials. It reminds me of the quote from Mark Twain, 'I didn't have time to write a short letter, so I wrote a long one instead.' It was obvious that the writers and editors of the course materials had gone to great lengths to ensure that the texts had a great clarity.

I'm sure that OU students anywhere have their own frustrations and challenges in pursuing their studies. In prison it was largely to do with delays in TMAs getting out through the prison censor and then getting feedback from the tutors past the Censor again. I don't actually know how much attention the prison authorities gave to the TMAs we wrote but we (being republicans) held to the conspiratorial viewpoint that everything we wrote would be photocopied and processed through Special Branch, or some other such security/intelligence body, and added to our files. In fact, in earlier years within the prison, it was this fear of the authorities gathering such information and thus building a detailed profile of the prisoner, that led the IRA camp staff to decide not to permit republican prisoners to use the prison-provided education facilities. By the early 1980s, however, this position had long since been abandoned and our view was that the prison authorities already knew all too well, from our actions, what our politics were about.

I always looked forward to the tutorials and tutor-counsellor sessions. They not only provided an opportunity to discuss the course materials but also to do this with someone from the outside world and someone who probably had a different political outlook than I had. We would meet for tutorials in the education room, which was positioned between the prison wings and the central control area of the H-Blocks. At times there could be several OU tutors and/or other teachers in the room, or the prison 'tuck shop' would arrive and set up in the room and prisoners would file out to it, which often led to bedlam.

Searches by the prison authorities also impacted tutorials. I recall one day waiting on Jenny to arrive for a tutor-counsellor meeting, seeing her walk up the front yard into the Block, followed a few moments later by a search team arriving into the Block. Moments later I spotted Jenny exiting the Block again. I got up to my window and called out to her and to her credit she came over to my window in the front yard to speak to me while the search team were filing past her. She told me that she had been informed by the Principal Officer in charge of the Block that a search was about to be conducted in the wing that I was housed in and that she would arrange an alternative date to meet. I asked her to go back into the Block and request that the search team search those cells first, including mine, which held prisoners who were due to attend classes or tutorials. She did as I asked, the Principal Officer facilitated the request, and I was able to meet with Jenny after my cell was searched. It was indicative of a change of attitude over the years as the prison authorities became more 'comfortable' with prisoners having access to the OU and other education courses. It was also reflective of a period of time when the prison began to 'settle down' after many years of strife.

Personal interaction with tutors and teachers

As republican prisoners we had a policy of being mindful of our behaviour when meeting with teachers, whether they were OU tutors or others. We were conscious that they had travelled some distance to get to the prison, that they then had to go through a lengthy process to gain admittance including a search procedure, then had to report to the Education Office, before finally being escorted to a particular Block by a prison guard. In light of this, we had a policy of asking a tutor/teacher, once we went out to the classroom, if they would like a cup of tea or coffee, a piece of toast, or a biscuit. We just saw it as good manners on our part in consideration of what they had just gone through to get to us. However, this basic social practice was regarded with some suspicion by the prison authorities. One tutor who I had for a course initially went to great lengths to refuse any offer of tea or coffee and it was only several visits later, once they had observed how other teachers in the classroom readily, and casually, accepted offers of tea/coffee and a round of toast that they told me how they had been 'advised' by the prison authorities when they first began to work in the prison. Apparently, they had been instructed not to accept anything from us because what might appear on the surface to be an ordinary, everyday thoughtful gesture, was really a way to slowly ingratiate ourselves with them and to eventually attempt to induce them into smuggling items into the prison for us!

Third World studies and Frelimo

One of the courses on offer from the OU in the early 1980s was Third World Studies and a comrade, Seán Murray, was studying it. Seán was also in charge of the IRA prisoners' education programme and I worked closely with him on it, eventually taking over from him when he was released from prison. At the time, one of the biggest challenges to us was how we could construct a uniform approach to study across the prison in the various H–Blocks. Such a programme of study would require written materials to be available in each H–Block and each of the four separate wings of the Blocks. There would be too much material to be able to hide it from the prison authorities and the regular searches they conducted but if it was to be sat openly in our cells it would be confiscated during those searches. Anything that included reference to the IRA, or Irish Republicanism, no matter how 'innocent', would attract the attention of the prison guards. It was then that we drew upon the materials from the OU Third World

Studies course. One of the conflicts looked at in that course was Mozambique and the guerrilla war waged by Frelimo (Frente de Libertação de Moçambique or Mozambique Liberation Front) so we wrote our educational programme as if it was about Frelimo, the war in Mozambique, and the role of Frelimo prisoners, substituting the term Frelimo for IRA, Mozambique for Ireland, and Frelimo prisoners for Irish republican prisoners. The documents were written up in prison-supplied notebooks, distributed throughout the republican wings in the prison, and sat openly in prison cells for years without the prison guards ever showing any interest in them (McKeown, 2001).

U221, The Changing Experience of Women

Within the Irish republican prisoner community, post-1981, there was a keen interest in feminism, certainly within a small group. We read feminist theories; we had female comrades imprisoned and ongoing dialogue with them via smuggled communications meant that a range of topics were often discussed and issues raised. We also had female friends and comrades on the outside who were to the fore in advocating a more feminist approach within the Republican Movement. The period of the blanket protest and hunger strikes had brought many of those women to the fore and they were now developing a more prominent role in terms of community development and political organisation and activism. I was therefore interested in studying the OU course, U221, The Changing Experience of Women. Two other comrades had already studied it and praised both it and the tutor, Joanna McMinn, very highly. The course, as its title suggests, looked at the role of women down through the ages in the context of domestic and public life. However, when I told an elderly aunt who came to visit me one day in prison what I was studying she was shocked; she thought the title referred to the menopause.

The U221 texts were excellent but of most importance was having Joanna as the tutor and being able to talk through the issues and how they manifested on the ground in a contemporary setting. We, in prison, could read feminist theories, but applying them to our material conditions and social relationships on the outside was more difficult, or we were more blind to some of the issues. Through discussions with Joanna I asked her if she would be willing to conduct informal classes with us as part of the prison Education Department's range of evening classes. She said she would if I, or one of the others who had already studied U221, Jackie McMullan, would co-facilitate such classes. We put the proposal to the prison Education Department for a 'Women's

Studies' class and it was accepted. The class ran for over two years and approximately 200 republican prisoners took part in it.

Final year of degree studies

I finished my degree studies with the OU in 1992. It was a special year for me. It was the year I was released from prison. Being a life sentence prisoner meant that release did not happen overnight; it was a process whereby I moved to a new prison – Maghaberry prison – a short distance away, where I was allowed out during the day to work, returning to prison in the evening, and allowed home at weekends. This process went on for three months before I was finally released.

Being a life sentence prisoner also means you never know exactly when you will be released, until you are actually informed by the prison authorities and the Northern Ireland Office. However, given a very successful campaign that republicans had waged regarding the release of life sentence prisoners, I was fairly certain that in 1992 I would be released. I was eager, therefore, to complete my degree studies before then, as I knew that once on the outside there would be many other things I'd want to do rather than pursue academic study.

In that year I took two courses; U205, Health and Disease, and DT200, Information Technology; Social and Technological Issues. Studying the two courses would mean that I had completed the required amount of eight full credits[4] for my degree. As soon as I received the course materials I began to study and to complete the TMAs well ahead of time as I knew it would be much easier to study while still in the H-Blocks. In June I moved to Maghaberry prison and, although I resented having to return to the prison each evening, after spending a day of freedom in Belfast, I also knew it was the only way I'd ever get my studies completed. I successfully completed them, and was also released.

And I thought that was that with academic studies and with the OU. I thought I'd be too busy engaging in so many activities that, up until then, I had only dreamed of and that I'd have no desire to study. However, I was out of prison only a relatively short period of time when I began to miss the regular application to study, learning new topics, and structuring my thoughts and responses in the writing of TMAs. It was around that time I was speaking with a friend and OU tutor, Mike Tomlinson, and I told him about how I'd like to write a book tracing the changes and developments that had come about within the republican prisoner community over the years; changes in our political outlooks and how we organised our command structures.

In the early years of the prison, republican prisoners had a much more conservative, even right-wing, Catholic, political outlook and very hierarchical command structures. In later years that changed to a much more left-wing, even Marxist, politics and the command structures reflected a much more collective leadership and egalitarian approach. Mike, who lectured at Queen's University, Belfast suggested I study for a PhD and that way I could get the book I wanted but also get the qualification. I didn't even realise until then that I could study for a PhD in that manner but decided that's what I would do.

I discussed the idea with Jenny (Meegan), who I still remained closely in contact with following my release, and she suggested that I enrol for the OU course, D803, Doing Prison Research, as it would assist me with my doctoral studies in terms of exploring various research methodologies. As always, it was excellent advice; I enrolled in the course. A central component of the coursework was to conduct a piece of research with some association to imprisonment and I choose the Women's Studies programme which I had organised in the prison with Joanna. I graduated that year (1994) with a Distinction in the Advanced Diploma in Criminology; Prison Studies and also commenced my doctoral studies at Queen's University.

Conclusion

Studying at Queen's was a very different experience from studying with the OU – I had to seek out my own materials and decide upon what was relevant to my research or not. They didn't arrive in carefully packaged regular mailings to me! But being used to 'distance learning' meant I was able to easily engage with the requirements of conducting doctoral studies through research.

My thesis, *Unrepentant Fenian bastards: the social construction of an Irish Republican prisoner community*, was completed in 1998 (see McKeown, 2001). A few weeks later, at the age of 42, I commenced the first real job I ever had, as Project Officer with a newly formed umbrella organisation for former IRA prisoners, Coiste na nIarchimí (Committee for ex-prisoners). The Good Friday/Belfast Agreement had been signed earlier that year and all remaining political prisoners were to be released over a two-year period. Times were changing.

Fast forward to the Sinn Féin Árd Fhéis (Annual General Meeting) in the Royal Dublin Society (RDS), Dublin, 2017. I was not there primarily to engage in the political discussions but to promote a calendar I had just published. The calendar was printed to commemorate the 40th anniversary of the start of the blanket protest in the prison in 1976. I had obtained an original blanket from the prison once it closed and it had lain in my attic for many years. I wanted to create something artistic from the blanket and decided to give it to a dressmaker and request that she make me items of clothing from it – a bow tie, a waistcoat, a tie. I then had a photographer take photographs of former prisoners who had participated in the protest, now wearing the garments. The photos were taken outdoors, in nature. The idea was to subvert the image from the time of the protest – of long hair, beards, and people wrapped in blankets. The photos were to look elegant.

I had been sitting for some hours at the stall allocated to me in the large hall of the RDS before I realised that the stall directly behind me was a promotional one for the OU. I was initially surprised at their presence at such a (party political) gathering but then it made sense to me; in terms of potential 'customers' there was a large pool to draw from, but also, many in the RDS had gone through the prisons, both north and south, and many of them were former OU students. I walked over and introduced myself but it turned out that I was already known to several of those at the stall. After some chat we took photos. It was all very casual, very 'normal', and somehow very fitting. The development of my political outlook and consciousness over many years was so much integrated with, and influenced by, my studies with the OU and the people those studies brought me into contact with, and now, in a much different context, in very changed times, the OU was still there, doing what it has done so perfectly over so many years. Long may it continue to do so.

Notes

[1] https://www.bbc.com/news/uk-northern-ireland-41271598.
[2] https://www.revolvy.com/page/Special-Category-Status.
[3] Royal Ulster Constabulary – the name of the Police Force in the north of Ireland at that time. In subsequent years they were reformed under the terms of the Good Friday Agreement to the Police Service of Northern Ireland following on from the report of the Patten Commission. https://cain.ulster.ac.uk/issues/police/patten/patten2001.pdfm.
[4] In later years the requirement was dropped to six full credits.

References

Bobby Sands Trust (nd) Website. www.bobbysandstrust.com/

Campbell, B., McKeown L. and O'Hagan, F. (eds) (1994) *Nor meekly serve my time: The H-Block struggle 1976–1981*, Belfast: Beyond the Pale.

Freire, P. (1996) *Pedagogy of the oppressed*, Harmondsworth: Penguin.

McKeown, L. (2001) *Out of time*, Belfast: Beyond the Pale.

VIGNETTE 8

My journey, my new life

Dan Micklethwaite

Learning is perhaps the most fundamental part of the human condition. From the moment we are born until our final breath, we take in, process and react to our worlds. Prior to finding myself in prison, learning was not something that I gave much consideration to. Learning in prison, however, quickly became an important aspect of my life. My introduction to The Open University has turned out to be more valuable than I ever imagined.

My journey as an indeterminate sentenced prisoner began in 2008. This induction into my new life was a truly harrowing experience; from such a position one simply cannot see a desirable future. Nor can one escape the futility of one's existence. Despite the depression and desperation that accompanies the start of a life sentence, the prison machine imposes its process. Part of this included the standard induction procedures that all prisoners go through. As a result, I was introduced to prison education.

In my experience it is an understatement to say that prison education is a hugely misused resource. I say this because education could be so much more. I have experienced a system that coerces prisoners into undertaking basic literacy and numeracy classes, in which many prisoners have no interest. This often becomes a combative and bureaucratic process in which the beauty and quality of learning is lost. Conversely, there is a glass ceiling for those prisoners who wilfully pursue educational betterment. While prisons generally provide a range of education classes, there is typically a progression limit of level 2; A–C grade GCSE equivalent. It would be an investment on a societal scale to expend more energy on the quality, meaning and experience of prisoner education. The Open University provides an example of how this can be done.

Within three months of engaging in standard prison education, I had reached the glass ceiling. I still had over a decade to serve until I would be considered for release. I undertook an Open University Openings course in psychology. Today, I hold a first-class honours BSc in Criminology and Psychological Studies, and an MSc in Criminology and Criminal Psychology (Distinction). I work as a full-time academic research associate, undertaking research and producing academic publications, and am in pursuit of a PhD. The Open University provided the cornerstone for my future and there are intricacies to my journey that have been profoundly meaningful.

As a prisoner a phrase that I often heard to describe the passage of a prison sentence is 'dead time'. This phrase is worth consideration. It denotes time trapped in a place against one's will. It denotes time out of a finite lifespan. It denotes time deprived of intimate relationships. It denotes time away from family and friends. Dead Time. Many of the things that make life meaningful are reduced to a purely symbolic quality. Ergo, the experience of life becomes dead. For most prisoners, there is the luxury of knowing this dead experience is for a limited period. Life sentence prisoners do not have this luxury, because they have no release date.

At the beginning of my sentence education provided a means of trying to make life meaningful. To my surprise I found that I enjoyed learning. Undertaking an Open University Openings course first served to whet my appetite. I applied for funding through the Prisoners' Education Trust (PET) and began a journey as an undergraduate in BSc Criminology and Psychological Studies. This became so much more than just another course in prison. It became a central coping mechanism for the stresses and trauma of my sentence. The hours locked in my cell spent reading course materials, taking notes and drafting assignments provided a much-needed distraction from the realities of prison life. This was a wholesome way to spend my time and it meant that my sentence could be productive. I was not wasting my life. My undergraduate ambition began to grow. Could I really achieve a degree? From this The Open University became more than a way to serve time, it became my future. I sought advice from the National Careers Service (sadly a valuable resource since removed from the prison system) and began to plot my sentence around my educational progression. Over the years I considered the possibility of many future careers. Keeping an open mind but also keeping focus. Notions of becoming a therapist, a psychologist or a university lecturer started to feel a little bit more possible with the passing of every successful module. The Open University provided me with hope. This has led me to working, now, in a forensic psychology research unit and enjoying work lecturing in university.

The impact The Open University had on the process of my rehabilitation cannot be overstated. The meaning and hope I derived from my study enabled the imagination of a new me, a *good* me. My study with The Open University played a significant role in the emotional transformation towards this new me. My undergraduate degree comprised two interconnected disciplines, Criminology and Psychology. My position as a life sentence prisoner meant that I lived in a criminogenic environment and I was required, by this environment to unpack and come to terms with the psychology of my crimes. My circumstances were such that I could apply my learning in the real world. Throughout the time of my undergraduate degree I resided in a prison-based therapeutic community. The experiences of being in therapy and of studying Criminology and Psychology proved to be symbiotic. My education helped me to understand my environment. It helped me to engage with the therapeutic process and so became part of my rehabilitation. I would often sit with my therapist (a psychoanalyst) discussing psychological topics and gaining his advice on due assignments and projects. The rehabilitative benefits of being in therapy were in no small part influenced by the understanding I developed through my learning with The Open University.

In my experience, The Open University proved to be an invaluable resource. The knowledge provided by the course materials is but one dimension of the ways in which The Open University aided both my academic development and my journey through the prison system. The Open University can play an active role not just in education but in improving prisoners' quality of life and prisoners' self-image. The Open University is a pathway for building better futures and, therefore, preventing future harms. This is a rehabilitative resource that should be made available to all.

13

Ex-prisoners and the transformative power of higher education

David Honeywell

Introduction

In this chapter I analyse the narratives of ex-prisoners who entered higher education to transform their lives. My studies reveal many underexplored challenges related to the desistance process that are generally overlooked in the academic literature. These include how the lengthy and sometimes apparently unending process of self-transformation involved in desistance from crime is for the individual concerned. I was aware of this through my own experiences as a former prisoner who used education as an escape from a dysfunctional life, yet despite gaining a Bachelor's and a Master's degree, it still took many attempts to become an accepted member of society. After completing an Open University (OU) foundation level course in 1997 while in prison, I was able to begin an undergraduate degree after my release. Even so, I found myself trapped between my old world and the new world I was attempting to transition towards. This has become easier with the passage of time but even with the transformative benefits of a university education, employment, relationships and friendships analysed by desistance academics, none of these were able to shield me from the painful and prolonged experiences of social and psychological liminality. Liminality is a feeling of being between two worlds, neither fully part of one or the other. These feelings of mine resonated with the respondents in this study and although there are many transformative benefits of education, it soon became apparent that liminality is a major hurdle for desisters. Education can enable individuals to move beyond the liminal stage, but in many cases there is always conflict where the past and present collide.

There are many studies on prisoner education but there still remains a dearth of research and discussion about ex-prisoners in education. This can be attributed to them losing contact with education, but also because many ex-prisoners find themselves experiencing barriers

(Pike, 2014). I interviewed 24 ex-prisoners (13 male/11 female) who had all entered higher education to transform their lives. Initially, my PhD study was heavily influenced by Anne Pike's (2014) Open University PhD study *Prison-based transformative learning and its role in life after release*, which found social rejection to be a major influence on the respondents' self-esteem. Pike's study gave me a platform from which to analyse not only prisoner education but also the experiences of prisoner learners after they are released from prison. I was also a subject situated within my own study as I shared similar lived experience of imprisonment, desistance and education as my respondents. In 1998 I was released from HMP Wealstun open prison with an unconditional offer to study a degree in criminology at Northumbria University after passing the foundation level OU course, Society and Social Sciences. This paved the way for me to become an academic and be in the position to be able to write this chapter.

Drawing on terminology used by desistance scholars such as Giordano et al (2002), higher education became my respondents' initial 'hook for change', where they were able to develop new identities as students (Pike, 2014). I recounted in my autobiography, *Never ending circles*, how between 1996 and 1997 while serving part of my prison sentence in HMP Acklington (now Northumberland) and HMP Wealstun I became acquainted with several life sentence prisoners who had all gained degrees through the OU. Their successes inspired me further and as a result of one of the lifers making contact with the prison OU coordinator, an interview was arranged. Having established my interests in criminology and sociology, it was suggested I study the D103 Society and Social Sciences foundation course. Then, through the combined support of the prison Education Department and the Leeds regional OU centre, as well as encouragement from others, I was able to embark on a course of study that would change my life forever.

On completing my foundation course, and nearing the end of my sentence, I was made an unconditional offer to study a criminology undergraduate degree at Northumbria University which also boosted my self-esteem. Until then I had no qualifications. It seemed like a big leap to go from having no qualifications to studying through the OU but because the materials they provide were designed in a very user-friendly way, it made the transition for me much easier.

Fifteen years later, while continuing to carve out an academic career for myself, it became clear to me that my 'insider' position as a researcher with lived experience of imprisonment provided me with insights, knowledge and understanding derived from years of living with, and among, criminals and inmates. This is an important point because an ex-prisoner's perspective on imprisonment, criminal stigma, labelling, the desistance process and the transformation of self is inevitably developed through their own experience. However, as Cullen (2003, cited in Jones et al, 2009, p 158) suggests, 'there's a risk of their perceptions being unintentionally biased'. It was essential to be mindful of the possibility of bias through continual self-reflection and understanding of its potential pitfalls. However, it could also be argued that complete objectivity in qualitative research is neither possible nor desirable. Another concern about 'insider research' is that it may unquestioningly accept all that insiders present, since being critical of their experience and knowledge may be taken to be a denial of its realities (Nind, 2014). This viewpoint corresponds with Liem and Richardson's (2014) assertion that there are limitations to studies that rely on ex-prisoners' accounts of desistance, and that there can be no way of actually knowing to what extent they have truly transformed.

There are increasing numbers of academic accounts that claim some forms of imprisonment, or some kinds of experience in prison, lead to self-change (see Schinkel, 2015; McNeill and Schinkel, 2016; McLean et al, 2017) and I also make this claim. Had it not been for my five-year prison sentence in 1995, I know I would not have followed a pathway of education. I argue that sharing this lived experience can validate some narratives because, as a researcher, I am wary of any partial or incomplete accounts of social phenomena. A researcher who has not experienced imprisonment may find it difficult to believe that imprisonment can provide positive change, but I know from my own experiences that this can and does happen. For me, the process of exploration cannot be passive or detached but is potentially reciprocal in that both the researcher and respondent are mutually implicated in the research questions.

Only two respondents of the 24 I interviewed had accessed the OU during their time in prison, for a variety of reasons. The majority of prison sentences were too short for prisoners to engage in a six-year OU degree but none had accessed any foundation courses either, as I had, while some already held degrees so they just continued their education after release.

The impact of discrimination, stigma and spoiled identities

Despite developing pro-social identities through the transformative process of higher education (see Darke and Aresti, 2016), my respondents continually encountered barriers which included further stigmatisation (Goffman, 1963). Goffman uses the term 'spoiled identity' to refer to the stigmatised individual as being made to feel like a social outcast, but I argue that sometimes the respondents unwittingly created this problem themselves. For example, disclosing too much about one's past can create stigmatisation from other individuals and from institutions. This occurred when some of the people I interviewed had not understood the implications of 'spent' and 'unspent' convictions as established by the Rehabilitation of Offenders Act 1974/2014 (for full guidance see Unlock, 2018). Unfortunately this misunderstanding resulted in several respondents being unfairly and painfully rejected by universities (Prisoners' Education Trust, 2017). Ex-offenders may encounter stigma and discrimination because of a naïve need or desire to share their experiences. They may do this by over-disclosing their pasts, perhaps as a way of redeeming themselves (Maruna, 2001) but also because their past remains part of their identity. But for some of the respondents in this study, the thought of being judged again for their past crimes was so distressing they did not disclose convictions through fear of rejection and undergoing further scrutiny which is explained in 'Debbie's' narrative:

> 'I went and applied for my PGCE [Postgraduate Certificate in Education] and it's the hardest thing I've ever done but I stayed on and did that. When they found out about my criminal record for that and it was in the same university centre, that was a little bit tougher [...]. I had to get a letter from 'Sarah' who is the CEO (of her current employment), explaining that I'd been here for four and a half years. It's my past and it's not a problem, Theresa had to write me a thing saying, "she excelled at all"!'

Debbie attempted to avoid stigma and overcome the barriers of entering higher education by withholding her past, but her past came to light when, after completing her degree, she decided to enrol on a teacher training course. Despite her proven commitment to study and the university where she had gained her degree her criminal past was scrutinised by a recruitment panel. She claims that it was as though she was being judged again for her past misdemeanours when all she wanted to do is move forward with her life:

> 'I felt very much like I'd been judged because of that. I got pulled into the office with the head and three people while

they scrutinised me. I get it. If I was going to be working with vulnerable people; they needed to be sure who they were putting there.'

There is no argument that, for certain courses, such as teaching in which adults are coming into direct contact with children and vulnerable people, a full disclosure of one's criminal background is imperative, but perhaps the problem here is not so much about policy but how individual cases such as Debbie's are handled by those making these judgements. Once the university eventually accepted Debbie's application, she successfully completed the PGCE which the university has since used as an example for other students to aspire to:

> 'I felt like I was under the spotlight at that moment in time. Having to rationalise why, what and why I wanted to do ... but they allowed me to [study the PGCE] and didn't find any fault. And after there was one day out of that year course, and it was over and done with and I was allowed to finish. They now use my files to show me round to everybody else so there you go.'

Debbie's present employers now see her as an asset to the organisation which has, in turn, led to increased self-confidence, self-respect and financial stability. Her past still invades her present at times but she explains that whereas previously she would have been frightened, she now has confidence.

Although Debbie had to face some hurdles at university, she did not have to endure total rejection, which is what happened in Melody's case. 'Melody', a 44-year-old student, had one of the most serious offending backgrounds yet, through studying in prison, proved that she was serious about changing her life and thus began her self-transformation. Yet despite this, she was initially rejected by the first university of her choice:

> 'I had done my "A"-level. I had done my GCSEs in jail. Started the "A"-levels, got released and my probation officer was really good, took me to college. Got "A"-levels in psychology, sociology and law, which I thought would be enough to get me in and I was just classed, being 25, as mature. Applied for a DIPSW [Diploma in Social Work] and it was "NO"! "Someone with an extensive criminal record like yours will never, ever, get in any university in

England or Wales." I've still got the letter. I've put it away for when I do get the degree.'

Aligning with much of the contemporary research (Pike 2014; Prisoners' Education Trust, 2017), Melody's narrative offers further evidence demonstrating discriminatory practices by universities. The university was more concerned about Melody's convictions than her academic abilities and achievements. As a result, she was forced to revert towards a period of liminality where she was neither rehabilitated nor a prisoner (Healy, 2010, 2014).

'Ruby' believes that she was rejected from five universities because of her criminal record. Ruby, 40, was involved in the sex industry and was a drug user. She now works as a substance abuse worker with other individuals with substance abuse issues. It was essential for Ruby to demonstrate her independence and gain a degree in criminology and sustain successful employment:

> 'Got rejected from five universities because I've a criminal conviction. I applied for social work and the reason I applied for social work was purely financial, because the pay is amazing. [The first] University wanted to know more about my convictions, but they'd already lost my UCAS form so there was no way I was sending a DBS [Disclosure and Barring Service – organisation providing information on convictions] through the post to the university. I ended up with a proper snotty woman asking me my convictions, which clearly, I'm not going to share. Didn't get a place. The second university didn't even acknowledge my application.'

The common denominator between Melody and Ruby's examples of being rejected by universities is that they both applied to study social work, which requires background checks for all applicants. Melody and Ruby then both enrolled on criminology degrees which were not qualifications for professional practice. This could be why students with criminal records gravitate towards social science degrees where there are fewer restrictions and but still opportunities for their experience to 'count' for something.

In some instances, respondents were treated more with contempt than being offered guidance, such as in Melody's case where she was told that with her extensive criminal record she will "never!" get in any university in England or Wales. She eventually proved them wrong, yet this rejection had a significant impact on Melody's sense of self and when she was asked how this affected her emotionally, this was her response:

Melody:	'I went and got wrecked [drunk]. Inside? I felt "f..k you!" I felt like going to rob someone, or shoot someone, you know?'
DH:	'So, it was anger?'
Melody:	'Yes definitely.'
DH:	'What about sadness though or anything like that? I'm trying to get a feel of your emotions.'
Melody:	'I would have probably hit someone before I burst into tears in them days. I've never been a crier. My anger would come out as violence instead of "boo hoo". Sadness – I would probably internalise it then become aggressive.'
DH:	'So, more frustration than anything then?'
Melody:	'Yes.'

Melody described how she became angry and frustrated as a result of being rejected and, as described in Matza's (1964) 'drift' theory, she drifts back into offending as her social bonds are weakened (see also McNeill, 2012). But the anguish and despair are not static emotions or simple episodes that pass. They sit within an existential process forming an ongoing emergence of identity. Melody's story includes a mixture of successes and unstable encounters, advances and setbacks. Being told she would never be accepted into any university due to her extensive criminal history, was made worse when, shortly after, she was rejected for a job application:

> 'I applied for a job at the local drug alcohol service. I think
> I got down out of sixty people, got to the last eight but
> didn't get that. I thought "bollocks to this"! I'm going
> back to crime!'

Ultimately this led Melody to consider re-offending, which is a common self-fulfilling prophecy in reaction to continual rejection which I know about from personal experience. I would often question what it would take to become accepted in society. Why, after achieving two degrees, was I still being rejected? And it was these questions that shaped the central theme of my PhD study that the desistance process is an ongoing and, for many, a never ending set of experiences, which include stigma, rejection and constant re-biographing (Maruna, 2001). Before my PhD study, I felt completely isolated, believing that no one else would be in this place of liminality, with one foot in the past and the other in the present – a person who existed between two social worlds (Healy, 2010, 2014) in which I belonged to neither.

Overcoming boundaries through education

Education does have its limitations though, for some individuals with serious offending backgrounds, such as 60-year-old 'Tom', who has a history of sex offences. The chance of going to a conventional university was not an option in Tom's case. The opportunity to enrol on an OU degree course enabled him to overcome this barrier. He was not able to interact with other students but, for Tom, the whole of aim of the OU was its transformative power and, despite the many barriers he has to face, he has made exceptional progress in his academic studies, which has boosted his self-esteem and given him the confidence to confront his past. Because the OU enables individuals to study through distance learning, the OU became the ideal route for Tom, and though education has not opened as many doors for him as it has for others, it has still given him an enriched sense of self. He studied sociology, social policy and criminology through the OU, achieving a first-class honours degree on release from prison. Since his release, and with additional support, he has completed a Master's degree in social research methods and, as Tom explains, education has completely transformed his sense of self:

> 'Once I started achieving education, it challenged my thinking about [how] I couldn't do anything, I was a worthless nothing. I was useless. All the self-esteem issues I had struggled with as a child growing up being told I was useless and couldn't achieve it […] I was now in the small percentage academically of others in the country. I could achieve … and I can look at my graduation photos and I could go back home and say "look what I did!" and that makes me proud. That totally transformed how I see myself.'

The psychosocial process of Tom's transformation has included a combination of education, psychotherapy and self-reflection on his past life experiences which caused him deep-seated trauma. Tom's narrative suggests that higher education had enriched his life to the extent that employment was a secondary concern for him. Moreover, it was about what education had done to improve his sense of self and, most importantly, a change in his own attitude and view towards himself. This sits within the third stage of Giordano et al's (2002) cognitive transformation process, whereby individuals see themselves in a different role as a 'replacement self' begins to emerge. Tom's experience exposes the narrowness of prison education being focused principally towards its utility for gaining employment, and supports the contrasting argument that prison education could emphasise its transformative benefits (Prisoners' Education Trust, 2017). Tom claims his decision to study through the OU was not just about anticipating the way his conviction for sexual offences would limit his study options at conventional university but also because of the concept of an Open University:

> 'I actually love the concept of The Open University because I think it's the best value for money you will get. The materials are second to none. The resources they have available, the work they do with the BBC, the programs they produce and they are all over the world. I think they are absolutely, they have superb materials. Most of the tutors are tutors at other universities anyway; they just do this as an extra. So, you get the best of all worlds. It's hard to [be] disciplined. It's hard to knuckle down and do it; it's hard to be very self-disciplined.'

Not everyone can leave prison with the possibility of continuing the roles they adopted in the prison education department. Once Tom was released from prison, he lost his status as an educator and, at the time of writing, has remained unemployed. This is largely because of his convictions but it also demonstrates the limitations of higher education and that it can only go so far in enabling individuals to transform their lives. Tom's earlier explanation, that education enabled him to view himself differently, is emphasised by McNeill and Schinkel (2016) as an essential element of the transition from the secondary stage of desistance to the tertiary stage of desistance. But there also needs to be a change in how others begin to view someone who is trying to change their lives and reintegrate, and tertiary, lasting, desistance depends not only on how desisters view themselves but also how they are viewed by others.

Clarissa, 41, had been a substance abuse user and eventually, through education, became involved in delivering workshops and seminars about her past experiences. She has also continued to work for the local council and has enjoyed delivering guest talks to college students about her previous struggle with substance abuse. Clarissa was a victim of child sexual abuse and developed problematic drug issues but, in later life, higher education provided her with opportunities, not least including accommodation where she was able to escape a volatile relationship:

> 'They [university] were ace! They used to have me in delivering sessions. They used to have me in delivering drug awareness sessions. I got a lot of confidence from that.'

Clarissa's experience has had a positive impact on her self-confidence and, although this is very encouraging for others in the same predicament, it clearly highlights the inconsistencies of universities' treatment of ex-offenders. Tom and Clarissa had both overcome being sexually abused, which has left psychological scars. In Tom's case, he went on to be a sexual offender himself, but although this has become a barrier for him finding employment, he has found education to be transformative, which has enabled him to develop a psychosocial transformation of self. Clarissa has continued to succeed through education and employment and, though her past experiences left an indelible mark on her, it has made her a strong person. In other words, individuals who overcome difficult times and transform their lives through education have the ability to present education as a milestone in their life.

Embracing student identities

Developing student identities was a liberating experience for the people I interviewed, which is consistent with Pike's (2014) study on prisoners in higher level learning, where the majority of prisoner learners developed and embraced their student identities while holding high hopes for a better future (Burnett and Maruna, 2004; Farrall and Calverley, 2006). Also, though Pike's initial findings suggest higher level learning provides a resilience factor which helps ex-prisoners cope with mounting barriers, later findings showed that those practical barriers could become overwhelming. For the prisoner learner, the student identity enables a transitional process which is consistent with cognitive transformation. It can take many years to re-establish an identity that will enable the ex-prisoner to fully reintegrate into society and re-evaluate their sense of self. Since being released from prison in

1998, it has taken a long time to reinvent myself as an academic. For the first ten years I tried to reinvent myself through many routes; as a personal trainer, as a freelance journalist and publisher, but was always haunted by my past convictions. As background checks increasingly became the criteria for employees, if I was ever to move up the career ladder, I would have to have my background scrutinised by uninformed individuals and go through the never ending cycle of being judged for the same crimes over and over again. I began to feel that I would never be accepted until, through my PhD study, I was catapulted into the world of teaching. Education allowed me to make a career for myself, but only by becoming part of an establishment, a university. In other words, the only way I would be able to transform my life through being accepted and fully integrated would be through the university culture. I would never be fully reintegrated into wider society because I no longer have anything to offer mainstream employment, therefore the academy has become the institution in which I am now defined. It seems it is just a case of adopting identities that fulfil students' aspirations (Laub and Sampson, 1993). Similar findings about the importance of prisoner/student identity can be seen in Pike's (2014) study, where prisoners felt that studying art, in particular, helped them to develop new identities.

The general consensus among many scholars interested in how people emerge from prison to develop better lives for themselves is to focus on the varying aspects of desistance. McNeill and Weaver (2010, p 71) conclude by arguing that:

> The desistance process seems to have common elements for all or at least most people – developing maturity, the emergence of new social ties which hold particular subjective significance for the individuals concerned and, sometimes, a renegotiation of personal identity.

The experiences of my interviewees support McNeill and Weaver's (2010) narrative because it is clear that they experienced many of the desistance elements the former refer to, such as maturing, developing new social bonds and the existential element of subjectivity, a new sense of themselves as worthy, rather than worthless, human beings. Despite the clear transformative benefits of education, there are still limitations, such as in Tom's case whereby, because his offences were sexual, he was more limited than the other respondents in what he was permitted to do once he had left prison in terms of employment and education. The OU enabled Tom to enter higher education but he has always had to remain in the cracks, at the margins of society. Even from my own perspective as an insider researcher with lived experience, there continue to be barriers. Over twenty years since being released from prison and three university degrees later, including a PhD, not everyone will welcome someone with my background. There continues to be stigmatisation within the academy (Prisoners' Education Trust, 2017) as well as wider society but, thankfully, with growing networks like the British Convict Criminology network (Aresti et al, 2012; Earle, 2016, 2018) and from the findings of my own PhD research, there is evidence of more people with convictions entering or wishing to enter higher education.

Conclusion

In this chapter I have tried to demonstrate the transformative benefits of higher education for a group of ex-prisoners from various backgrounds and, though the transformative benefits are clear, for some of the respondents there were many ongoing barriers. It is accepted that education can be a significant factor in the journey towards desistance (see Darke and Aresti, 2016), yet people with convictions who want to pursue or continue their education still encounter discrimination from the very institutions that claim to be inclusive. In 2017, the Prisoners' Education Trust highlighted a significant failure by universities towards people with criminal convictions but at present some are still very discriminative, which was supported in my own study. Also we have seen that some respondents found prison to be a positive experience (McNeill, 2014) where they began to reflect and make changes through education and, as McLean et al (2017) argue, there are increasing numbers of accounts of prisoners experiencing self-change in prison. This is in complete contrast to what one would expect, but, as Aresti et al (2010) discovered, during such painful experiences some prisoners may encounter an existential experience which makes them reassess their lives. This challenges Goffman's (1961) 'total institution' concept of prisoners experiencing the stripping down of identities because some of the people I interviewed were able to develop new identities through prison education (see also Pike, 2014).

References

Aresti, A., Eatough, V. and Brooks-Gordon, B. (2010) 'Doing time after time: an interpretative phenomenological analysis of reformed ex-prisoners' experiences of self-change, identity and career', *Psychology, Crime & Law*, 13(3): 169–90.

Aresti, A., Darke, S. and Earle, R. (2012) 'British convict criminology: developing critical insider perspectives on prison', *Inside Time*, August: 26.

Burnett, R. and Maruna, S. (2004) 'So prison works, does it? The criminal careers of 130 men released from prison under Home Secretary, Michael Howard', *Howard Journal*, 33(4): 390–404.

Darke, S. and Aresti, A. (2016) 'Connecting prisons and universities through higher education', *Prison Service Journal*, 225: 26–32.

Earle, R. (2016) *Convict Criminology – Inside and Out*. New Horizons in Criminology. Bristol: Policy Press.

Earle, R. (2018) 'Convict criminology in England: developments and dilemmas', *British Journal of Criminology*, 58(6): 1499–516.

Farrall, S. and Calverley, A. (2006) *Understanding desistance from crime*. Crime and Justice Series. London: Open University Press.

Giordano, P.C., Cernkovich, S.A. and Rudolph, J.L. (2002) 'Gender, crime, and desistance: toward a theory of cognitive transformation', *American Journal of Sociology*, 107(4): 990–1064.

Goffman, E. (1961) *Asylums: Essays on the social situation of mental patients and other inmates*, Harmondsworth: Penguin.

Goffman, E. (1963) *Stigma: Notes on the management of spoiled identity*, Englewood Cliffs, NJ: Prentice Hall.

Healy, D. (2010) *The dynamics of desistance: Charting pathways through change*, London: Routledge.

Healy, D. (2014) 'Becoming a desister: exploring the role of agency, coping and imagination in the construction of a new self', *British Journal of Criminology*, 54(5): 873–91.

Jones, R.S., Ross, J.I., Richards, S.C. and Murphy, D.S. (2009) 'The first dime: a decade of convict criminology', *The Prison Journal*, 89(2): 151–71.

Laub, J.H. and Sampson, R.J. (1993) 'Turning points in the life course: why change matters to the study of crime', *Criminology*, 31: 301–25.

Liem, M. and Richardson, N.J. (2014) 'The role of transformation narratives in desistance among released lifers', *Criminal Justice and Behavior*, 41(6): 692–712.

Maruna, S. (2001) *Making good: How ex-convicts reform and rebuild their lives*, Washington, DC: American Psychological Association.

Matza, D. (1964) *Delinquency and drift*. New York: Wiley.

McLean, R., Matra, D. and Holligan, C. (2017) 'Voices of quiet desistance in UK prisons: exploring emergence of new identities under desistance constraint', *Howard Journal*, 56(4): 437–53.

McNeill, F. and Schinkel, M. (2016) 'Prisons and desistance', in J. Bennett, B. Crewe and Y. Jewkes (eds) *Handbook on prisons*, Cullompton: Willan Publishing, pp 607–21.

McNeill, F. (2012) 'Four forms of "offender" rehabilitation: towards an interdisciplinary perspective', *Legal and Criminological Psychology*, 17(1): 18–36.

McNeill, F. (2014) 'Three aspects of desistance?', Discovering Desistance blog, http://blogs.iriss.org.uk/discoveringdesistance/2014/05/23/three-aspects-of-desistance/.

McNeill, F. and Weaver, B. (2010) *Changing lives? Desistance research and offender management*, Glasgow: SCCJR Project Report.

Nind, M. (2014) *What is inclusive research?*, London: Bloomsbury Academic.

Pike, A. (2014) *Prison-based transformative learning and its role in life after release*. PhD thesis, The Open University.

Prisoners' Education Trust (2017) 'Boxed in? Applying to uni with a criminal record', www.prisonerseducation.org.uk/news/applying-to-uni-with-a-criminal-record.

Schinkel, M. (2015) 'Hook for change or shaky peg? Imprisonment, narratives and desistance', *European Journal of Probation*, 7(1): 5–20.

Unlock (2018) 'Unlock for people with convictions.' www.unlock.org.uk/.

Prison choices: taking a degree or packing tea?

Alan Jermey

My Open University journey began after being found guilty of murder at 41 and given a life sentence with a minimum tariff of 16 years for a crime I did not commit. I found myself at HMP Belmarsh, certainly not one of the more attractive or forward-thinking prisons in the UK, with officers wanting to maintain their 'harsh' reputation. There was little choice of activities and I was immediately assigned to packing tea and cereal packs.

That was not for me, so I discovered a 'little oasis', the Education Department. I found my way onto a level 3 counselling course, which included study of Freud and Maslow's work in the psychology field. Nearing the end of the course, I asked the tutor if she felt I was bright enough to study towards a degree in psychology. There was a positive response and she introduced me to the distance learning coordinator. Not a widely promoted position at Belmarsh!

The whole process of being on remand for 10 months and then a six-week trial certainly drained me and the guilty verdict left me at the lowest I have ever felt, not knowing what I was going to do with the next 16 years. With support from the distance learning coordinator and the counselling tutor (a qualified psychologist), I found myself enrolled onto DD101, Introducing the Social Sciences, in 2009, with an objective of completing a degree in psychology. I was a keen sportsperson and understood how a positive mindset can help your performance. However, let's just say the facilities at Belmarsh were rather basic.

The initial module was rather daunting: "Here are some books, read them"; "The Education Department have got some DVDs, watch them, take notes and write some essays." Sounds simple doesn't it! Now the reality – we were not allowed DVD players, Playstations or X-boxes (despite what the *Daily Mail* tells its readers!). By this time, I had progressed to working in the gym and had to liaise with the distance learning coordinator to wheel in a TV and DVD player for an hour at a time to watch and take notes, then refer back to coursework.

It wasn't long until I got transferred to HMP Whitemoor, where things were slightly better organised. My initial tutor would not travel so I transferred to another and found myself chasing deadlines. Fortunately, DD101 was completed and my next module was DSE212, Exploring Psychology. Now we were getting somewhere. The coursework was interesting and the tutor very helpful and motivational, travelling

2–3 hours to get to my tutorials. A great experience, and the tutor even sent me a good luck card before the exam, a nice humane gesture.

Passed DSE212 – good coursework but the exam let me down. On to DD307, Social Psychology: Critical Perspectives on Self and Others, again a great subject and perhaps the perfect environment to study it! My first initial tutorial was over the phone but after completing two tutor-marked assignments (TMAs), I was advised that my tutor had been taken ill. The replacement gave the impression that I was dumped on them and that they would not be able to give me much support other than to mark the TMAs. Part of the module required a research study, I chose 'close relationships'. Again, a difficult subject in an all-male prison, but I adapted the research to gym partners, 'spotting' each other while weight training, supporting and motivating each other. Trying to get access to recording equipment to interview subjects required security clearance.

To compound things further, during the module there was an altercation between two fellow inmates who decided to pull shanks (knives) in the classroom and have it out with each other. After the dust had settled, we were not allowed back into the room as it was a 'crime scene' and my coursework had been contaminated with blood. I'm sure that was an interesting email, requesting duplicate exam booklets due to them being covered in blood! To sum this module up, great course but a disaster, and it was the one that I was looking forward to!

The next module was SD226, Biological Psychology: Exploring the Brain. Wow, this was in-depth. I moved to HMP Swaleside, a B-Cat. prison within the first few weeks of this course, so I thought hopefully things would get better. The new tutor did come and visit me. First tutorial was in a room that could only be described as a storage facility. Clearing off the dust from the desk and chairs made a great first impression on the tutor, who admitted it was the first time that he had covered the module and was not too familiar with the material. I did struggle with this module due to my limited scientific knowledge, but passed, and moved on.

Next came a conundrum, having initially set out to complete a degree in psychology, I was advised that two modules were not available to those in secure environments. Therefore, I could select modules of my choice to complete an Open degree, or fit my modules into another named degree. The obvious choice was 'criminology and psychological studies'. Initially I thought I had no interest in criminology. I was advised by the OU coordinator to try it and he said I would find it really interesting and it might be an alternative career to become a lecturer with experience of both sides of the fence.

It was with a certain amount of trepidation and reluctance that I agreed, and started DD208, Welfare, Crime and Society. However, I must admit the subject matter was captivating and drew me in. My tutor was very enthusiastic and I completed the module. I just had DD301, Crime and Justice to complete, and a final free choice for my last 30 credits. I kept the same tutor and submitted the first two TMAs, got transferred to HMP Coldingley and found myself in a three-man cell, not the best conditions when you need to study there, when your cell mates are arguing over *EastEnders* or football on the TV! I decided to defer the module, giving me time to get established in a single cell.

The new tutor was truly inspirational, a human rights lawyer from London, very enthusiastic and motivational. He attended all the tutorials in person, even when the prison was locked up for training; he got the Education Department to get me out for the tutorial, so he didn't have a wasted journey. The result was an overall distinction, a reflection of how good the tutor was and the hard work that I had put in.

The story doesn't quite end there. I was persuaded to have my graduation ceremony at HMP Coldingley and, rather reluctantly, I agreed. The date was set, invites were sent out and then the prison had an outbreak of norovirus, so I didn't know whether it was going to go ahead or not. With 24 hours' notice, permission was granted but only a few prisoners were allowed to attend. Despite the circumstances, it was an opportunity for my family and friends to see a positive side of prison. Personally, it was great to see my mum and dad feel proud again, I hadn't seen my dad shed a tear in a long time!

My outside probation officer attended the graduation, ironic that she had completed the same degree and obtained the same mark. She commented that she was impressed that I was able to work without any online resources, as she completed much research via the internet. Ruth McFarlane was also present and complimented me on my 2:1.

However, my journey has not finished. I am studying towards a Master's degree in Development Management and investigating the possibility of completing a doctorate when I get to D category. Education has helped me progress through my time in prison, setting me objectives to achieve and a way to keep my brain functioning well in what can be a very numbing, or should I say dumbing, experience, where there is little to stimulate the grey matter.

Surely in the 21st century, it is a crime that more is not done to improve every prisoner's education. If we are truly to believe in rehabilitation and second chances, then more help is needed. Knowledge is power and if we are to be given a second chance, more needs to be done about promoting education in prisons, particularly above level 2 English and maths. I read in many papers that there are jobs available for people with the right qualifications and skills. Why not give us these, so we are able to rejoin society and become valid members of society? Maybe I was lucky that I bumped into that counselling tutor, otherwise I might still be in a workshop packing tea and cereal packs.

14

What the OU did for me

Erwin James

Before I went to prison I'd never heard of The Open University. University, as far as I was aware, was a sort of big college where 'posh' people went to learn to be doctors, lawyers, pilots or politicians. It wasn't a place for unimportant people, and even less important people like me. I never had what might be termed in conventional terms a 'social circle' – there was nobody I'd ever known during the journey of my life who had been to university. None of my family were particularly educated, certainly not beyond secondary school. Convicted of murder and condemned to a life sentence in 1984 the idea that I might ever attend any kind of university, apart from the university of crime, and one day live a meaningful, contributing life was as remote as it was fanciful.

My life before prison had been one long catalogue of dysfunction and chaos. It had been a painful life, painful, for me for sure – but, more pertinently, painful for other people because of me. All these years later I still remember the calm that came over me as the judge, Justice Otton, pronounced sentence, "Life imprisonment, take him down."

The wooden steps leading from the number one courthouse at London's Old Bailey were steep and narrow. But all I felt as I was escorted down to the cells below was a huge sense of relief that I did not have to go back out on those streets again. After a few hours in an iron-barred holding cell underneath the court known as 'the cage' reserved for those who, on paper and in the eyes of the media and the public, were among the most dangerous in the country, I was taken under heavy escort as a Category A prisoner to Wandsworth prison in the south of the city.

Stripped and searched in the reception area and handed my prison garb of stripes and denims and a bedroll, along with a plastic mug, knife, spoon and fork, soon I was being marched along the corridors, clanging through steel gate after steel gate, finally ending up in a solitary cell on 'D2' – the landing designated for 'Cat. A's.

I knew that I deserved all that was coming to me. I had no thoughts of 'rehabilitation' – no ambitions or aspirations. I was too numb to be concerned about the three sets of iron bars across the window high up on the back wall which made it difficult even for gloom to penetrate. A small wooden table, a steel cot bed and a wooden chair furnished the grim, 10 ft × 6 ft space. The smell of human waste from under the bed led me to my plastic toilet bucket and the cell walls, covered in flaking emulsion paint, crawled at night with scuttling cockroaches. During the 23 hours of daily 'bang up' the cell doors were opened for only minutes at a time, just long enough to collect food and water, or to empty the 'slop bucket' in the communal sluice along with several dozen other men. Despite the brevity of our interactions during times of unlock, violence regularly manifested in the toilet recesses. We were allowed one shower a week and one change of socks, underwear and shirt. Exercise on the yard was limited to half an hour a day, so long as the weather was not 'inclement' – a word I'd never heard before I went to prison. Inclement weather, as determined by the mood of the prison guards, meant that fresh air was a scarce commodity.

The truth is I never expected to live again, at least not with any purpose. Had the death penalty been on the statute books I would undoubtedly have received it. I was so full of failure and self-loathing that I know in my heart I would not have minded. I was 27 years old, ill-educated, inarticulate and plagued with chronic social inhibitions. As far as I was aware I had no skills or abilities that might be useful to society. If I thought about the future at all I could only see a long black tunnel with no light at the end of it. The early weeks and months of my imprisonment provided no clues that a life spent in prison could ever remedy my deep-rooted inadequacies.

Long hours, days, weeks and months in isolation can have a profound effect on an individual's thinking. I began to wonder if I'd been born bad. Did I choose to be bad? Or was I made bad? I never knew until then how powerful the mind's image mechanism could be. My dreams, day and night, were vivid. I traced the long winding path that had led me to that prison cell. My impoverished parents had left Scotland as teenagers in the 1950s and hitchhiked south searching for a better life. They toiled at low-paid jobs and saved and four years after I was born they bought a tiny smoke-blackened terraced house on a hill in a small Yorkshire town. My sister was born when I was six. I remember a happy, loving, secure family experience – me, an inveterate smiler always dressed in my favourite cowboy suit, my sister, rosy cheeked and hair a mass of curls – until one Friday night my mother was killed when the van she was a passenger in crashed into a lamp post. The driver, who was drunk, was also killed and my father, the other passenger, had to be cut from the wreckage.

The father that emerged from hospital some weeks later however was not the caring, loving father I remembered. In his place was a violent, selfish, grief-stricken drunk. His abusive relationships with a succession of women after my mother's death, all single mothers with children of their own, left little room for me and my baby sister. When his violence towards me became too much to bear I moved out onto the streets. I was 10 years old. Over the preceding three years I'd changed from a happy, trusting little boy, into a furtive, dishonest, anxious survivor.

A burglary conviction sent me to a council-run children's home aged 11, where I lived for the next four years in a community of around 25 boys – a mishmash of orphans, victims of abuse and kids like me who had been convicted of relatively petty crimes. The best I can say about the experience was that at last I was going to school regularly. I was a surly, incommunicative student in most subjects – one teacher describing me, commented in a school report that I had, 'a chip on both shoulders' – yet I shone in English. It appeared that it was something for which I had a natural aptitude, sharing the top spot in the class with a boy called Michael, who I now understand suffered from a form of autism. It was always a race between Michael and me to get our hands up first in spelling lessons.

Whenever I took my report card back to the home at the end of term, however, nobody thought to acknowledge that I might have achieved something with my A grades in English composition and comprehension. There was no abuse that I knew of in the home. But neither was there any encouragement or sense that any of us in there would amount to very much. In our little world none us thought that we might grow up to be train drivers or astronauts. In the end I left school when I left the home, aged 15, with no academic or vocational qualifications. From then on I only ever had a very poor view of my intellectual abilities.

At 16 I was back on the streets, trying to figure out who I was and where I belonged in life. As I drifted around the country I worked: on building sites; with road laying gangs; as a factory hand; and washed up in restaurants. But I also committed more crime. Alcohol brought some relief from my anxieties, but it also unleashed bouts of unbridled rage. Like my father I became a violent, selfish drunk. Criminal damage, assault, burglary, vehicle theft – drunk tanks, police cells, young offender prisons – my court convictions mounted with each year that passed. I slept rough, sometimes for weeks at a time, in garden sheds, graveyards, motorway service cafes. The more frustrated I became with my failing life, the less I cared about the victims of my crimes. I looked at people who apparently lived meaningful and purposeful lives in their nice houses and watched them driving their nice cars and I wondered, "How does anyone get to live like that?"

Booze, crime and violence led me down the darkest road and into the company of another failed individual. Operating from a London squat we began committing drunken crimes together. Burglary, smash and grab raids, mugging, robbery and finally murder. Two men dead. Two families grieving. Before he sentenced us both to life Justice Otten described me as "brutal, vicious and callous".

But were either of us born bad? Were we made bad? Or did we choose to be bad? These questions had never occurred to me until I was banged up in Wandsworth. There was and never will be any excuse for my crimes or anyone else's – but I started to realise that how any of us become who we become is a complicated process, dependent on so many variables. Deep gnawing thoughts dominated my thinking. I was never so grateful that I could read. Every Saturday morning we were taken six at a time to the prison library where we could choose six books. This was the most exciting hour of the week. Even though the choice was limited my desperation for reading material was great. I needed escape and so mostly I read Western paperbacks. *Edge: The Loner* was my favourite. When I grew tired of Westerns I tried novels by Stephen King, ghost stories and then history books, which to my surprise I found I enjoyed the most.

After a year I was transferred to my first long-term high-security prison. On my new wing there were convicted fraudsters, drug dealers, burglars and robbers alongside some of the most high-profile, and according to the courts, most dangerous offenders in the country, including terrorists, serial killers, child abductors and torturers. In the accepted way of the UK prison system we all rubbed shoulders together. We were a grim club, with barely a spoon of hope between us.

It was there I met the psychologist whose job was to assess the dangerousness and the risk to the public that any of us posed or might pose when and if we were ever to be released. Her name was Joan, a small, mousy haired lady, with a ready smile and a kind word for all. With no guards in sight she would call us up to her office, a converted cell on the wing, so she could make her assessments. During one call up she said to me, "You know we're all born loveable?" I said, "Even me?" She said, "Of course. None of us can choose the life we are born into. We're all born with the potential to become who we are meant to be, to have fulfilling and contributing lives." Before then, as well as thinking about my own life journey, I'd started to think about the journeys of my fellow prisoners. We were all strangers with relative failings and dysfunctions and it appeared relevant to me, somehow, that so many of us had had a limited education, been through state care, had alcohol, drug or mental health issues. Joan gave us hope.

When I said to her that many other people have problematic and damaging upbringings but don't commit crime. She said that generally people reacted to the same circumstances in different ways. "We are all individuals," she said, "and that's how we think, act and react – as individuals." I had never tried to blame my criminal behaviour on anyone else. As far as I could see I was just who I was. I had made the choices that led me through the prison gates. Joan said that good choices and decisions depended on good circumstances and good information. "Most decisions are made instinctively," she said. "If you are in a good place in yourself, in your life, the chances are you'll make good decisions, leading to good actions. But if you are not, the potential for harm and distress to be done to others as well as yourself as a result of bad decision is high."

Joan told me that I owed it to my victims to try to live the best way I could and to try and achieve something meaningful with the life I had left. I knew I could never make amends, that my slate would never be clean. "But you are bright," she said, "you have to educate yourself." By then I was nearly 30 years old. The thought of sitting behind a desk in a classroom held no appeal at all. "But I'm too thick for education," were my exact words. "Nobody is thick!" she said, rather irritably. "Everybody has the ability to learn." It took a while, but eventually, with Joan's words ringing in my ears, I took a tentative step towards the prison Education Department, initially only to please her, to acknowledge her good intentions and put an end to her gentle but firm cajoling. "I'll give it a try," I'd said to her, without the slightest inkling that when I walked into the English teacher's classroom that dark November evening it would irreversibly change the course of my life.

The English teacher was young and pretty and gave me good marks for my work. After several months she held me back at the end of a class and said, "I'm putting you in for an exam." Though I loved the class, the 'homework' she gave us to complete in our cells and anticipation of her comments on my work, my insecurity and sense of inadequacy quickly kicked in. "Are you sure?" I said, "Do you think I could pass?" She thought I was joking. But I did pass, English 'O'-level, with a Grade A – and like an overgrown child I couldn't wait to get to Joan's office a few days later to show her my certificate. "I told you," she said. "We all have potential remember …"

I worked in the workshops by day, but in the evenings I joined other classes, history, geography, maths. Soon I had a clutch of certificates. But there were challenges sustaining an attitude to learn. The vagaries of prison life are perplexing and varied. Riots, protests, killings, self-harm and suicides – yet among the chaos, debilitation, human corrosion and corruption, through education I saw possibilities. Teachers were my salvation.

Despite my apparent ability with English I'd never had the desire to write outside a classroom. It was the prison chaplain's wife who first gave me an inkling that I might have a talent for writing. Her name was Grace and she had volunteered to run an evening class once a week in the Education Department on the perils of drinking too much alcohol. Similar to Joan, Grace was an open-hearted woman who treated everyone as equal. The content of the course didn't matter too much. An hour and a half in her company was enough to make a prisoner feel like a human being again – for a while, anyway.

Grace also used to give us 'homework' to do in our cells. (Is alcohol a stimulant or a depressant? What are the damaging effects of overindulgence? How many units of alcohol can a man safely drink per week? How many for a woman?) After the fourth or fifth session, she pulled me to one side and thanked me for the effort that I had made with my homework – and then she said: "Can I ask you, do you write?" An odd question it seemed. "Well, yes …" I said. She smiled, acknowledging my puzzlement and then said: "No, do you write? Are you a writer?" This time it was my turn to smile. "Oh no," I said, "no, not at all."

A writer? If anyone else had asked me such a question, I would have thought that they were making fun of me. But Grace had been sincere. With just a few hundred words of my untidy handwriting in her hands, Grace had really thought that I might be a writer. For a fleeting moment I wondered that if my life had taken a more stable and secure path, could I actually have been a writer?

My call-ups with Joan continued. We talked about the benefits of education – and she lent me books by authors such as Solzhenitsyn and Dostoevsky. Flaubert and de Maupassant followed. Then at the end of one session she said to me, "Have you ever considered higher education, studying for a degree?" By then I had heard of The Open University and I knew that several men on my wing were studying for degrees with the OU. But despite my modest academic success so far, I still could not get past my deep-rooted sense of inferiority. Even when I passed an exam, the niggling thought that always dampened my sense of achievement was that I'd only been given a pass because I was a prisoner. I told Joan I would think about I but didn't take it any further. When she retired, she Joan left me a copy of Solzhenitsyn's *Cancer ward*, along with a card in which she had written: "Today is the first day of the rest of your life. Make it count."

A month or so after Joan left, the head of the prison Education Department came to my cell. "We believe you are capable of studying to degree level," he said, "and we'd like you to apply to enrol on an Open University course." I found out later that this invitation had been suggested to him by Joan. It's hard to describe how this conversation made me feel. Humble, excited, frightened – of failure. I told him I would think about it. After looking at Joan's little card for a while I decided I'd have a go. I had nothing to lose but time.

The day I went to his office to say I would indeed like to enrol with the OU, he smiled, shook my hand and said, "Wonderful! We'd like you to study Sociology." Immediately my heart sank. "But," I said, "I've lived Sociology. I need colour! Please can I study the Arts?"

I could barely contain my excitement when my first parcel of OU study material arrived. A102, the Arts foundation course, introduced me to Philosophy, Art History, Literature and Music. I still had to work in the workshops during the day, but in my cell at night I read about Socrates and Jeremy Bentham and listened to Mozart on my little cassette recorder. I was introduced to Joseph Wright of Derby, and Thomas Gradgrind, the anti-hero of Charles Dickens' *Hard times* and his frightening obsession with facts. I relished the challenge of completing my monthly tutor-marked assignments (TMAs), then waited with bated breath for their marked return, invariably looking for complementary comments about the quality of my writing as well as a decent mark.

Every few months an OU tutor would visit to give me a tutorial. Gradually my confidence built so that I was sure he was not just humouring me with his grade As and Bs – and of course, the occasional C.

I decided to concentrate on history. Over the next few years my OU journey took me from classical Greece and the Peloponnesian war, through the Augustan age of Rome, culture and belief in Europe in the Middle Ages, the Reformation, the Age of Enlightenment, Victorian Britain, and finally a comparative study of Great Britain and the US from 1860 to 1970. Along the way I gained a reputation in the various prisons in which I was located for being able to "write a good letter". Fellow prisoners would ask, usually through mutual associates, if I could assist with parole representations, letters to probation officers or social services, or just wing applications to the governor. TMAs were a wonderful apprenticeship for somebody providing a writing service.

Life on the concrete and steel of the landings could be bleak and often merciless. But we are blessed in our prisons by the number of well-motivated people who work in them who want people like I was then to succeed in finding a better way to live. Without Joan and Grace, some good prison governors, officers, teachers, probation officers and volunteers, I'd never have discovered that education, and writing in particular, would free my mind to the extent that being bound became my means of liberation – liberation from a past that was more constricting than any prison sentence ever could be.

I took a Diploma course in European Humanities in 1993 and graduated with a BA in 1994, ten years after my sentence began. I declined the prison governor's offer of a ceremony. In the light of my past criminal actions any celebration of my achievements, I decided, would be inappropriate. The confidence that my education gave me, however, allowed me to get involved in prisoner representation groups, charity fundraising events and prison magazine projects while working as a hospital orderly, gym orderly, workshop hand and yard cleaner. I wrote to newspapers complaining at the crass portrayal of prison life with which the media generally misinformed the public. "Most of us deserve to be here," I'd write, "and there are opportunities for lives to be changed. But tell the public the truth. These places are not 'holiday camps.'" The only reply I ever received was from the *Independent*. The features editor thanked me for my letter, "So could you write a piece for us, about the reality of prison life?" Another life-changing moment had arrived.

My article was titled 'Rough justice in the jailbirds pecking order'. I was exhilarated when I saw my actual words in the paper, but I was even more amazed when a cheque arrived in the post for £160. I wrote more letters to newspapers. I began to reflect that perhaps, if my life had been different, I could have been a journalist. I even dreamed that maybe it was not too late. On the strength of my article in the *Independent* the Prison Service supported my enrolment onto a distance learning course in journalism. "Such stuff as dreams are made on…"

The chances, in fairness, of such a dream becoming a reality were slim. The vagaries of prison life persisted and still I wrote. An article I sent on spec to the *Guardian* was published in 1998 – and then in 1999 an extraordinary stroke of fortune occurred. A warm, good-natured probation officer paid me a visit. Richard expressed an interest in how I spent my time in prison. "Education mostly, er, and I like to write," I said. He seemed impressed. "My next door neighbour is a writer," he said, "His name is Ronan Bennett." I knew that Ronan Bennett was an Irish writer who had been imprisoned when he was 18 years old for a murder he hadn't committed and had spent two years in Long Kesh prison in Northern Ireland before he was exonerated.

I'd read a book that Bennett had helped to write called *Stolen years* by Paul Hill, one of the people convicted of the Guildford pub bombing of 1974 who was sentenced to life imprisonment – and later cleared of all charges and released after serving 15 years. I had also read a novel by Bennett called, *The second prison*. We talked about Ronan Bennett's writing. Clearly I was a fan. "Why don't you drop him a line?" Richard said. I did and so began an earnest correspondence. A year or so later I had a message from the landing officer to call Ronan. "It's urgent," said the officer.

When I called him Ronan told me that he had been talking to an editor at the *Guardian*. "He's looking for a serving prisoner to write a regular column about prison life for the paper," he said, "and I've told him about you." Ian Katz was then the editor of *G2*, the paper's features section. I sent him some articles that I thought might work as columns. He wrote back to me and then came to see me. "Well, you can write," he said, "but I need to know more about you and about why you are in here."

It was a tense visit. I'd never met a newspaper editor before. He was a family man, a professional man who exuded integrity. Instinctively I respected him. I hated having to discuss the worst aspects of myself with him – but I wanted him to know me and to trust me and so I opened up and told him the truth. "But I've used my time well," I said, "I've even got a degree, with the OU." It suddenly occurred to me that without realising it, all those years of study and writing I had been preparing for opportunity – and now opportunity had come knocking. I could not have been any better prepared. I wondered after the visit whether Katz would still want me to write for him. It was a big responsibility he was taking on, a big risk, to his reputation and to that of his newspaper.

Each day following Ian Katz's visit I waited anxiously for the post. A week passed before my name appeared on the letter board outside the wing office. I stuck my head in the door and saw an envelope on the desk bearing the *Guardian* logo. "Cheers Guv," I said as the landing officer passed it to me. I raced back to my cell and tore it open. Katz was polite but brief. "It was nice to meet you," he wrote, "We'd like you to write three columns of 800 wds to start. We'll call it *A life inside*."

The governor responsible for lifers was unimpressed when I asked for his approval to write the column. "I'll give you 50 small nos or one big no but the answer will be the same," he said, "I suggest you get another hobby." We argued. He stonewalled. I picked up the evidence of my modest writing achievements that I had spread on his desk and began slipping them back into my folder. I was about to slope out of his office when I remembered the distance learning journalism course I had done with the support and encouragement of the Prison Service. "Hang on a minute," I said. I pulled out the course diploma and showed it to him. "You encouraged me to do this." He looked a little shame-faced, lowered his eyes and said, "We didn't expect you do to any real journalism."

Persistent and determined I wrote to the Home Office, supported by Ian Katz and eventually the then prisons minister Paul Boateng agreed I should be allowed to write the column. "I'm content for this to go ahead," were his precise words. The inaugural column appeared in February 2000, entitled: 'How Beggsy fell out with Bob' – a little vignette about a fall-out over a newspaper between two prisoners in neighbouring cells. It was the first column of its kind in the history of British journalism. I received £20 a month from the *Guardian* for phone cards so I could telephone in my copy to the copy takers from the wing phone booth. The money the paper paid me for the column went to charity. I wrote the column from my prison cell for four and a half years and then in August 2004, exactly twenty years to the day since I had been taken into custody, the parole board ordered my release.

When I stepped out through the prison gate on that hot August day and breathed free air for the first time in two decades I had no sense of triumph. Those twenty years barely made a dent in the debt I owed to my victims. But I had done my best and now I had to learn to live again. The difference in my circumstances from when I entered the prison system could not have been greater. I'd gone in with nothing to show for my 27 years but hopelessness and misery. Now I'd emerged as a professional writer, a journalist for a national newspaper no less.

But there were still fears to overcome, not least was the fear I felt the first time I stood opposite the old *Guardian* building at 119 Farringdon Rd, wondering if I could really cross that road. I'd been invited in to write on the features desk. The nearer I got as my bus trundled through the busy London traffic the more my sense of excitement diminished, replaced with a heightening sense of trepidation. The people I would be sitting with and working alongside were the kind of people I used to look at when I lived on the streets and wondered how to become like them. As far as I knew they had all been to university and they were graduates. When I finally stepped off the kerb, I knew that the only thing that gave me the courage to take that step, was not the fact that I could write, that I was a paid writer, or that I had a regular by-line in one of the most famous newspapers in the world – it was because I was a graduate, an Arts graduate with The Open University. That's what the OU did for me.

Appendix: Study with The Open University

Have you been inspired by the stories in this book? Are you considering OU study yourself?

Unlike other universities, the OU does not have entry requirements to study most of its undergraduate qualifications and there are no tests to gain entry – in fact, more than 40 per cent of new OU undergraduate students in the UK don't have the formal qualifications they'd need to go through a traditional university application process.

The OU has changed the lives of more than 2 million people, bringing them new knowledge, skills, interests and inspiration, and helping them to achieve new goals. We are the UK's largest university, with more than 180,000 students. This includes learners in prisons and secure environments.

The OU offers qualifications in a broad range of subjects and provides access to a range of educational opportunities, from short introductory modules to longer, broader modules leading to degrees and other recognised qualifications.

For more information on courses visit our website www.open.ac.uk and for specific information about our work in prisons go to www.open.ac.uk/secure-environments or speak to your prison education manager.

The Open University: What's Stopping You?

Index

Page numbers in **bold** type refer to tables.

community, and prison education
172–3
'conscientisation' (Freire) 87
Conservative governments 75, 78, 96
Convict Criminology 141–2, 145–6,
148, 149, 206
Council of Europe 12
cover image 1, 9
Crewe, B. 98
'criminal capital' 99
Criminal Justice Act 1967 53
criminology 75, 141–2, 178
see also Convict Criminology
Criminology and Psychological Studies
degree, OU 98, 173, 191, 192
Crosby, James 62
Crosland, Anthony 55
Crowther, Geoffrey 54
Crumlin Road Gaol, Belfast 37, 39, 40
Cummines, Bobby 62
Cunneen, Chris 78
Cusson, M. 97

D

D35, Crime, Order and Social Control
course, OU 133
D102, Foundation Course in the Social
Sciences 182
D103, Society and Social Sciences
foundation course, OU 196
D317, Social Psychology: Personal
Lives, Social Worlds course, OU
121
D803, Doing Prison Research course,
OU 188
Daniel John 56
Davies, Bob 57
DD101, Introducing the Social Sciences
course, OU 209
DD102, An Introduction to the Social
Sciences course, OU 130–1
DD208, Welfare, Crime and Society
course, OU 210–11
DD301, Crime and Justice course, OU
211
DD301, Crime and Punishment course,
OU 102
DD307, Social Psychology: Critical
Perspectives on Self and Others
course, OU 133, 210
de Baroid, Christophe 36
'dead time' 192
'depth' of imprisonment 98, 101, 171
desistance 4, 14, 105, 196, 197, 201–2,
205, 206

academic study as catalyst for 100
challenges to 195
literature on 99–100
precipitating factors 97
digital resources, access to 3, 11,
14–15, 19–20, 23, 24, 26, 47–8,
58–9, 87, 118, 132, 133, 135,
160, 177, 178, 209
milestones **16–17**
DIPSW (Diploma in Social Work)
199–200
Discovering Desistance blog (McNeill)
103
discrimination, impact of 197–202
domestic violence 112
Downes, D. 175
'drift' theory 201
drug-related crime 112–13, 114,
125–6, 139
see also substance abuse issues
DSE212, Exploring Psychology course,
OU 132, 209–10
DT200, Information Technology;
Social and Technological Issues
course, OU 187

E

Earle, Rod 1–9, 73–93
ED209, Child Development course,
OU 131
Educating Rita 65
education 2
as a human right 12
and social class 111
see also adult education; higher
education; prison education;
universities
employment
barriers to amongst prisoners 105,
133
impact of discrimination on
197–202
impact of higher education on
prospects for 14
Encyclopaedia Britannica 54
Engineering courses 31–2
EPIC (Ex-Prisoners Interpretative
Centre) 44
'Eris' (vignette) 95–6

F

family relationships 126–7, 132, 160
Farley, H. 18
Farrall, S. 102

'tightness' of imprisonment 98, 101, 171

Time to Think (OU oral history archive) 3, 6, 33

TINA ('there is no alternative') doctrine 81

Tomlinson. Mike 187

'total institutions' 206

transfers, impact of on prisoner students 24–5, 47–8, 56, 58

Troubles, the, Northern Ireland 3, 6
    see also Long Kesh, Northern Ireland

tutors 7–8, 18–19, 24, 55–6, 96, 131, 182–3, 185, 210, 211, 219
    face-to-face tutorials 8, 18, 48, 118
    and prison security 184
    telephone tutorials 8, 48

Twain, Mark 183

Tyler, T. 168

U

U205, Health and Disease course, OU 117, 187

U210, The English Language: Past, Present and Future course, OU 121

U221, The Changing Experience of Women course, OU 186–7

UCL (University College London) 83

UDA (Ulster Defence Association) 37, 42

Universal Design for Learning 23

universities
    1950s expansion of 52
    critical analysis 81–9
    and neoliberalism 82–3
    and prison education 84–7
    see also higher education

University College Galway 44

University of Al-Quaraouiyine, Morocco 83

University of Bologna, Italy 83

University of Kent 173

US
    imprisonment 74, 88–9
    see also Cold War

UVF (Ulster Volunteer Force) 37, 39, 40, 42, 44

V

VC (Virtual Campus) 20, 59

violence in prisons 127–8, 214

VLE (Virtual Learning Environment), OU 20, 23

W

Wacquant, L. 101, 106

war on drugs, US 89

Watts, Jackie 64

Weaver, B. 102, 103, 104, 205

'weight' of imprisonment 98, 101, 168, 171

Weinbren, Dan 1, 2, 3–4, 51–70, 82

Western Europe, OU students in 57, 59, 61–2

Westminster University 141, 148

Whitemoor Wide Web 20

Wilde, Oscar 143, 146

Wilson, Harold 52, 53, 54, 55

women prisoners, substance abuse, health and mental health issues 113–14

Woods, Norman 61

'working' prisons 15, 18

Y

Y161, Introducing Environment course, OU 123

Youle, Chris 60

Z

Zimbardo, P. 140